**YOU CAN'T ALWAYS SAY WHAT YOU WANT**

The freedom to think what you want and to say what you think has always generated a pushback of regulation and censorship. This raises the thorny question: to what extent does free speech actually endanger speech protection? This book examines today's calls for speech legislation and places it into historical perspective, using fascinating examples from the past 200 years, to explain the historical context of laws regulating speech. Over time, the freedom to speak has grown, the ways in which we communicate have evolved due to technology, and our ideas about speech protection have been challenged as a result. Now more than ever, we are living in a free speech paradox: powerful speakers weaponize their rights in order to silence those less-powerful speakers who oppose them. By understanding how this situation has developed, we can stand up to these threats to the freedom of speech.

Dennis Baron is Emeritus Professor of English at the University of Illinois at Urbana-Champaign. He is a frequent commentator on language issues in the national media and has written a number of popular books, including *What's Your Pronoun?* (2020).

# YOU CAN'T ALWAYS SAY WHAT YOU WANT

## *The Paradox of Free Speech*

### Dennis Baron

University of Illinois, Urbana-Champaign

# CAMBRIDGE
## UNIVERSITY PRESS

University Printing House, Cambridge CB2 8BS, United Kingdom

One Liberty Plaza, 20th Floor, New York, NY 10006, USA

477 Williamstown Road, Port Melbourne, VIC 3207, Australia

314–321, 3rd Floor, Plot 3, Splendor Forum, Jasola District Centre,
New Delhi – 110025, India

103 Penang Road, #05–06/07, Visioncrest Commercial, Singapore 238467

Cambridge University Press is part of the University of Cambridge.

It furthers the University's mission by disseminating knowledge in the pursuit of
education, learning, and research at the highest international levels of excellence.

www.cambridge.org
Information on this title: www.cambridge.org/9781009198905
DOI: 10.1017/9781009198882

First published 2023

Printed in the United Kingdom by TJ Books Limited, Padstow Cornwall

A catalogue record for this publication is available from the British Library.

ISBN 978-1-009-19890-5 Hardback

*for Iryce*

# Contents

# Figures

# Table

# Foreword

Free speech is guaranteed by law in the United States, yet there are always exceptions. You may have "the freedom to think as you will and to speak as you think," but there are always some things that you want to say but can't.* We revel in our free speech. We taunt anyone who tries to shut us up with, "It's a free country. I can say whatever I want." Yet it's never really "free speech," it's more like "free speech, but."

This is a book about our freedom of speech and the legal "buts" that complicate it. Laws protect or limit the words we use, or at least they *try* to do so, because statutes that protect free speech often generate attempts to limit that freedom, and laws that limit what we say prompt us to get around those limits.

Whether it's a broad law establishing an official language, a narrower one forbidding threats or obscene speech, or a statute that defines a single word, like *tomato* or *marriage*, breaking language laws has consequences. Penalties may range from a slap on the wrist to serious fines and long jail terms. The prominent American socialist and frequent presidential candidate Eugene Debs was sentenced to ten years in prison for protesting American participation in the First World War. Debs knew that the 1918 Sedition Act criminalized speaking against the war, yet he exercised his right to say what he thought and went to jail for his beliefs.

Attempts to regulate language in the United States go back to its founding. After the United States won its independence from England, Noah Webster proposed that the new nation drop English and adopt

---

* The elegant phrase in quotes is from Justice Louis Dembitz Brandeis' concurrence in the Supreme Court case of *Whitney* v. *California* (1927), which we'll look at in more detail in Chapter 3.

what he called "Federal Language," though he later changed the name to *American English*. Federal language yoked two common Enlightenment notions: that language was national and that it was perfectible. Webster set out to make American English not just independent, but also better than the original, an upgrade to English 2.0. But some of the "improvements" Webster championed in the schoolbooks and dictionaries that he published were quirky. He spelled words to better reflect their pronunciation or, rather, his pronunciation. Webster was from New England, and so in his dictionary *deaf* became *deef*, because that is how he and his neighbors said the word. Webster also rewrote *bridegroom* as *bridegoom*, to signal the word's derivation from Old English *guma*, a word meaning variously "adult male, boy, or servant." Webster's speller was a hit, and some of his spellings became standard in the United States, like *ax, plow, honor, center,* and *gray*. But many of the "improvements" he put in his dictionary, like *deef* and *bridegoom*, proved too eccentric for most people. Although New York's Philological Society promoted *federal language* in a procession celebrating the Constitution in Philadelphia in July 1788 – no doubt because Webster was a founder and mainstay of the group – Congress never adopted Webster's Federal English or made his *American Spelling Book* the national textbook.[1] Nor has the United States ever designated English as its official language. Yet federal, state, and local governments repeatedly supported the idea of official English, and they frequently passed laws both defending and forbidding what Americans can say or write.

Manipulating language is a way of manipulating people, and it's not just the law that shapes our words. Parents routinely correct children's speech, pushing them toward preferred forms, even punishing them for swearing or saying "ain't." The concept of a *swear-box* or *swear jar*, a container into which one puts a coin to atone for each instance of swearing, originates in the late nineteenth century in England; it is not unknown in American families today, though given the amount of swearing both in private and in public, its effectiveness has always been limited. Friends police one another's words to force consensus or affirm a group identity. And employers may compel workers to follow prepared scripts in order to protect the brand and increase profits. Or they may silence employees to protect trade secrets and discourage complaints on social media. Failing to follow the company's language rules could lead to reprimands, fines, and even unemployment.

Teachers may mold language as well, pressuring students to model standard grammar, accents, and vocabulary, and grading them down when they fail to do so. Webster, a failed lawyer, tried his hand at teaching, which led him to his career as a prescriber of correct English. Teachers in the mold of Webster argue that using Standard English will lead to social and economic success, though as linguists point out, there is no single agreed-upon language standard. Plus, the supposed standards are not innate features of language, not more logical, more effective, or more beautiful than any other variety of speech. Nor does mastering them guarantee success. The "standards" are merely the forms presumed to be in use by elite groups of speakers and writers, a presumption not always backed up by evidence.

The social control of language is a vast topic best left for other volumes. *You Can't Always Say What You Want* focuses instead on the *legal* control of language. Webster was not alone in holding contradictory, even paradoxical, views of language: on the one hand, he argued that the words Americans use create a national identity. On the other, he insisted that American English must be perfected, modified, and policed in order to bring that much-desired national identity into existence. As we'll see in the pages that follow, the connection between language and nation is at best nebulous. Even before the United States gained independence, Americans knew that their English was diverging from the British variety, and it was clear to them that their own English varied from New England to the Southern states. The British generally frowned on words perceived to be American (many still do so today). So did some Americans, though others chose to celebrate the American language, even to enshrine it in the law. Controlling what we say and write often becomes a way to protect the national identity – the brand. At least that is what supporters of official language laws contend. And laws forbidding certain kinds of speech, like swearing, threatening, or lying, enforce ideas about class, race, gender, and appropriate behavior, even though the speakers of a language may ignore or actively rebel against these norms. Despite the laws and the cajoling of parents and teachers, of employers and friends, people continue to swear and threaten one another; they still say "ain't"; they violate language taboos; and in the words of the fictional Dr. Gregory House, "Everybody lies."

*You Can't Always Say What You Want* focuses on the history of several key free speech issues: political speech, obscenity, threats, official language, and compelled speech, in order to provide some background to the current threats to free speech in the United States, with references where applicable to freedom of expression in Britain and in the European Union (EU). Although liberal democracies like these have generally expanded speech rights over the years, that is no reason to be complacent. Some laws do broaden speech protections, but others continue to chip away at these hard-won freedoms.

As we look at the laws that protect or limit speech, we'll consider as well how courts interpret statutes, particularly those laws that deal with language use. Originalism, a method popular in American legal circles today, seeks to determine what reasonable people understood the Constitution and the early laws of the United States to mean at the time they were enacted. But as we'll see, that original meaning may be difficult or impossible to recover, and so other legal scholars prefer to read a law both practically and flexibly, understanding the meaning of older laws in light of present conditions in order to achieve an outcome that promotes the common good.

Although the scope of this book is broad, there are aspects of language law that I have not had room to address. These include defamation, a topic too varied and complex to be treated here, yet one with important connections to the freedom of speech and of the press. Case in point: former vice presidential candidate Sarah Palin sued the *New York Times* for defamation, claiming that the *Times* recklessly disregarded the truth when it printed a 2017 editorial mistakenly connecting her political rhetoric with a 2011 mass shooting in Arizona, even though the newspaper quickly corrected its error. But both the judge and the jury rejected her argument that the *Times* had acted with malice, finding instead that the newspaper had made an honest mistake, which it quickly corrected.[2] She failed to convince the courts to reverse the precedent set in the 1964 Supreme Court decision in *New York Times* v. *Sullivan*, that public figures must prove in a defamation suit that damaging misinformation about them wasn't simply an honest mistake, but was instead the result of "actual malice" on the part of the writer.

Other areas I do not address include blasphemy, not a current problem in the West but one which remains an issue – sometimes a life or death issue – in many parts of the world; and commercial speech, including the laws of intellectual property and of trademark and copyright. I do not cover the expanding field of forensic linguistics either, with topics as varied as the linguistic structure of police and courtroom interrogation; the impact of the common mis-translation and mis-transcription of witness testimony or patient interviews; document verification and author identification; and the identification or exoneration of suspects or defendants through linguistic analysis of their speech or writing. In the interests of brevity, I must leave a deeper exploration of these important aspects of language law to other books and other scholars.

# Acknowledgments

First, a nod to truth in advertising: I am not a lawyer. I do not even play one on TV. But I have been writing about the history of language control and language law for over forty years, everything from spelling and grammar reforms to Constitutional interpretation; from gender pronouns to official English; from the ways that technologies of reading and writing channel the behavior of speakers and writers, to the ways that these technologies are shaped by what we say and write.

Many people and institutions provided invaluable help as I developed this book. The John Simon Guggenheim Memorial Foundation generously supported me as I drafted my manuscript, and the University of Illinois at Urbana-Champaign granted me valuable time for research and writing. Librarians and archivists at the University of Illinois, the Library of Congress, Yale University, Arizona State Library, the State Historical Society of Iowa, the Phoenix Police Museum, the Newberry Library, the Bodleian Library, the British Library, the University of Chicago Library, and the Chicago History Museum, all generously granted access to their collections, both in person and virtually, and helped me to locate important but elusive materials. Special thanks to my daughter and favorite librarian, Rachel Baron Singer, then at the University of Michigan Library, who found legal records for me that I could not locate on my own. And to my son, Jonathon Baron, who helped me access and photograph rare materials at Yale. A shout out, too, to the many students and colleagues over the last few years who have patiently listened to my musings (and a few rants) about language and law, and who have offered gentle but necessary corrections. Thanks, too, to Charles Dyke and Jeffrey Kaplan, my fellow co-conspirators writing the *Linguists' Brief* in *District of Columbia* v. *Heller* (2008), and especially to the late Richard W. Bailey, valued co-author on our brief, a no-nonsense mentor about all things linguistic, a tireless booster, and, always, a friend. Thanks, as well, to Helen Barton, at Cambridge University Press, for encouraging me in this project over the past few years; for never hesitating to tell me to revise; and for shepherding the book through production in the midst of the pandemic. And thanks as well to her able assistant, Isabel Collins, and to Laura Simmons, Lyn Flight, Santhamurthy Ramamoorthy, and all the others at the design, production, and marketing teams at Cambridge for their valiant efforts to perfect my manuscript, to design this book, and to bring it to you. An editor once told me, no book is ever finished until you find a mistake in the printed version. Reader, those mistakes I acknowledge mine.

Finally, my thanks to Iryce, my wife, for decades of unflagging encouragement and support during the many setbacks and reboots that are endemic to life, to writing, and to writing this book in particular at a time when free speech has come under stress across the political spectrum.

## CHAPTER 1

# Free Speech, But …

THE DEFENSE IN FORMER PRESIDENT Donald Trump's second impeachment relied in part on the assertion that his speech at a rally on January 6, 2021, was protected by the First Amendment.[1] Trump spoke for more than an hour to a crowd of thousands outside the White House, at a rally that he himself had been promoting for months, one that he had promised would be "wild." Trump repeated the lie that the 2020 presidential election had been stolen from him. He used the word "fight" twenty separate times. And he promised his supporters that he would march with them down Pennsylvania Avenue to the Capitol to "stop the steal."

When he finished speaking, Trump did not join the 10,000 who marched to the Capitol. And while the world watched in horror, hundreds of them broke into the Capitol building, where they attacked police, ransacked offices, and roamed the hallways looking for lawmakers to punish. They erected a makeshift gallows on the Capitol grounds. Some rioters shouted "Hang Mike Pence" as they marched through the building, a response to Trump's insistence that the vice president had been too weak to stop Congress from counting the Electoral College ballots that would confirm Joe Biden as president.

The events of January 6 have been called a riot, an insurrection, an act of domestic terrorism, or, by some of Trump's more ardent supporters keen to erase the memory, a peaceful demonstration that got a little out of hand. In the weeks and months that followed, more than 725 were charged with offenses ranging from trespass and resisting arrest to assault with a deadly weapon to seditious conspiracy, a crime which carries a maximum penalty of twenty years in prison.[†] The Capitol invasion left 7 dead, including 3 police officers, 140 officers injured, some seriously, and $1.5 million in property damage.[2] And it left this question: Did Donald Trump incite the riot that day, or were his words protected by the Constitution?

It has become common in the past few years for the American conservatives to reject any criticism of their words by invoking their freedom of speech. And they're quick to label any criticism of their positions "cancel culture," an attempt to deprive them of their First Amendment speech protections. The far right similarly rejects firearms regulations as violations of their Second Amendment right to keep and bear arms, as long as the guns in question belong to conservatives and not progressives. They defended Trump's words as peaceful and they rejected the notion that the rioters were armed, or even rioting. Although police confiscated a significant number of guns and other weapons from the invaders of the Capitol, and millions watched the riot unfold on TV, Senator Ron Johnson, of Wisconsin, told a Milwaukee radio interviewer, "This didn't seem like an armed insurrection to me."[3] Representative Andrew S. Clyde, of Georgia, went further, calling the Capitol riot a "normal tourist visit."[4] Normalizing the events still further by referring to them as constitutionally protected free speech, in February, 2022, the Republican National Committee declared the January 6 insurrectionists "ordinary citizens engaged in legitimate political discourse."[5]

District of Columbia law makes clear that the rioters' weapons did not have Second Amendment protection. But were Trump's words constitutionally protected speech? The relevant part of the First Amendment states, "Congress shall make no law … abridging the freedom of speech." It turns out that "no" in the Constitution doesn't always mean "no." As we'll see in the chapters that follow, fighting words and threats have never been

---

[†] The rarely used but serious charge of seditious conspiracy is detailed in 18 US Code § 2384: "If two or more persons in any State or Territory, or in any place subject to the jurisdiction of the United States, conspire to overthrow, put down, or to destroy by force the Government of the United States, or to levy war against them, or to oppose by force the authority thereof, or by force to prevent, hinder, or delay the execution of any law of the United States, or by force to seize, take, or possess any property of the United States contrary to the authority thereof, they shall each be fined under this title or imprisoned not more than twenty years, or both."

protected speech. And for much of American history, political speech wasn't guaranteed protection either. Criminal or seditious conspiracy are not protected. Neither is incitement to riot. The unanswered question hanging over the events of January 6 is this: Did Trump's words incite the violent acts that followed? And if they did, can he be held accountable?

Freedom of speech is never absolute. Justice Oliver Wendell Holmes said in *Schenck* v. *United States* (1919), the Supreme Court's first free-speech decision, "The most stringent protection of free speech would not protect a man in falsely shouting fire in a theatre and causing a panic." We'll look at *Schenck* in detail in Chapter 3, but in affirming the convictions of two First World War draft protestors, the *Schenck* court ruled that speech posing "a clear and present danger" to the nation can't hide behind the First Amendment.

In Trump's second impeachment, the former president's lawyers invoked two different First Amendment decisions: *Watts* v. *United States* (1969) and *Brandenburg* v. *Ohio* (1969). We'll examine both of these cases in detail later on as well, but neither case furnishes a good defense for the former president. Robert Watts, referring to then-President Lyndon Johnson, said, "If they ever make me carry a rifle the first man I want to get in my sights is LBJ." Watts wasn't about to shoot anyone – people laughed as he aimed an imaginary rifle at an imaginary Johnson. The US Supreme Court found that Watts' words, though hyperbolic and perhaps ill-chosen, posed no danger to the president. They did not cause a riot. They did not encourage anyone to harm the president, or anyone else. Instead, the Court declared that what Watts said was protected political speech, a peaceful protest against what he considered an unjust war.

*Brandenburg* also fails to protect Trump's words. Ku Klux Klan member Clarence Brandenburg invited a local TV reporter to film a "rally" of a dozen men wearing sheets in a remote Ohio field, where they burned a cross and made threats against Jews and Blacks. But the Supreme Court reversed Brandenburg's conviction because his words, though hateful, were spoken to a small group in a remote location, where they could have no broader impact. They were not likely to produce what the Court termed "imminent lawless action."

The words of Watts and Brandenburg were protected because their tiny audiences did not and could not act on what the speakers said. In

3

contrast, Trump spoke to a crowd of thousands primed for action. Many of the listeners, by their own testimony, were waiting for his command to attack an unprotected Capitol. Trump urged them to fight and told them to march. Although his lawyers insisted that Trump meant "fight" in a figurative sense, many in the crowd literally marched and they literally fought. It was textbook imminent lawless action. Trump's lawyers insisted that his speech was hyperbolic. He didn't mean for anyone to break the law. But Senate minority leader Mitch McConnell, a long-time Trump supporter, disagreed. McConnell, who had been trapped inside the Capitol by the mob, acknowledged that Trump's words were practically and morally responsible for the Capitol riot.[6]

We'll consider a speaker's intent in more detail when we look at threatening speech in Chapter 5, but for now there is lots of evidence suggesting Trump's state of mind. There is his long record of violent rhetoric in his private conversations, his public speeches, and his Twitter posts (after January 6, the social media platform blocked him). He never seemed to care when his words caused chaos or damage to individuals, to financial markets, to America's trading partners, or the nation's allies around the world, even to Americans trying to cope with the Covid-19 pandemic. At various times he told his audiences to rough up protesters and lock up his opponents. He suggested drinking bleach or trying unproven drugs to fight the coronavirus. Some people followed those instructions. And for months he had promulgated the "big lie," urging his followers to reclaim an election he insisted had been stolen from him.

All of this led up to Trump's rally in Washington on January 6 to "stop the steal," and to the riot that followed. In light of the Supreme Court's rejection, in *Terminiello v. Chicago* (1948), of the heckler's veto – banning speech because of fears that the audience might respond violently – it would appear that Trump's speech that day could not have been prevented by authorities who feared that the crowd would overreact.[7] But even if the president's words, and those of his then-attorney Rudy Giuliani and other speakers that day, were constitutionally protected, the police should have been prepared for the lawlessness that followed.

Trump himself did not engage in violence, even if he egged others on. After promising rally-goers that he would accompany them to the Capitol, he returned to the White House. There his reported actions further revealed his state of mind.[8] He was said to be delighted watching the Capitol riot on TV. He did nothing to rein in his followers, despite pleas from advisors that he intervene. He ignored warnings of danger and urgent requests for help from political allies like Senator Tommy Tuberville and House minority leader Kevin McCarthy, who, like Mitch McConnell and Vice President Pence, were trapped in the Capitol. He even encouraged the mob to go after Pence. Hours later, as police began to get things under control, Trump posted a video asking rioters to go home. But even then he repeated his charges of a stolen election and told the rioters that he loved them. In the days that followed, rioters defended their actions by saying that they were only following Trump's orders. All this suggests his intent.

As the Supreme Court acknowledged in *Watts*, political speech can be raw, rowdy, belligerent, in your face. As long as it remains speech, it enjoys First Amendment protection. But once speech is accompanied by lawless action, it is no longer protected. And in any case, freedom to speak doesn't protect speakers from the consequences of their speech. When Trump's words were directly followed by rampage, unlawful entry, property damage, injury, and death, there seems no way to give those words First Amendment cover. And the question remains for those who still insist Trump was simply exercising his right to free speech like any other American, shouldn't a president know better?

The First Amendment guarantees the right to speak. It also guarantees the right of the people *peaceably* to assemble to petition the government to redress their grievances. But the right to speak and protest doesn't mean you can stop the members of Congress from carrying out their constitutionally mandated duty to count the Electoral College ballots on January 6. Similarly, the right to keep and bear arms doesn't mean you can violate local gun laws and it certainly doesn't mean you can use weapons to assault or threaten other people.

It is a free country, to be sure, but experience and the law show that we can't always say what we want. That doesn't make free speech a myth, but it shows that the freedom to speak is never absolute. As the events of January 6 reveal, wrapping yourself in the First Amendment doesn't make what you said protected speech. And wrapping yourself in the Second Amendment doesn't mean you can strap on your guns to storm the

Capitol. Nor does it mean that you can use your right to speak and bear arms in order to silence someone else.

Two forces threaten free speech in America: people who assert their free speech rights in order to suppress the speech of others; and people who exercise their right to bear arms to silence whoever they do not like. Both forces invoke the Constitution to drown out the voices of the poor and the powerless, the very minorities whose rights the Constitution would normally guarantee. One claims that the First Amendment guarantees them a speech platform which they can use to silence their critics. The other insists that the Second Amendment guarantees their right to bring a gun to the state legislature or to a political demonstration, or even to a voting booth to silence anyone with whom they disagree. There is a third force eroding free speech as well, one I will look at briefly in my concluding chapter: the increasing erosion of our privacy that accompanies recent advances in digital technologies. These threats do not make free speech an illusion. But they do remind us that the right to speak – a right embedded in the fabric of democracy – must always be defended. And they reveal a gap between popular definitions of free speech and the legal understanding of the right to speak.

## FREEDOM OF SPEECH IS NEVER ABSOLUTE

The First Amendment reads, in part, "Congress shall make no law … abridging the freedom of speech, or of the press; or the right of the people peaceably to assemble, and to petition the government for a redress of grievances."[‡] The meaning of *no law* seems plain enough: you do not need a dictionary to tell you that *no* means "no." But in practice the First Amendment means, "Congress may make *some* laws abridging the freedom of speech." In other words, even though it is a free country, you can't always say what you want.

There are laws against all sorts of speech. Massachusetts, Michigan, Oklahoma, and Rhode Island are just some of the states with "no public

---

‡ The amendment also protects the free exercise of religion, a guarantee that merits its own study, but since my concern in this book is with language, I will address religion only when it relates to protected and unprotected *speech*.

swearing" laws currently on the books. They are not quaint holdovers from a more prudish time: the week before I drafted this paragraph a Georgia woman was jailed for cursing in an elementary school within earshot of the children.[9] Federal law makes it illegal to threaten someone on social media. And it used to be against the law in the United States to criticize the president, to protest a war, even to sing a song in a language other than English.

The First Amendment also protects Americans from compelled speech. You can't be forced to say something against your will, like the Pledge of Allegiance. But just as the government may prohibit some speech, it may also compel certain kinds of speech. If you want a government job, you can be forced to sign a loyalty oath. The Constitution requires the president to take the oath of office before assuming their duties. And police must read an arrested person their rights. The government may compel product labels and warnings. And here's an irony: the Fifth Amendment protects the right to remain silent, but in 2013 the Supreme Court ruled that a prisoner must speak in order to invoke that right to silence.[10]

In fact all sorts of laws, rules, and regulations tell us what we can and cannot say or write, and violating them may be costly:

- Criticizing the president in 1798, or writing anything false, scandalous, or malicious about the government, could mean jail time and a $2,000 fine (that's about $40,000 or £30,000 today).
- Protesting the war in 1918, or saying anything disloyal, profane, scurrilous, or abusive about the US government or its policies, could get you twenty years and $10,000 (about $160,000 or £117,500 now).
- Teach a German song in 1920 in a Nebraska private school? You'd be fined up to $100 ($1,200 or £880 today), with up to thirty days in the county lockup.
- Don't even think about traveling to New York from the Italian Riviera in 1929 with a copy of *Lady Chatterley's Lover* stashed in your luggage. You would be relieved of the racy novel at the pier, not by a pickpocket looking for a thrill but by a Customs Agent.
- Broadcast a comedy routine in 1973 about seven dirty words you can't say on the air, and the FCC might fine the offending radio station or, worse yet, revoke its license.

- Wear a jacket with an obscenity about the draft written on it inside the Los Angeles County courthouse in 1968, as Paul Robert Cohen did, and you will get sixty days for disturbing the peace.
- The US Supreme Court later reversed Cohen's conviction because his anti-war message was protected political speech, but don't even think of wearing clothing with anything political on it when you visit the Supreme Court today or you'll be fined, imprisoned for up to sixty days, or both.[11]

Although this list of don'ts is hardly exhaustive, the First Amendment does guarantee free speech, and when it comes to political speech, that guarantee is particularly robust. Today you can freely criticize a president or a war, or voice your opinion on any matter of public concern. It is legal to sing a song in Spanish, or Farsi, or Navajo. It is legal to swear on cable TV, or on the Internet. And *Lady Chatterley's Lover* is not only legal, it's got 100,000 ratings, averaging 3.5 stars, on Goodreads.

What the First Amendment does not protect is your right to speak on social media. The First Amendment only limits government attempts to regulate speech. The Constitution doesn't typically concern itself with private speech controls – the kind imposed online, as well as by employers, schools, or social and religious groups. So Donald Trump was wrong to complain in 2020 that social media was violating his free-speech rights and trying to "cancel" him by flagging some of his more misleading tweets, or when those platforms banned him for the lies he posted on January 6. Facebook and Twitter are free to regulate what users upload to their platforms. When Trump's supporters proclaimed on Fox News that they were being silenced, it was clear they still had a platform on America's most popular news network. These speakers crying "cancel culture," who've already amassed large audiences, are essentially trying to cancel their critics, who typically command much smaller audiences.

The second threat to our free-speech rights is another constitutional amendment. In 2008, the US Supreme Court ruled that the Second Amendment protects an individual's right to own a gun.[12] That led the state of Virginia to allow people to carry guns openly. And that set up a conflict between the First and Second amendments when armed protestors tried to silence counter-demonstrators at a 2017 rally in Charlottesville, Virginia.

The First Amendment says free speech may not be abridged. The Second Amendment says the right to keep and bear arms shall not be infringed. Both amendments are framed as absolutes, but in practice both are contingent: it is constitutional to abridge some speech, and some gun ownership can be regulated. Still, it is possible to invoke your right to speak in order to suppress speech with which you disagree, and as armed demonstrators in Charlottesville, Virginia, Portland, Oregon, Kenosha, Wisconsin, Lansing, Michigan, and the District of Columbia have shown, it is increasingly likely that someone with a gun can prevent you from speaking.

Self-defense and free-expression are surely essential rights. So is the right not to be shot or shouted down. No matter how rude, insulting, extreme, or unpopular it may be, speech with any degree of social value is still protected in the United States by the First Amendment. And though assault with a deadly weapon remains a crime, the Supreme Court has also determined that the Second Amendment guarantees everyone the right to tote a gun, perhaps the most common deadly weapon there is. Other countries do not follow America's lead in protecting either words or guns. The United Kingdom and the European Union value free speech, but they also criminalize racist, sexist, and hateful language. And every other modern democracy is appalled at America's determination to hang on to personal weapons, particularly those designed to inflict massive harm with minimal effort.

Although the constitutional amendments guaranteeing freedom of speech and the right to bear arms were ratified along with the rest of the Bill of Rights in 1791, the early United States was far less permissive about words or weapons than it is now. In the few nineteenth-century challenges to gun control laws, courts had no problem upholding laws that banned the possession of the kind of knives, handguns, and concealable swords frequently used, not for military ends, but for brawling, murder, and mayhem. As for the First Amendment, courts also saw no paradox between the Constitution's broad protection of speech and laws banning all sorts of speech, from profanity and obscenity to perjury and political protests. Even criticizing the president, always a popular pastime, could lead to an arrest.

The words of these amendments haven't changed, but our understanding of them has. During the twentieth century, the courts broadened what counts as speech protected by the First Amendment. In 1917, you could be fined or thrown in jail for calling Woodrow Wilson a bad name or opposing America's entry into the First World War, speech that wouldn't raise an eyebrow today. Although obscenity is still illegal, what counts as obscene has narrowed to the point where, today, you can import *Lady Chatterley* or any other book you want, as long as you do not try to sneak more than 100 ml of shampoo past airport security. And in 2008, the Supreme Court found that the Second Amendment means the opposite of what the courts had understood it to mean since 1791. Instead of supporting state militias, that amendment now guarantees the right of individual Americans to own pretty much any weapon for any lawful purpose. We looked at the January 6 riot in DC, where carrying guns is illegal. Now let's look at Charlottesville, where guns are legal. There the guarantees of the First and Second amendments clashed dramatically, and people died.

## THE AMENDMENTS MEET IN CHARLOTTESVILLE

The First Amendment guarantees the right to speak and the Second, the right to keep and bear arms. As part of the Constitution, these rights of speech and gun ownership are equal in value: one does not trump the other. But in August, 2017, when white supremacists with assault rifles marched into Charlottesville, Virginia, to hold a "free speech rally," the constitutional balance between speech and self-defense shifted, and the guns won.

Here's what happened. Under the banner "Unite the Right," Jason Kessler, a newcomer to the white supremacy movement, called on American Nazis, Klansmen, and other right-wing extremists to come to Charlottesville to protest the removal of a statue of Confederate General Robert E. Lee from Lee Park, recently renamed Emancipation Park.

Kessler applied to the Charlottesville Department of Parks and Recreation for permission to hold a "free speech rally" for about 400 people, "in support of the Lee monument."[13] But once Parks and Recreation approved the permit, Unite the Right took to social media to invite thousands of protestors to join their white supremacy crusade: "This is an event which seeks to unify the right-wing against a totalitarian Communist crackdown, to speak out against displacement level immigration policies in the United States and Europe and to affirm the right of Southerners and white people to organize for their interests just like any other group is able to do, free of persecution."[14]

Media reports suggested that more than 2,000 protestors might show up in Charlottesville for what the Southern Poverty Law Center was calling the "largest hate-gathering of its kind in decades." Many right-wing extremists announced that they would come armed (Virginia permits carrying firearms openly), and rally organizers enlisted nativist militias and motorcycle gangs to protect them from the Charlottesville "Communists" they opposed. Fearing violence and seeking to better manage the crowds of protestors and counter-protestors, the city moved the event away from centrally-located Emancipation Park, to McIntire Park, both larger and further from downtown, to facilitate crowd control. In response, Kessler, backed by the Virginia chapter of the American Civil Liberties Union (ACLU), sued Charlottesville, invoking the demonstrators' First Amendment rights to speak, assemble, and petition the government, and asking to return the rally to Emancipation Park. Demonstrators sought protection for their words, but for insurance they brought their guns to town.

On April 11, the day before the scheduled rally, the District Court granted Kessler's request. That night, neo-Nazis exercised their free speech rights by marching triumphantly through the University of Virginia campus in Charlottesville, armed with tiki torches from the local garden center, shouting antisemitic and racist slogans, and threatening anyone who got in their way. And on April 12, thousands of Unite the Right supporters, many of them waving guns and dressed in battle fatigues, rallied at Emancipation Park.

In Charlottesville, the speech of counter-protestors exercising their own right to speak and assemble proved useless against this display of right-wing firepower, and violence erupted. Normally police separate protestors from counter-protestors at rallies to minimize clashes. But Charlottesville police seemed unwilling or unable to do this. When authorities eventually declared the demonstration a threat to public safety, it took two hours to clear the park, and it took longer still for police to wrest control of downtown Charlottesville from the protestors. One marcher fired his gun into a crowd as he left the park. Another drove his car into a crowd of counter-demonstrators, killing one and injuring nineteen. And two police officers died when their surveillance helicopter crashed.

Much of the nation recoiled at the violence in Charlottesville. The day after the rally, a crowd chased Jason Kessler as he tried to hold a press conference; questions were raised about police inaction; and many public figures expressed dismay at then-President Trump for blaming the Charlottesville violence on both sides, when all accounts showed that it was Kessler's followers who carried lethal weapons and instigated the most serious incidents. For a time, the nation seemed to have had enough of racists hiding behind the Constitution. A second white supremacist "free speech" rally on Boston Common a week later drew, not the promised hordes of demonstrators, but only about fifty, enough to fit inside the Common's bandstand, while 20,000–30,000 peacefully assembled in the nation's oldest park to register their disapproval of the alt-right's racist message.

No one owns the First Amendment. Its protections extend to every side of every controversy, and free speech is a traditional rallying cry in American politics regardless of your point of view. Partisans on the right and left from Berkeley to Boston to the halls of Congress loudly assert their right to speak while blaming their opponents for trying to silence them. And many in the broad political center wonder if extreme speech of any kind really does merit constitutional protection, whether it is the speech of rabid white supremacists like Richard Spencer, who coined the term "alt-right" to sanitize the particular brand of hate speech on display in Charlottesville, or the generally anonymous "black bloc" anarchists who deny government authority. Free speech is stretched to its limits when the "speakers" carry torches or guns or chemical sprays and engage in threatening behavior.

In its lawsuit against Charlottesville, the ACLU contended that by moving the demonstration from a park directly connected to Unite the Right's message, city authorities had succumbed to the heckler's veto. In the end, there was no heckler's veto in Charlottesville, where the authorities let the white supremacists say and do pretty much whatever they wanted. But speech was chilled by the "Second Amendment veto" used by the followers of Kessler and Spencer: when there is a showdown between the First and Second amendments, the people with guns tend to silence those who are unarmed.

At another "free speech" rally forty years earlier, there was no legal way to exercise a Second Amendment veto. In 1978, American Nazis marched to support what they called "White Free Speech" in Skokie, Illinois, a city with a majority Jewish population that included a significant number of Holocaust survivors. The marchers wore Nazi uniforms, carried Nazi flags, and displayed swastikas. As in Charlottesville, they had a permit for their protest. As in Charlottesville, the courts – prompted by the ACLU – let the march go ahead. And as in Charlottesville, the courts ruled that a heckler's veto could not stop the Nazis from exercising their First Amendment rights, because even hateful and unpopular speech is protected by the Constitution. The courts reasoned that anyone offended by the marchers' message could turn away, although some of the judges apologized to the residents of Skokie for having to endure the pain and insult of a Nazi presence.[15] And so the Nazis marched legally, as they did in Charlottesville. But Illinois did not permit carrying weapons openly, and in Skokie, the Nazis did not have guns.

In Charlottesville, however, the Nazis, the Ku Klux Klan, and other white supremacists could bring their weapons to the park or carry them openly downtown, threatening anyone who might oppose their "message" of white supremacy. Emboldened by the relaxation of gun control after the 2008 *Heller* decision, right-wing protestors have exercised their Second Amendment vetoes not just in Charlottesville, but at a number of "stop the steal" demonstrations after the 2020 presidential election.[16] But even though openly carrying a gun is permitted in Virginia, brandishing one is not. State law forbids holding or waving a weapon "in such a manner as to reasonably induce fear in the mind of another of being shot or injured."[17] But it is not necessary to wave a gun in someone's face to silence them. Simply having one in your hand, on your hip, or bulging in your pocket or purse, is enough to convince most people that they are in a space where the First Amendment does not apply.

The ACLU has always opposed violence, but it has also consistently warned against allowing hecklers to silence speech. In a 1934 pamphlet urging that American Nazis be allowed to speak at New York City's Madison Square Garden despite the fear of violence at their rallies, the organization outlined the position it would later take in *Kessler* v. *City of Charlottesville*:

> To those who urge suppression of meetings that may incite riot or vio-
> lence, the complete answer is that nobody can tell in advance what meet-
> ings may do so. Where there is reasonable ground for apprehension, the
> police can ordinarily prevent disorder ... If and when Nazi meetings result
> in breaches of the peace, their organizers can be prosecuted under the
> criminal law ... Short of that, their freedom to carry on their agitation
> should be unrestricted.[18]

That was an unpopular position to take at a time when violence had become a regular feature of Nazi rallies in Germany, violence that would result in the murder of millions of Jews and others on the streets and in death camps, not to mention the slaughter on the battlefields of the Second World War.

Two days after Charlottesville, the Virginia ACLU similarly insisted, "Our lawsuit challenging the city to act constitutionally did not cause violence." Later, the organization argued that they could not have foreseen that violence because, before they agreed to take his case, they made Jason Kessler swear "in court papers that he intended the rally to be 'peaceful' and 'avoid violence,'"[19] a statement that suggests the defenders of free speech were well aware that Kessler and his crowd were spoiling for a fight. In that 1934 pamphlet, the ACLU defended its controversial position: "We do not choose our clients. Lawless authorities denying their rights choose them for us." Similarly, the Virginia ACLU insisted that they defended Unite the Right only because the government illegally interfered with the protestors' right to speak. But the ACLU has never felt bound to accept every free-speech case that comes its way. Just five days after Charlottesville, ACLU Executive Director Anthony Romero announced that the organization would no longer back the speech rights of "hate groups seeking to march with firearms" and that in the future, it would screen its clients more carefully "for the potential of violence at their rallies."[20]

The events of Charlottesville raise two important questions:

1. When does the right to bear arms conflict with the right to speak one's mind?
2. When do words cross a line from protected to unprotected speech?

To answer these questions requires us to understand how courts go about interpreting our laws. We will start by looking at how the Second Amendment right to bear arms has been interpreted from its first draft, in 1789, until the Supreme Court determined in 2008 the meaning that paved the way for First and Second amendment showdowns. The Second Amendment consists of a single, twenty-seven word sentence. Seeing how judges have moved from one understanding of that sentence to its opposite offers a lesson in legal meaning-making. And that, in turn, will lead us to the main focus of *You Can't Always Say What You Want*: the many attempts to define and limit the right to speak and write.

We will see that there is an ever-shifting line between protected and unprotected speech for political speech, obscene speech, and threatening speech which can leave speakers at a loss to know when they've crossed that line. Each attempt to separate protected from unprotected speech solves some problems but raises new ones. That is true of many legal landmarks. *District of Columbia* v. *Heller* affirmed an individual right to own weapons, but it did not address whether states can ban guns at protests and rallies. Instead, the *Heller* court suggested that there are many "sensitive" places where guns may be prohibited, like courtrooms, schools, or government buildings – even after *Heller*, you still can't bring weapons into the Supreme Court. But *Heller* did not say anything about keeping guns out of bars or sports arenas, where spirits often run high. As a result, states vary on what they will or will not permit: Maryland and Alabama ban guns at rallies and demonstrations, but Virginia does not.[21] It remains to be seen how American courts will treat attempts to restore a balance between the right to speak and the right to bear arms, but it is clear that Charlottesville has raised an issue that *Heller* did not foresee, an issue that is not going to go away anytime soon. In 1919, the Supreme Court observed that the First Amendment would never protect someone falsely shouting "fire!" in a theater and causing a panic. After Charlottesville, it is time to recognize that bearing arms at a political protest is a similar recipe for disaster that should not be permitted under any interpretation of the Second Amendment.

## A MATTER OF INTERPRETATION

To recap, both the First and Second amendments are framed as absolutes: "Congress *shall make no law* ... abridging the freedom of speech"; and "the right of the people to keep and bear arms, *shall not be infringed*." Even so, the courts always interpret these rights as relative: there are some words and weapons that remain outside the law. Obscene speech, threats, and fighting words are not included in the First Amendment's broad protections. Nineteenth-century courts found that the Second Amendment did not guarantee the right to own a Bowie knife (sometimes called an Arkansas toothpick) or a sword in a cane, and no modern court would protect your right keep and bear a rocket-propelled grenade or an improvised explosive device. Figuring out which words and weapons are OK and which are unprotected requires reading between the lines, reading what Akhil Reed Amar calls "America's unwritten Constitution."[22]

Interpreting the law – finding what it allows or prohibits – is not always easy, but it is always necessary, and it is a never-ending process. The Supreme Court has repeatedly modified its understanding of the First Amendment to shift the line between protected and unprotected speech, and it has even modified its 2008 spin on the Second Amendment, striking down some gun regulations but permitting others to stand.[23] Current events suggest that the Court may eventually be asked to consider what happens when the two amendments clash, as they did in Charlottesville in 2017, or when armed protestors marched on the Michigan State House to protest the public-health lockdown in 2020. Not to mention January 6. That will require revisiting many previous interpretations of speech and arms protections.

Understanding laws, like understanding anything spoken or written, is both subjective and subject to revision. Even so, the law remains a coherent system that is both stable enough to function well at any given point in time, while flexible enough to meet new demands and circumstances.

Any system dependent on interpretation presents the possibility of multiple meanings, some of them inconsistent with others. This may lead to misunderstanding and disagreement. In some contexts we tolerate this ambiguity. For example, it is easy for us to accept competing interpretations of literature because there is no easy way to know what Hamlet means when he asks, "To be or not to be?" Competing interpretations of sacred texts are common, too, though disagreement over the tenets of a faith can result in new sects, new religions, even holy wars.

In contrast, we expect consistency from the law: its meaning should be clear and constant and it should apply equally to all. And yet conflict over legal meaning is also normal. Lawyers contest everything from the broad application of a statute, to the significance of a word in a contract, to the second comma in the Second Amendment. And they routinely argue over the definition of a word in a law. In 1893, for example, the Supreme Court was asked to decide whether tomatoes should be defined as fruits or vegetables so an importer could pay the appropriate tariff. The court ruled that tomatoes were vegetables because, even though scientists classified them as fruits, ordinary people thought tomatoes were vegetables.[24] But ordinary meaning is not always obvious. In *Heller*, the Supreme Court ruled that the phrase *bear arms* in the Second Amendment ordinarily means, "carry a gun" and has nothing to do with soldiering, even though pretty much everyone since the 1790s considered the phrase to be military. Even today, soldiers bear arms; hunters carry guns; criminals pack heat.

It turns out that law, like every other form of language, is never absolute, never wholly unambiguous, never completely transparent or explicit. Like all forms of language, laws require interpretation, and interpretations are subject to challenge and reinterpretation. When Judge Learned Hand wrote, "It will be necessary, first, to interpret the law," he was explaining a section of the 1917 Espionage Act that criminalized antiwar protest. But he was also saying that a law doesn't have meaning until a court interprets it. Complicating this is the fact that there are many ways to read a law – strictly, loosely, pragmatically, ideologically. They do not all produce the same results, and no single approach, or combination of approaches, is required. Judge Hand found that the Espionage Act protected antiwar protests, but his interpretation, which we will look at in more detail in Chapter 3, was immediately rejected by an appeals court that saw nothing wrong with suppressing speech in wartime. But attitudes change, and courts today would be more likely to agree with Hand that the First Amendment permits nonviolent opposition to a war.

The ongoing cycle of interpretation and reinterpretation and the conflicting methods of legal interpretation do not make the law hopelessly relative or perilously unstable. Rather, they are a normal part of how law functions. The stability of law depends not on its words, not even on choosing the one right method of legal interpretation, but on the willingness of society to be bound by law, to accept legal interpretation, to acknowledge the need to challenge an interpretation from time to time, and to accept the idea that when things change, interpretations may have to be modified or even rethought completely to accommodate new circumstances. If we didn't reinterpret the law, or replace old laws with new ones, we would still be living under slavery, women could not vote, and no one would have the right to remain silent.

Even the framers recognized that we must live with laws whose meaning is not always easy to uncover. James Madison responded to complaints that the proposed Constitution for the new United States was not clear enough by comparing law to scripture. Madison argued that the deity's ideas are perfectly straightforward, but we poor mortals, prone to error and misreading, come along and muddy the text. If religion seems hard, he concluded, then interpreting law is even harder: people write the law, not gods, and language itself is not always up to the job of conveying complex ideas.[25]

There will always be laws that were not written as precisely or with as much foresight as they should have been, if only because writers are human, and they – we – all make mistakes. There will always be instances where the application of a law will be contested, where the meaning of its words will be disputed. Some 6 percent of early Supreme Court decisions were not unanimous, a sign that founding-era judges disagreed about statutory meaning from the outset. The framers themselves argued over the Constitution's meaning, not only while they were drafting it, but immediately after it was ratified as well. Jefferson and Hamilton disagreed about whether or not the Constitution authorized a federal bank.

Madison and Jefferson disagreed with John Adams about the constitutionality of the 1798 Sedition Act.[26] If these learned patriots had different understandings of the founding document that they had debated, drafted, and edited till they got the text just right, then as Madison might put it, mere mortals like us shouldn't be surprised that we, too, contest its meanings.

## "WHEN *I* USE A WORD, IT MEANS JUST WHAT I CHOOSE IT TO MEAN – NEITHER MORE NOR LESS"

That is how Humpty Dumpty defines interpretation in Lewis Carroll's *Through the Looking Glass*. We all have opinions about what a law means, but it is the courts that get to prescribe meaning. Why laws need interpretation, and why judges should be the ones to do this, was articulated as long ago as the sixteenth century. Edward Saunders, a sergeant-at-law (the equivalent of a Queen's Counsel in England today), observed in the case of *Partridge* v. *Straunge and Croker* (1553) what Madison later echoed in *Federalist* 46, that laws may indeed be unclear. According to Saunders, the words of a statute are but sounds – he called them "the verberation of the air." The words, mere images of the law, have no meaning until they are interpreted, and according to Saunders this must be done in a way that brings the greatest benefit to society:

> If the words of [a statute] are obscure, they shall ... be expounded most strongly for the public good. For words, which are no other than the verberation of the air, do not constitute the statute, but are only the image of it, and the life of the statute rests in the minds of the expositors of the words, that is, the makers of the statutes. And if they are dispersed, so that their minds cannot be known, then those who may approach nearest to their minds shall construe the words, and these are the sages of the law, whose talents are exercised in the study of such matters.[27]

Interpretation is necessary to recover the law's true meaning, its spirit. And that spirit, says Saunders, will ensure the public good. For Saunders, here's how to interpret a law whose meaning isn't clear. First, ask the legislators who wrote the laws exactly what they meant. When that is not possible – they may be dead or otherwise unavailable – then get judges to "construe the words," because that is what these sages of the law are trained to do.

As we will see in more detail in the next chapter, American constitutional interpretation falls into two broad schools: originalists seek to determine the document's original public meaning: what a reasonable person would have understood the Constitution to mean at the time that it was enacted. On the other side are those who see the Constitution, not as a "suicide pact" forcing us to do something harmful and destructive, but as a living document flexible enough to adapt to changing circumstances, and they seek a practical interpretation that benefits the public good today. In any case, most modern commentators agree with the general position of Sergeant Saunders, that when it comes to legal meaning, the letter of the law is just the beginning. As legal scholars William Baude and Stephen Sachs put it, "In legal interpretation we start with written words and somehow end up with law. The question is what happens in between."[28]

Understanding the spirit of the law, what its words are actually saying, comes only from "what happens in between," an act of interpretation. Few of us get to draft the laws which govern us, and few of us get to serve as judges. But in some way, we are all interpreters of the law. The relationship between words and the law is debated regularly in the press, on social media, and at the dinner table. These discussions cover topics of broad interest: Should a book like that be in a library? What does "marriage" mean? Could a Facebook post get you arrested? Can't we make everyone speak English?

Even when such questions are "settled" by the courts, they continue to resonate. Because who may marry, carry a gun, read a book, or get locked up for tweeting, remains a matter of public interest and may affect us personally, it is vital that we understand how judges read the language of the law. Their interpretations create the legal authority that, in turn, governs the language that we use, specifying who may speak and who may be punished for speech; what may be published and what censored. Laws may even tell us what to say, and whether we have to say it in English.

The goal of *You Can't Always Say What You Want* is to help readers understand these two important, frequently interconnected acts – how judges parse the words of a statute and how statutes regulate language by sorting protected from unprotected speech. Grounded in linguistics, history, and legal analysis, the book places contemporary issues of free speech and banned speech in their historical perspective, illuminating how judges figure out what the law says, then explaining how the law shapes and limits what we can say. We will look at subversive language, strong language, angry language, foreign language, and required language, to illustrate two ways that we interpret the language of the law. We do so ideologically, to force the law to conform to our sense of what it should mean, whether that sense is liberal, conservative, or something in between; and we do so through linguistic analysis, determining how the words, phrases, clauses, and sentences of the law work together to generate meaning. Whether we are talking about strict construction, the conservative philosophy that laws mean only what they meant when they were enacted, or a pragmatic, results-oriented philosophy, the liberal view that laws must be adapted sensibly to accommodate unforeseen conditions and changing circumstances, we are interpreting laws to make the words – the verberation of the air – fit the case at hand.

This doesn't make the law unreliable, and it should not cause anyone to lose faith in the legal system or in our freedom to think as we will and to say what we think. Instead, it should broaden our insight and deepen our understanding of just how the law really works: practical interpretation within a larger framework of tradition leavened by changing circumstance. That is what I hope to show as we look at the shifts over time in our understanding of how laws mediate what we can and cannot say and write.

The conflicts over legal interpretation that I will discuss in the following pages reveal a fundamental paradox: we demand stability from the law in ways that set it apart from other forms of language use, but legal authority depends on interpretation, an act that is always subjective, contingent, continually evolving. The meaning of any text or utterance is constructed not just from its words, but also through exchanges between speakers and hearers, writers and readers. In addition, although the decisions of judges may seem final, court rulings frequently require further interpretation, sometimes revision, occasionally, reversal. This should not be surprising, for it is how all language works: understanding text is always a matter of interpretation, and no interpretation is ever final.

## CHAPTER 2

# Guns and Grammar

A man in the pursuit of deer, elk and buffaloes, might carry his rifle every day, for forty years, and, yet, it would never be said of him, that he had *borne arms*, much less could it be said, that a private citizen *bears arms*, because he has a dirk or pistol concealed under his clothes, or a spear in a cane.

*Aymette* v. *State of Tennessee*, 1840

The First Amendment didn't clash with the Second in Skokie in 1978, but it did in Charlottesville in 2017. That is because the white supremacists who came to Charlottesville carried guns. In *District of Columbia* v. *Heller* (2008), the Supreme Court defined the meaning of the right to keep and bear arms for the first time, and that definition, which protected an individual's right to carry a gun, led the state of Virginia to permit people to carry guns openly in public.§ The presence of those weapons threatened public safety and left the speech of anyone without a weapon unprotected.

---

§ When an appeals court ruled that the District of Columbia's decades-old ban on handguns violated the Second Amendment, the District's Attorney General asked me to support their appeal to the Supreme Court by writing an amicus brief explaining the structure and meaning of the amendment at the time that it was ratified, in 1791. The linguists Richard W. Bailey and Jeffrey Kaplan joined me, and the attorney Charles Dyke assisted in drafting the brief. Opponents of the gun ban presented their own grammatical analysis to support their claims. Although this chapter has its origins in what the Supreme Court called "the Linguists' Brief," and the *Heller* decision turned on more than linguistic arguments, I offer here a broader, retrospective analysis of the way in which the courts interpreted the language of the Second Amendment as they established the legal meaning that set up a potential conflict with the First Amendment. I add as well some important updates to our understanding of the meanings of *keep arms* and *bear arms* that were not readily available when *Heller* was decided in 2008.

The Second Amendment reads, "A well regulated Militia, being necessary to the security of a free State, the right of the people to keep and bear Arms, shall not be infringed." It presents a case of dueling meanings, guaranteeing either a collective right of the American people to maintain armed militias, or the individual right of every American to carry a weapon. In *Heller*, the Supreme Court examined the amendment's structure, a complex sentence introduced by an absolute clause. The Court looked as well at its most-disputed words, *militia* and *the people*. And it determined the meaning of its central phrase, *the right to keep and bear arms*.

For two centuries after the ratification of the Bill of Rights, the wording of the Second Amendment was not problematic. Courts generally assumed that it guaranteed the right of the states to arm militias. But 217 years after ratification, the Supreme Court decided that its original, plain, and public meaning guaranteed the right of individuals to own a gun. The shift from the earlier view that the amendment guaranteed a collective right to weapons for community defense, to the current one, that the amendment guarantees an individual right for personal self-defense, demonstrates that legal meaning-making, like interpretation in general, is a contingent, subjective, evolving, and sometimes contentious process, particularly when guns are involved. And sometimes that process of interpretation seems remarkably distanced from the facts.

In *Heller*, a majority of the justices found that the first part of the amendment, the militia clause, could be ignored. In addition, those justices found that the phrase *bear arms* is not limited to military contexts: it simply means "carry a gun."[1] Both of these readings are problematic, and because for much of this book we will be looking at how courts interpret the language of the law and how specific laws control what we can and cannot say and write, analyzing how the Supreme Court came to its decision in *Heller* offers an important insight into how courts determine legal meaning, and how that meaning impacts our lives. It also seems a perfect way to begin this study of the paradox of free speech.

## THE MILITIA CLAUSE AND BEARING ARMS

A well regulated Militia, being necessary to the security of a free State, the right of the people to keep and bear Arms, shall not be infringed.

The first words of the Second Amendment, called the militia clause, offer the amendment's rationale. No other constitutional amendment begins with a justification, and as the House and Senate revised the amendment over several weeks in the summer of 1789, the militia clause persisted from the first draft to the sixth and final version, the one that was passed by Congress and sent to the states for ratification. The persistence of the clause through multiple drafts suggests that the framers wanted us to pay attention to it. As for the phrase *bear arms*, Justice Scalia wrote in his *Heller* opinion that founding-era sources used the words unambiguously "to refer to the carrying of weapons outside of an organized militia." That is simply not the case. The epigraph to this chapter, from an 1840 Tennessee Supreme Court case about the right to bear arms, clearly states that the idiomatic phrase *bear arms* has nothing to do with hunting or self-defense. In addition, a review of several large databases of eighteenth- and nineteenth-century texts that were not readily available to the *Heller* court in 2008 shows that at the time that the Second Amendment was being drafted, the plain, ordinary, common, natural, and original meaning of *bear arms* was "carrying weapons in war" in connection with military service, or in other forms of organized group offense, defense, or rebellion.[2]

By discounting the militia clause and redefining the meaning of *bear arms*, the Court rejected the position that most earlier courts had taken on the Second Amendment. Take *Aymette*, for example. A nineteenth-century Tennessee law made it a misdemeanor for a person to wear, "any bowie knife, or Arkansas tooth-pick, or other knife or weapon ... under his clothes, or keep the same concealed about his person." In 1840, William Aymette was convicted of carrying a concealed Bowie knife. Aymette appealed, arguing that the state's weapons ban violated his right to keep and bear arms, as guaranteed by the state constitution. But the Tennessee Supreme Court found that the amendment referred only to military weapons, not those used for private self-defense or criminal activity.[3]

In his ruling, Judge Nathan Green observed that the phrase *bear arms* could never describe a hunter, let alone a private citizen with a hidden "dirk or pistol":

A man in the pursuit of deer, elk and buffaloes, might carry his rifle every day, for forty years, and, yet, it would never be said of him, that he had *borne arms*, much less could it be said, that a private citizen *bears arms*, because he has a dirk or pistol concealed under his clothes, or a spear in a cane.

Green went on to specify with some energy that although the Second Amendment permits weapons useful for the militia, it does not permit Tennessee residents to own *personal* weapons which are easily turned to crime and violence:

They need not, for such a purpose, the use of those weapons which are usually employed in private broils, and which are efficient only in the hands of the robber and the assassin. These weapons would be useless in war. They could not be employed advantageously in the common defence of the citizens. The right to keep and bear them, is not, therefore, secured by the [Tennessee] constitution ... The legislature, therefore, have a right to prohibit the wearing, or keeping weapons dangerous to the peace and safety of the citizens, and which are *not* usual in civilized warfare, or would not contribute to the common defence.

Texas had a similar weapons ban and, in 1872, when William English asked the Texas Supreme Court to reverse his conviction for carrying a pistol while intoxicated, Judge Moses B. Walker observed that "the 'arms' referred to in the second amendment to the United States constitution are the arms of a militiaman or soldier," and not "the deadly weapons spoken of in the statute ... pistols, dirks, daggers, slungshots, sword-canes, spears, brass-knuckles and bowie knives. Can it be understood that these were contemplated by the framers of our bill of rights? Most of them are the wicked devices of modern craft."[4] Walker continued in the same tone:

To refer the deadly devices and instruments called in the statute "deadly weapons," to the proper or necessary arms of a "well-regulated militia," is simply ridiculous. No kind of travesty, however subtle or ingenious, could so misconstrue this provision of the constitution of the United States, as to make it cover and protect that pernicious vice, from which so many murders, assassinations, and deadly assaults sprung, and which it was doubtless the intention of the legislature to punish and prohibit.

One early Second Amendment case reached a different conclusion. In 1846, in *Nunn* v. *State*, Georgia Chief Justice Joseph Henry Lumpkin found that the amendment's words mean exactly what they say: "The right of the whole people, old and young, men, women and boys, and not militia only, to keep and bear arms of every description, not merely as are used by the militia, shall not be infringed, curtailed, or broken in upon, in the smallest degree."[5]

*Nunn* was an outlier. Even *Heller*, affirming an individual right to own weapons, did not consider that right absolute. And as we will see repeatedly, even though the First Amendment begins, "Congress shall make no law abridging the freedom of speech," courts have not considered speech protections to be absolute either. More consistent with pre-*Heller* judicial interpretation was *Andrews* v. *State* (1871), in which the Tennessee Supreme Court picked up where it left off in *Aymette*. In *Andrews*, Judge Thomas J. Freeman noted that no state could ban weapons that served the dual purpose of self-defense and national defense, but the state was free to regulate weapons not useful for war "for the public good … with a view to prevent crime."[6] Freeman thought it was fine to ban the handguns, swords, and knives popular with criminals. Like Judge Walker before him, Freeman laced his opinion with the kind of rhetorical flourishes that accompany a number of Second Amendment cases, including *Heller*, where passions on both sides run high:

> No man can be permitted … to gratify his whim or willful desire to use a particular weapon in his particular self-defense. The law allows ample means of self-defense, without the use of the weapons which we have held may be rightfully proscribed by this statute. The object being to banish these weapons from the community by an absolute prohibition for the prevention of crime, no man's particular safety, if such case could exist, ought to be allowed to defeat this end. Mutual sacrifice of individual rights is the bond of all social organizations, and prompt and willing obedience to all laws passed for the general good, is not only the duty, but the highest interest of every man in the land.

The view that banning the weapons of crime was both constitutional and necessary for the public good persisted into the twentieth century.

Although the Supreme Court did not explicitly interpret the Second Amendment in *United States* v. *Miller* (1939), it did find that a federal ban on sawed-off shotguns was constitutional because soldiers did not use them, only mobsters did.[7] The central figure in that case, Jack Miller, could have stepped right out of a 1930's gangster film. He was a getaway driver and general all-around hoodlum turned FBI snitch.[8] Miller had been convicted of transporting an unregistered sawed-off shotgun across state lines in violation of federal law. He appealed, claiming that the National Firearms Act, passed in 1934 in response to a wave of high-profile mob killings like the St. Valentine's Day massacre, conflicted with his Second Amendment right to keep and bear arms. An appeals court agreed, reversing Miller's conviction. The government appealed that decision, and while the Supreme Court was considering the case, Miller disappeared. At his criminal trial, Miller had testified against the rest of his gang, and a month after his bullet-riddled body turned up in an Oklahoma field, the Supreme Court reinstated Miller's conviction. True, Miller's sentence now had to be limited to time served, but the Court felt the need to affirm the constitutionality of the Firearms Act:

> In the absence of any evidence tending to show that possession or use of a "shotgun having a barrel of less than eighteen inches in length" at this time has some reasonable relationship to the preservation or efficiency of a well regulated militia, we cannot say that the Second Amendment guarantees the right to keep and bear such an instrument. Certainly it is not within judicial notice that this weapon is in any part of the ordinary military equipment, or that its use could contribute to the common defense ... With obvious purpose to assure the continuation and render possible the effectiveness of [the militia], the declaration and guarantee of the Second Amendment were made. It must be interpreted and applied with that end in view.

Toward the end of the twentieth century, however, the National Rifle Association (NRA) promoted a new strand of legal thinking, the individual rights model, which discounted the militia clause and argued that the Second Amendment had just one guarantee, that "the right of the people to keep and bear Arms, shall not be infringed." Judge William

Garwood reinforced this individual rights interpretation in a supplement to his opinion in *United States* v. *Emerson* (2001),[9] and the US Department of Justice quickly adopted Garwood's interpretation as the original, plain meaning of the amendment.[10] These actions set up a conflict with the earlier collective defense model, prompting Judge Stephen Reinhardt, of the Ninth Circuit Court of Appeals, to declare in *Silveira* v. *Lockyer* (2002) that the Second Amendment's text was ambiguous, and that its plain meaning was not plain at all.[11]

After examining the amendment's language and its legal history, Reinhardt opted for the traditional, collective rights interpretation. In contrast, Judge Laurence H. Silberman, of the District of Columbia Circuit Court of Appeals, adopted the NRA's interpretation in his opinion in *Parker et al.* v. *District of Columbia* (2007), the case that would eventually reach the Supreme Court as *Heller*. Throwing out the District's ban on handguns, Silberman argued that the "preambulatory" militia clause was grammatically independent from the amendment's operative main clause, that the need for a well-regulated militia has nothing at all to do with a citizen's right to keep and bear arms.[12]

One of the roles of the Supreme Court is to resolve conflicting interpretations of the Constitution. The clash between the Ninth Circuit and the DC Circuit over the Second Amendment's meaning let the Supreme Court step in and resolve the dispute. In its decision in *Heller*, a divided Court adopted the new individual rights reading, insisting that this was, in fact, the amendment's original meaning. The Court disconnected the two halves of the amendment, explaining that the militia clause, which furnishes a rationale for the operative clause, cannot limit the scope of the right to keep and bear arms. In other words, the militia clause is there; it just doesn't count. What the Court said in *Heller* is that the Constitution guarantees the right to own all sorts of weapons for self-defense, hunting, and sport, or any other lawful purpose. And that made it possible to carry guns at protest marches in Virginia, where the presence of weapons all but guaranteed unlawful violence and suppression of speech. It is clear, however, that the framers always intended the Second Amendment to be read as a whole, and they knew that *bear arms* meant "to carry weapons for an organized, military purpose."

## WHAT DID THE FRAMERS MEAN?

We must interpret the Second Amendment in the final form that was ratified by the states, but given its conflicting readings, looking at how Congress revised the amendment's wording from James Madison's proposal on July 8, 1789, until it was presented to the states for ratification in September of that year, confirms the significance of the militia clause and reinforces the military meaning of *bear arms*. Here's Madison's original wording:

> The right of the people to keep and bear arms shall not be infringed; a well armed and well regulated militia being the best security of a free country: but no person religiously scrupulous of bearing arms shall be compelled to render military service in person.[13]

As Madison's version made its way through the House and Senate, text was added, rearranged, and removed (see Table 2.1). Although the record of the Congressional debate is sparse, we can see from the clearly documented chain of revisions that a few minor edits resolved unnecessary repetition, but two rewrites actually changed the amendment's structure. Madison's original had the militia clause in second place. In the first revision, a House select committee moved the militia clause to the front of the amendment, making it more noticeable. The militia clause kept its initial position through four more revisions, a sign that Congress intended it to inform our understanding of the right to bear arms.

Madison's first draft also had a final clause explicitly exempting conscientious objectors from bearing arms for military service. That clause, with its unmistakable military context, was also revised several times to clarify its wording, but on August 17, Representative Egbert Benson, of New York, moved to strike it, arguing that "this humane provision should be left to the wisdom and benevolence of the government. It [is] improper to make it a fundamental in the constitution." The House rejected Benson's motion, 22:24, but strong sentiment against the conscientious objector provision in particular, plus a sense that specific exemptions from military service should be left to the states, may be why two weeks later in version 5, the Senate dropped the measure protecting Quakers. A sixth

**Table 2.1** The six versions of what would become the Second Amendment

| Versions of the Second Amendment |
| --- |
| 1. The right of the people to keep and bear arms shall not be infringed; a well-armed and well-regulated militia being the best security of a free country: but no person religiously scrupulous of bearing arms shall be compelled to render military service in person.<br>[Madison's original draft, presented to the House on July 8, 1789.] |
| 2. A well-regulated militia, composed of the body of the people, being the best security of a free State, the right of the people to keep and bear arms shall not be infringed, but no person religiously scrupulous shall be compelled to bear arms.<br>[Version in the report of the House select committee, July 28.] |
| 3. A well-regulated militia, composed of the body of the people, being the best security of a free State, the right of the people to keep and bear arms shall not be infringed, but no person religiously scrupulous shall be compelled to bear arms in person.<br>[House version approved August 20.] |
| 4. A well-regulated militia, composed of the body of the People, being the best security of a free State, the right of the People to keep and bear arms, shall not be infringed, but no one scrupulous of bearing arms, shall be compelled to render military service in person.<br>[Version approved by House and Senate, August 24.] |
| 5. A well-regulated militia, being the best security of a free state, the right of the people to keep and bear arms, shall not be infringed.<br>[Senate version, September 4; Senate debates were secret.] |
| 6. A well-regulated militia, being necessary to the security of a free state, the right of the people to keep and bear arms, shall not be infringed.<br>[Approved by the House and Senate, September 9, 1789, and sent to the states for ratification.] |

and final Senate version sharpened the wording of the militia clause – why bother if it wasn't important? – and a few days after that, the House approved the final text that we now know as the Second Amendment.[14]

## THE MEANING OF *BEAR ARMS*

In his opinion in *Heller,* Justice Scalia stated that the natural meaning of *bear arms* is simply, "carry a weapon" – it has nothing at all to do with armies. According to Scalia, only the phrase *bear arms against* is military. But that is clearly wrong. Madison's original draft of the Second Amendment uses the unmodified *bear arms* twice: "The right of the people to keep and *bear arms* shall not be infringed," and "no person religiously scrupulous of *bearing arms* shall be compelled to render military service in person." In the first revision, the latter phrase becomes "no person religiously scrupulous shall be compelled to bear arms." The third and fourth drafts have, "no person religiously scrupulous shall be compelled to bear arms in person." At the last minute, Congress dropped the conscientious objector clause, but the military sense of *bear arms* in the remaining text is inescapable. That is because nonmilitary uses of *bear arms* – not just *bear arms against* – are not just rare in the founding era, they're virtually nonexistent. Searching new linguistic databases not available to the *Heller* court yields dramatic results. Of the 281 instances of *bear arms* in the Corpus of Founding Era American English (COFEA), and the 1,572 instances in the Corpus of Early Modern English (COEME), only a handful are not clearly military.[15] Critics object that the texts collected in COFEA and COEME do not represent the ordinary meanings of words and phrases because they did not address ordinary readers. But newspapers, which do address ordinary readers, confirm the data from the other corpora. Ordinary people in the late eighteenth century, both in the United States and in England, got news of the American Revolution, the Declaration of Independence, the Constitution, and the amendments to the Constitution that formed the Bill of Rights, from newspapers. An additional search for instances of *bear arms* from 1700 to 1800 in five digitized newspaper databases confirms that the phrase rarely appears outside of a clearly military context.[16]

But we should not need big data to tell us this. "Bear arms" has never fit comfortably with the language of personal self-defense, hunting, or target practice. Writing about the Second Amendment in 1995, the historian Garry Wills, echoing *Aymette*, put it succinctly: "One does not bear arms against a rabbit."[17] But that is not all. During oral arguments in *Heller*, Solicitor General Paul Clement claimed that *bear arms* means "to carry them outside the home." Justice David Souter challenged this: "But wait a minute. You're not saying that if somebody goes hunting deer he is bearing arms, or are you?" Clement replied, "I would say that and so would Madison and so would Jefferson." Souter was not convinced: "In the eighteenth century, someone going out to hunt a deer would have thought of themselves as bearing arms? I mean, is that the way they talk?" Clement finally conceded that no, that was not the way they talked: "Well, I will grant you this, that 'bear arms' in its unmodified form is most naturally understood to have a military context."[18] Souter did not need to point out the obvious: "bear arms" appears in its unmodified form in the Second Amendment.

*Bear arms* is a common phrase compared with *keep arms*, which only occurs about twenty-five times in founding-era sources, but even then, its connotation is primarily military. To be fair, though, the Second Amendment protects the right "to keep and bear arms," a combination of words that does not seem to occur before Madison used it in the amendment. It is not clear whether Madison intended *keep arms* and *bear arms* to mean different things, or whether he felt that *keep* and *bear* would reinforce one another, much like other commonly paired words in legal discourse, such as *on or about, cease and desist, assault and battery,* or *breaking and entering* (yes, there are fine legal distinctions between the terms of each pair, but their goal seems to be to eliminate loopholes, and so they function as if they were synonyms). Both sides in *Heller* tried to explain the odd pairing of *keep* and *bear,* frankly without much success, but despite the conclusions in *Heller, keep and bear arms* remains one of those problematic legal phrases that should have been clarified *before* it was put into the Constitution.

### *HELLER* AND LEGAL INTERPRETATION

Here, again, is the text of the Second Amendment:

> A well-regulated Militia, being necessary to the security of a free State, the right of the people to keep and bear Arms, shall not be infringed.

The Supreme Court started with these twenty-seven words and wound up with law. What changed to prompt a shift away from the collective rights interpretation? Why did the courts, and perhaps the national mood, swing from reading the Second Amendment as bolstering a collective right to arm a militia for the defense of the community, to something quite opposite, the individual right to carry a gun? Certainly, our understanding of the language of other parts of the Constitution has shifted drastically over time. Slavery, once legal, was finally barred. Voting rights that were initially reserved for men eventually extended to women as well. Some of this was done by Constitutional amendment, some by statute, some by new interpretations of existing law. For example, the First Amendment guarantees free speech, but through reinterpretation, the legal boundaries between protected and unprotected speech have shifted drastically over the past century. Rights have even been read into the Constitution – like the right to privacy – that appear nowhere in the text.

The Second Amendment, like any other document, legal, literary, religious, commercial, or personal, is not understood through its words alone. Even the most literal interpretations of the Constitution are conditioned by reading between the lines. Interpretation always feeds on experience and assumptions, many of them shared, some of them subjective, some even idiosyncratic. What changed specifically with the reinterpretation of the Second Amendment was a mood – encouraged by the arguments and political clout of the pro-gun NRA – a growing sense of paranoia in the nation, a fear of crime, a fear of terrorism, even a fear of the government itself. This may not be a majority view. The public response to the growing number of mass shootings favors gun control. Even so, a poll taken a few months before the Supreme Court's *Heller* decision indicated that close to 75 percent of Americans already thought that the Constitution guaranteed an individual's right own a gun.[19]

In *Heller*, the Supreme Court ruled that Washington, DC, could not impose a total ban on handguns, because Americans have an inherent right to self-defense, and handguns are currently their self-defense weapon of choice. But, like the right to privacy, the right to self-defense is never explicitly mentioned in the Constitution, and *Heller*'s interpretation of the right to bear arms resolved only some of the Second Amendment's ambiguity. The Court did not rule out all gun restrictions, only total bans on handguns. As Justice Scalia put it, "We do not read the Second Amendment to protect the right of citizens to carry arms for any sort of confrontation, just as we do not read the First Amendment to protect the right of citizens to speak for any purpose."[20]

To find the meaning of the Second Amendment's words, the Supreme Court considered evidence from the dictionaries and grammar books and other documents from the framers' day as well as the present time. It weighed other evidence as well, including the Second Amendment's legislative history, the constitutions of the individual states, legal precedents involving Second Amendment questions, and commentaries by legal scholars on the amendment's history and meaning. In the end, the Court split 5:4 along ideological lines. In 2008, the conservative majority found the DC handgun ban, enacted in 1975, to be unconstitutional. The liberal minority, reading the same twenty-seven words, came to the opposite conclusion.

When nine jurists who have spent their professional careers interpreting the law differ so drastically on the meaning of a single sentence, we are forced to conclude that meaning depends more on the reader than on the words. To paraphrase the slogan of the NRA, *words don't make meaning, people do.* There are many contexts in which a single sentence can have multiple, equally valid interpretations. But when it comes to the Supreme Court's interpretation of the Second Amendment, majority rules. The reading preferred by five justices becomes the law of the land. The interpretation of the remaining four becomes a legal footnote. But even after *Heller*, the semantic uncertainties of the amendment's wording continue to muddy whatever plain meaning it may have: the Court declared that total bans on handguns are out; but what about bans on assault rifles? Or bans on carrying guns, whether openly or concealed? Or background checks? Or restrictions on other kinds of arms (remember, not all arms are guns)? Lawsuits are now making their way through the courts seeking to clarify many of these questions.

As scholars like Judge Richard Posner have observed, each side in *Heller* argued from a position usually adopted by the other: the liberals took an originalist position, seeking to understand the amendment as the framers did; the conservatives preferred to read the Second Amendment loosely, as part of a living constitution where meaning can also reside between the lines of the text.[21] That is what Justice Scalia did when he located the founders' intent by purporting to read their minds: "The prefatory clause does not suggest that preserving the militia was the only reason Americans valued the ancient right; *most undoubtedly thought* it even more important for self-defense and hunting ... self-defense ... was the central component of the right itself."[22] It may be that, if polled, most Americans in the 1780s "undoubtedly thought" that guns were "even more important" for hunting and self-defense than for state security, but although the Second Amendment explicitly mentions the militia, it is silent on the question of shooting game or intruders. In *Heller*, the Court made policy by stressing the need for personal ownership of powerful guns in order to fight the current epidemic of urban crime which the founders never mentioned and surely never foresaw.

Conservative jurists insist they focus on the text and nothing but the text as they seek to discover the original public meaning of the Second Amendment. But it is not clear that the amendment ever had a single shared meaning, or, if it did, whether that meaning is recoverable. That is true of any text, not just legal ones. The best we can hope for when investigating an older text is to examine how it was discussed around the time it was written and to use historical sources to glean the meaning of any difficult or ambiguous words or phrases. Even so, there is no guarantee that a reasonable reader in 1791 would interpret the Second Amendment in the same way as their equally reasonable neighbor. When the Supreme Court said that it had determined the original public meaning of the Second Amendment, its reading, like any linguistic interpretation, involved both an examination of the text and a certain amount of guesswork.

The overall impact of *Heller* on gun regulation is still unclear. A skeptical Posner warned, "The only certain effect of the Heller decision ... will be to increase litigation over gun ownership." Such litigation is ongoing, with several cases in the US circuit courts challenging various state arms regulations. One of these, *New York State Rifle and Pistol Association v. Bruen* (20-843) will be decided by the Supreme Court in the 2021–22 term, after this book has gone to print.

English common law and American jurisprudence have always supported the public regulation of weapons. As early as 1328, the English Statute of Northampton (2 Edw. 3, c. 3) banned "rid[ing] armed by night nor by day" without royal permission, and from the seventeenth century to the present, the American colonies, and later the states, passed many statutes banning the carrying of weapons either openly or concealed – none of which were seen to conflict with the natural right of individual self-defense.[23] Even Justice Scalia tempered his opinion in *Heller* by noting that gun regulation remains both possible and, in some cases, even desirable:

> The Court's opinion should not be taken to cast doubt on longstanding prohibitions on the possession of firearms by felons and the mentally ill, or laws forbidding the carrying of firearms in sensitive places such as schools and government buildings, or laws imposing conditions and qualifications on the commercial sale of arms.

Scalia suggested that a ban on guns in federal buildings would be constitutional, and it is very likely that he would have found DC's ban on openly carrying weapons during the invasion of the Capitol on January 6 a permissible regulation. In addition, lower courts are starting to rely on corpus evidence that *bear arms* is first and foremost a military term, as the Vermont Supreme Court did in 2021 when it upheld the state's ban on large-capacity magazines.[24] But the reasoning of the *Heller* majority does not hold out much hope that linguistic data will have much impact on a Supreme Court that is even more conservative today than it was in 2008, and the confrontations between the First and Second amendments that we saw in Charlottesville and later, when right-wing protesters stormed the state house in Lansing, Michigan, will continue to occur.

In 1857, *New York Tribune* editor Horace Greeley wrote, "there may be no very intimate connection between guns and grammar."[25] Greeley wasn't thinking about the Second Amendment, but his words sum up what happened in *Heller*, where each side considered the grammar of the Second Amendment. In the end, it was the presumed need for guns, not the findings of grammar, that steered the Court's majority to conclude that the DC gun law had to go. In one of his stand-up routines, the comedian Eddie Izzard quipped, "the National Rifle Association says that, 'Guns don't kill people, people do,' but I think the gun helps."[26] As the Supreme Court follows up *Heller* with additional rulings on what kinds of gun regulations are constitutional, even if it rejects linguistic data confirming the Second Amendment's military concerns, it should also consider the growing national sentiment that gun regulation *is necessary to the domestic security of a free state*. There seems no other effective way to reduce the growing number of mass shootings, a phenomenon unknown in any other democracy.

And effective gun regulation comes with a bonus feature: keeping guns out of public places will protect speech. A federal judge ordered the city of Charlottesville to permit the protest against the removal of Robert E. Lee's statue from a city park, even though demonstrators might be armed, because the Supreme Court ruled that the potential for violence is not a sufficient reason to abridge First Amendment guarantees.[27] In *Brandenburg v. Ohio* (1969), the Court said that authorities may step in only when speech threatens *imminent lawless action. Heller*, and the subsequent decision in *McDonald* v. *City of Chicago* (561 US 742, 2010), which applied the Second Amendment to the states, addressed the right to keep guns *at home* for the purposes of *self-defense*. The Court has not yet ruled on whether the Second Amendment protects a right to carry guns outside the home for any lawful purpose. But demonstrators did not bring their guns to Charlottesville, or to later protests in Kenosha and Lansing, or to the January 6 insurrection in the District of Columbia, for self-defense or to protect their right to speak, to assemble *peaceably*, or to petition the government for a redress of grievances. They brought them as a show of force, leaving the speech (and safety) of those who remained unarmed at risk. The clash between First and Second amendment protections is generating much discussion in legal circles.[28] But the central question remains unresolved: Do guns at protests guarantee the safety of armed speakers and their right to speak, or do they threaten imminent lawless action and nullify free speech?

## CHAPTER 3

# A Clear and Present Danger

The people shall not be deprived or abridged of their right to speak, to write, or to publish their sentiments.

From the first draft of the First Amendment,

June 8, 1789, *Annals of Congress*, 451

Guns or no guns, political speech is now the most strongly-protected form of speech in the United States. But that has not always been the case. Although the First Amendment was ratified in 1791, and some lawmakers feared that the 1798 Sedition Act might conflict with constitutional free-press guarantees, the Supreme Court didn't hear a First Amendment case until the waning days of the First World War. The First Amendment flatly states, "Congress shall make no law … abridging the freedom of speech, or of the press; or the right of the people peaceably to assemble, and to petition the government for a redress of grievances," but in that case, *United States* v. *Schenck* (1919), the Supreme Court ruled that Congress may in fact prohibit speech in order to preserve the republic.[1]

After *Schenck*, the general trend of First Amendment rulings has been liberalizing, with more and more speech moved into the protected category. But protections can also be withdrawn, or at least diluted. In *Tinker* v. *Des Moines* (1969), for example, the Supreme Court protected speech in public schools.[2] But later decisions narrowed *Tinker's* scope, placing more and more types of student speech outside the First Amendment's shield. During a classroom discussion of the Charlottesville riot shortly after it happened, a student in my class reported that her Skokie, Illinois, high school prevented her from submitting an essay to a city-wide contest because even after thirty-seven years her topic – why the Nazis should not have been allowed to march there in 1978 – remained too controversial. For her, as for most students whose right to speak has been abridged, taking the school to court was not a realistic option. In the end, a surprising amount of American speech remains either unprotected or in a limbo where speech is protected, but speakers aren't in a position to claim that protection. All this makes people think they can't always say what they want.

## THE PARADOX OF FREE SPEECH

It may seem paradoxical, but freedom of speech and the control of speech are always intertwined. Speak out, especially on something controversial, and someone – government, church, school, parent, troll, or terrorist – may try to correct you, stop you, punish you, or even shoot you. And despite the large body of legal rulings, the border between protected and unprotected speech is seldom clear or stable, which may leave speakers unsure about what they can say and when. Laws may protect speech, but they always leave some speech unprotected. In addition, the First Amendment applies only to government regulation of speech: words in the private sector are typically unprotected, which makes employers generally free to fire anyone who says or writes something that they don't like.

Governments see no irony in simultaneously defending and banning speech. The US Supreme Court, the ultimate guarantor of free speech, bans political speech in or near the court building: a person may not "(1) parade, stand, or move in processions or assemblages in the Grounds; or (2) display in the Grounds a flag, banner, or device designed or adapted to bring into public notice a party, organization, or movement."[3] Recently a federal appeals court upheld the constitutionality of this speech ban because "the Court's plaza ... is a 'nonpublic forum,' an area not traditionally kept open for expressive activity by the public."[4] In addition, the Court promulgates its own rules banning protests, political speech, and even religious speech, both indoors and out:

No person shall engage in a demonstration within the Supreme Court building and grounds. The term "demonstration" includes demonstrations, picketing, speechmaking, marching, holding vigils or religious services and all other like forms of conduct that involve the communication or expression of views or grievances, engaged in by one or more persons, the conduct of which is reasonably likely to draw a crowd of onlookers. The term does not include casual use by visitors or tourists that is not reasonably likely to attract a crowd of onlookers.[5]

It's a most ingenious paradox: what the First Amendment protects, the Supreme Court prohibits. Still, the United States has broader speech protections than other democratic nations. Hate speech is constitutionally protected in the United States. In contrast, British law has long defended free speech, but it now criminalizes insults to race or religion, which can get offenders up to seven years imprisonment, and online harassment is punishable by a fine and up to five years in prison.[6] France echoes these restrictions and in addition punishes anyone who celebrates or excuses a terrorist act with up to five years in jail and a €75,000 fine (roughly $86,000 or £64,000). Imagine the impact of such a regulation on the right-wing social media response in the United States after January 6. France also criminalizes hate speech. Article 11 of the European Union Charter of Fundamental Rights frames both the right to free expression and the right to be safe from verbal abuse as relative, not absolute, and these at-times competing rights are routinely balanced on a case-by-case basis: "1. Everyone has the right to freedom of expression. This right shall include freedom to hold opinions and to receive and impart information and ideas without interference by public authority and regardless of frontiers. 2. The freedom and pluralism of the media shall be respected."[7] The official explanation that accompanies Article 11 explains:

The exercise of these freedoms, since it carries with it duties and responsibilities, may be subject to such formalities, conditions, restrictions or penalties as are prescribed by law and are necessary in a democratic society, in the interests of national security, territorial integrity or public safety, for the prevention of disorder or crime, for the protection of health or morals, for the protection of the reputation or rights of others, for preventing the disclosure of information received in confidence, or for maintaining the authority and impartiality of the judiciary.

## *JE SUIS CHARLIE*

A confrontation between free speech and guns in Paris two years before Charlottesville highlights some differences between the American and European approach to speech and weapons. On January 7, 2015, gun-wielding terrorists attacked the Paris offices of the satirical French magazine *Charlie Hebdo*, killing twelve, including editors and cartoonists. *Charlie Hebdo* – "Charlie Weekly," in English – is named after the cartoon character Charlie Brown, but its contents bear no resemblance to the gentle humor of the *Peanuts* comic strip. Rather, *Charlie Hebdo* is an over-the-top satirical magazine bent on skewering ideologues, politicians, and the generally humorless, and it had gone too far, in the eyes of the attackers, whose rampage was payback for cartoons and articles lampooning the Prophet Muhammad. Over the course of three days, two groups of terrorists killed a total of seventeen people, injured others, and took still others hostage. The attacks moved from the offices of the journal to the streets of Paris, and finally, to a kosher supermarket at the edge of the city. Much of the world denounced this brutal attack on a magazine that few people had read, but whose well-publicized excesses had at one time or another infuriated many who were now supporting it. Three years earlier, for example, the French government condemned *Charlie Hebdo* for re-publishing controversial Danish newspaper cartoons satirizing Islam, cartoons which sparked death threats to newspapers and deadly riots in the Muslim world. But now, French president François Hollande was expressing outrage over the murder of *Charlie*'s cartoonists. On January 11, four days after the attack, millions rallied at the Place de la République in Paris, in the squares of other French cities, and in cities abroad as well, to reassert their commitment to free speech. *Je suis Charlie* – "I am Charlie" – became the chant of the day.

World leaders joined Hollande at that rally on January 11 to condemn violence and defend the universal right to speak one's mind. They, too, were Charlie, although at the same time both Hollande and British PM David Cameron, balancing free speech with the public safety, increased their governments' online surveillance, not just of terrorists and anyone who might be supporting terrorists, but of everyone else as well, just in case they might become terrorists. This despite the fact that such monitoring

**The old anarchist says, "I've got a pencil and I know how to use it."**

**3.1** The old anarchist says, "I've got a pencil and I know how to use it." Cartoon drawn by the author the day after the *Charlie Hebdo* attacks.

could discourage non-terrorists from speaking their minds online and drive actual terrorists to hatch their plots through more secretive channels.

Free speech is a powerful, even a magical slogan, but as *l'affaire Charlie Hebdo* shows, in practice it is never absolute. For a few days, the spirit of January 11 prevailed. Everyone expressed their commitment to free speech. The pencil became mightier than the Kalashnikov as political cartoonists mourned their murdered colleagues with an outpouring of cartoons depicting well-sharpened No. 2s triumphing over censorship and hate. The message resonated: the resistance of artists is not futile.

But *Charlie* fever proved all too brief. On January 14, just a week after the Paris massacre, the magazine's surviving staff published a new issue with a cover depicting a cartoon Muhammad shedding a tear and holding a sign that read, "Je suis Charlie" under a banner proclaiming, "All is forgiven."[8] The cover sparked renewed threats against the magazine for daring once again to depict Muhammad, even though the new context was not satirical. Many of those who had condemned the murder of the cartoonists began to temper their response: free speech is important, to be sure, but cartoons insulting religion invite serious consequences. Pope Francis expressed this shift in sentiment when he told reporters that he didn't condone the deadly riots triggered by *Charlie Hebdo*'s latest issue, but, pointing to the aide standing next to him, he added, "If my good friend Dr. Gasparri says a curse word against my mother, he can expect a punch. It's normal. It's normal. You cannot provoke. You cannot insult the faith of others. You cannot make fun of the faith of others."[9]

With *Charlie* once again making waves, "l'esprit du 11 janvier" began to evaporate, and the cry of "free speech" morphed into "free speech, but ..." Increasingly, people began to murmur, "It's too bad that innocent bystanders were killed, *but* these cartoonists should have censored themselves." United for a week, the French were suddenly one no longer, as public concern for protecting speech and the lives of cartoonists was replaced by calls to preserve order, and apologists for the anti-*Charlie* violence began to recast it as a regrettable, a predictable, even a necessary response to provocative speech.[10] The novelist Salman Rushdie, who became a target of Muslim fundamentalists after publishing his novel *The Satanic Verses* in 1988, remained one of the few public figures still condemning the murder of artists for exercising their right to speak: "The moment somebody says, 'Yes I believe in free speech, BUT,' I stop listening ... The moment you limit free speech, it is not free speech."[11]

*Charlie Hebdo* – whose masthead proudly labels it a *"journal irresponsable"* – eventually resumed regular publication, with the editors acknowledging that their new-found friends would soon desert them. Millions may rally for free speech for an afternoon, but in nations like France, where speech is mostly free, most of the time, and where hate speech is illegal, freedom of speech is just too abstract a cause to champion every day, especially when some of that speech threatens public order. The French historian Emmanuel Todd condemned the spirit of January 11 as a hysterical expression of religious, racial, and ethnic hatred by France's entrenched, right-leaning middle classes.[12] And American cartoonist Garry Trudeau, once the target of censors for his progressive and often-controversial "Doonesbury" comic strip, complained that

*Charlie* had wandered "into the realm of hate speech" and implied that the violent response to their lampooning was to be expected: "What free speech absolutists have failed to acknowledge is that because one has the right to offend a group does not mean that one must. Or that that group gives up the right to be outraged."[13]

In May, the writers' group PEN American Center honored *Charlie Hebdo* with its Freedom of Expression Courage Award for 2015. Announcing the award, the writers' organization stated, "It is the role of the satirists in any free society to challenge the powerful and the sacred, pushing boundaries in ways that make expression freer and more robust for us all."[14] This prompted more than 200 writers to denounce PEN's choice and boycott the award ceremony. They did not condone the murder of cartoonists and innocent bystanders, but – there's that *but* again – they did condemn *Charlie* for speech "intended to cause further humiliation and suffering" to the "marginalized, embattled, and victimized" underclass of French Muslims who are already victims of French colonialism.[15]

To be sure, many prominent writers supported the PEN American award to *Charlie*. Defending free speech once again, PEN chapter president Salman Rushdie argued that "the execution of the cartoonists is the hate crime." There is a fine line to be drawn between fighting words and the heckler's veto, as Adam Gopnik suggested when he praised the courage of the *Charlie* cartoonists in the face of terror. Gopnik reminded writers: "The idea that we should be free to do our work and offer our views without extending a frightened veto to those who threaten to harm us isn't just part of what we mean by free expression. It's what free expression is."[16]

As Rushdie and others have noted, it is important to read *Charlie Hebdo* in the long tradition of French journalistic satire, and *Charlie* has always been an equal-opportunity offender. Contrary to the claims of its critics, the journal targets, not France's marginalized and oppressed minorities, but autocratic politicians and fundamentalists of every religious persuasion, those powerful public figures who seek to silence their opponents and impose their beliefs by force. Religion is a frequent subject for the defiantly secular journal which makes its home in an unabashedly secular country, but *Charlie* vigorously attacks France's racist, ultra-right-wing Front National as well. According to Dominique Sopo, president of France's SOS Racisme, "the journal denounces racism and the hate of Muslims every week ... [resolutely attacking] racists, antisemites, and islamophobes."[17]

In the end, despite the well-publicized dissents, the *Charlie* journalists who accepted the PEN America award received a standing ovation at the May 5 banquet. In his remarks, surviving *Charlie* editor Gérard Biard said, *tout court*, "Being shocked is part of democratic debate. Being shot is not."[18] And over the course of the following year, *Charlie* continued to satirize and offend Muslims, Catholics, the French, and pretty much everybody else. On the anniversary of the attacks, the magazine's cover depicted God dressed as a terrorist, with the caption, "The assassin is still at large." Fearing reprisals, the *New York Times* obliquely identified the figure in the cartoon as "a bearded man"; the Vatican newspaper quickly condemned it; and the Associated Press and other news media decided the image was too offensive to reprint.[19]

## FREEDOM OF SPEECH IN WARTIME

We can see from *Charlie Hebdo*, Charlottesville, and more recently, from the Black Lives Matter protests and the attempts to overturn the 2020 US presidential election (though not the many down-ballot conservative wins in that same election), that stressful times put extra pressure on speech, pressure which may weaken its protection. But free speech has always been a contingent right. Speech in wartime has not enjoyed the same protections as peacetime speech. Eighteenth-century American legislators had no problem reconciling state and federal speech protections with state bans on obscene speech, and they freely limited political speech as well. Seven years after the First Amendment was ratified, Congress passed the Sedition Act, whose specific goal was to abridge the freedom of speech, and of the press, ostensibly to prepare for the possibility of war with France after the French Revolution. In practice, though, the Sedition Act offered a pretext to arrest the many domestic critics of the Adams administration for dissing the government:

If any person shall write, print, utter or publish … any false, scandalous and malicious writing or writings against the government of the United States, or either house of the Congress of the United States, or the President of the United States … such person … shall be punished by a fine not exceeding two thousand dollars [$2,000 in 1798 would be about $40,000, or £29,500, today], and by imprisonment not exceeding two years.[20]

During the House debate over the Sedition Act, opponents claimed that the bill would violate constitutional guarantees of free speech and a free press, while supporters replied that governments surely had the right to defend themselves against attack, whether physical or verbal.[21] Both James Madison and Thomas Jefferson argued that the Sedition Act violated the First Amendment, but they did so anonymously, to avoid the unpleasant consequences of the law. Another signer of the Declaration of Independence, Supreme Court Justice Samuel Chase, ignored the First Amendment's speech protections as he doled out convictions for sedition in his role as head of a federal circuit.[22] Ultimately, Jefferson allowed the Alien and Sedition Acts to expire when he assumed the presidency in 1801, and more than a century would pass before the Supreme Court revisited free speech and the First Amendment. But when, after the outbreak of the First World War, the Court took up a series of cases springing from opposition to American participation in the war, it supported the government's insistence that speech protections could be suspended in times of national emergency.

## SPEECH IN OUR TIMES

The First World War brought a new crackdown on speech critical of the US government. Hundreds were arrested for offenses ranging from calling President Woodrow Wilson a bad name to very real cases of spying or disrupting military operations. Iowa went so far as to ban the use of foreign languages for the duration of the war. In later chapters we will look more closely at presidential name-calling and what happened to nonanglophones in Iowa. In this chapter we will consider what happened to speakers who criticized the war and the military draft.

One of the most prominent early voices against the war was Wisconsin Senator Robert M. La Follette, a progressive Republican who attacked war profiteers and delivered a passionate defense of free speech in wartime in the Senate:

> The citizen and his representative in Congress in time of war must maintain his right of free speech. More than in times of peace it is necessary that the channels for free public discussion of governmental policies shall be open ... Our government, above all others, is founded on the right of the people freely to discuss all matters pertaining to their government, in war not less than in peace, for in this government the people are the rulers in war no less than in peace.[23]

La Follette survived a drawn-out attempt by hawkish colleagues to expel him from the Senate, but many of the others charged with sedition wound up in jail.

The United States entered the First World War in April, 1917. One month later Congress passed the Selective Service Act, establishing a nationwide draft to provide troops for the war effort. And in June it passed the Espionage Act, which targeted spying but also banned interfering with conscription and sending subversive materials through the mail.[24] Punishments for these wartime offenses ranged from small fines to death. A sedition amendment, added to the law in 1918, made it easier to prosecute any sort of criticism of the government, including negative comments about the war or even calls for a swift peace.[25]

From 1917 to 1919, some 2,000 people were prosecuted for violating the Espionage Act and almost 900 were convicted, including the well-known socialist and frequent presidential candidate Eugene Debs, as well as two members of Congress, one of whom was re-elected while in prison.[26] Two hundred prosecutions involved speech issues.[27] In addition, several states passed laws banning movies with supposedly pacifist tendencies.[28] For example, in a 1917 California case aptly titled *United States* v. *The Spirit of '76*, Robert Goldstein was sentenced to ten years in prison for producing a silent film, "The Spirit of '76," portraying a fictional romance between King George III and an American Quaker woman. Although it depicted such iconic events as Paul Revere's ride, censors condemned

"The Spirit of '76" as unpatriotic for portraying the 1778 Wyoming Massacre in Pennsylvania, with scenes of British soldiers bayonetting babies and shooting women. The movie was seized at a screening in Chicago, and after an attempt to show it in Los Angeles, Goldstein was arrested for interfering with military operations in violation of the Espionage Act. At his trial, the prosecution claimed that since men in the audience could be eligible for the draft, watching depictions of British atrocities could persuade them to oppose the war. Trial Judge Benjamin Bledsoe agreed, condemning the subversive nature of "The Spirit of '76":

> The disposition and purpose of the whole play in its deeper significance is to incite hatred of England and England's soldiers ... so to excite or inflame the passions of our people, or some of them, as that they will be deterred from giving that full measure of co-operation, sympathy, assistance, and sacrifice which is due to Great Britain, simply because of the fact that Great Britain, as an ally of ours, is working with us to fight the battle which we think strikes at our very existence as a nation.[29]

Bledsoe found that the free speech protections of the First Amendment did not apply to a film that would be at best objectionable if shown in peacetime, but whose exhibition during a time of national peril amounted to treason:

> [Speech] which in ordinary times might be clearly permissible, or even commendable, in this hour of national emergency, effort, and peril, may be as clearly treasonable, and therefore properly subject to review and repression. The constitutional guaranty of "free speech" carries with it no right to subvert the purposes and destiny of the nation.

Unfortunately, no copy of the film survives, and so it is impossible to assess exactly how controversial the scenes in question might have been.

### *THE MASSES* AND THE MAILS

Another war-related case, much-discussed in literary circles at the time, concerned *The Masses*, a socialist monthly which combined satire, political cartoons, and cultural criticism, leavened with irreverent humor, essays, poems, and contemporary fiction. *The Masses* was edited by the poet Max Eastman, and its contributors included such well-known writers as John Reed, Dorothy Day, Vachel Lindsay, Louis Untermeyer, Carl Sandberg, Sherwood Anderson, and Bertrand Russell. In 1917, the New York City postmaster declared *The Masses* unmailable under the Espionage Act, citing political cartoons and poems in its August issue that criticized the draft and American involvement in the war. Since the magazine depended on subscriptions for its survival, the editors promptly went to court to obtain an injunction against the postmaster. In retaliation, police arrested Eastman and the other editors for violating the Espionage Act by interfering with the draft.

The relevant portions of the Espionage Act read:

Whoever, when the United States is at war, shall ... willfully obstruct the recruiting or enlistment service of the United States, to the injury of the service or of the United States, shall be punished by a fine of not more than $10,000 or imprisonment for not more than twenty years, or both [H.R. 291, Title 1, section 3; it was a hefty fine: $10,000 in 1917 would be about $185,000, or £135,900 today].

Another section of the law banned sending antiwar materials through the mails:

Every letter, writing, circular, postal card, picture, print, engraving, photograph, newspaper, pamphlet, book, or other publication, matter or thing, of any kind, containing any matter advocating or urging treason, insurrection, or forcible resistance to any law of the United States, is hereby declared to be nonmailable [penalties included a fine of up to $5,000, imprisonment for up to five years, or both].

The indictment against Eastman, his editors, and one contributor, charged that they "did conspire together ... unlawfully and willfully to cause ... insubordination, disloyalty, mutiny and refusal of duty in the military and naval forces of the United States ... by means of the publication ... of articles, poems, cartoons and pictures."[30] According to defendant Floyd Dell's wry account of the trial, presided over by a very patient Judge Augustus Hand, Max Eastman jumped from his seat and stood to attention when a band stationed at a Liberty Bond booth in the street outside the courtroom struck up the national anthem.[31] Another defendant, cartoonist Art Young, showed his own brand of irreverence when the prosecutor questioned him about his intent in drawing antiwar cartoons:

> He thought their meaning was perfectly clear. They spoke for themselves, he said. "What did you intend to do when you drew this picture, Mr. Young?" Intend to do? Why, to draw a picture – to make people laugh – to make them think – to express his feelings. For what purpose? For the public good. How did he think they would effect such a purpose? Art scratched his head. He did not think it was fair to ask an artist to go into metaphysics. Had he intended to obstruct recruiting or enlistment by such pictures? No, he hadn't been thinking of recruiting or enlistment at all! He couldn't see what possible connection those pictures had with obstruction of recruiting or enlistment. He mentioned a little picture of [the prosecutor] Mr. Barnes which the jury had seen; and he suggested that maybe someone would think that he had drawn that picture to discourage Mr. Barnes from enlisting! The ordeal over, Art Young went back to his seat, and fell into an exhausted slumber.[32]

After two mistrials, the prosecutors dismissed all charges against the staff. But the magazine itself was not as lucky. *The Masses* lawsuit against New York City postmaster Thomas G. Patten for banning it from the mails brought a temporary injunction from Judge Learned Hand, who summarized the charges leveled by Patten against four of the magazine's cartoons:

> The first is a picture of the Liberty Bell broken in fragments. The obvious implication ... is that the origin, purposes, and conduct of the war have already destroyed the liberties of the country. It is a fair inference that the draft law is an especial instance of the violation of the liberty and fundamental rights of any free people. The second cartoon shows a

**3.2** After he woke from his nap, Art Young drew this cartoon of himself asleep during the "trial for his life." *The Liberator,* June, 1918, p. 11. Courtesy of the Newberry Library.

cannon to the mouth of which is bound the naked figure of a youth, to the wheel that of a woman, marked "Democracy," and upon the carriage that of a man, marked "Labor." On the ground kneels a draped woman marked "Motherhood" in a posture of desperation, while her infant lies on the ground. The import of this cartoon is obviously that conscription is the destruction of youth, democracy, and labor, and the desolation of the family. No one can dispute that it was intended to rouse detestation for the draft law.[33]

Hand prefaced his reason for granting the injunction against the Post Office by stating the role of the judiciary in this case: "It will be necessary, first, to interpret the law, and, next, the [magazine's] words and pictures."[34] Many judges used a "bad-tendencies" test to abridge speech under the Espionage Act: a speaker could be punished if their words could cause others to commit an illegal act. But Hand warned that to interpret the Act so broadly would criminalize large quantities of historically protected speech, clearly not the intent of Congress.

Conscription

**3.3** "Conscription," by Henry J. Glintenkamp. *The Masses*, August, 1917, p. 9. The second of the four cartoons characterized as nonmailable by the Post Office. Another of Glintenkamp's cartoons showed death measuring a soldier for a coffin. Glintenkamp fled the country to avoid prosecution. Courtesy of the Newberry Library.

After interpreting the law, Judge Hand interpreted the words and pictures in the magazine, finding in each case no violation of the Espionage Act. He observed that, although it is constitutional to ban speech that advocates illegal acts, the Espionage Act cannot be used to censor speech that merely criticizes government policy, and nothing in *The Masses* incited its readers to break the law. Hand said of the cartoons and poems at issue:

> They fall within the scope of that right to criticize either by temperate reasoning, or by immoderate and indecent invective, which is normally the privilege of the individual in countries dependent upon the free expression of opinion as the ultimate source of authority.[35]

In Hand's view, the Espionage Act targeted only the explicit advocacy of illegal action, not criticism of the draft that could hypothetically convince someone to dodge it, because such a position criminalized all unpopular political speech. That cannot be done in peacetime, nor can it be done in time of war:

> To assimilate agitation, legitimate as such, with direct incitement to violent resistance, is to disregard the tolerance of all methods of political agitation which in normal times is a safeguard of free government. The distinction is not a scholastic subterfuge, but a hard-bought acquisition in the fight for freedom ... If one stops short of urging upon others that it is their duty or their interest to resist the law, it seems to me one should not be held to have attempted to cause its violation. If that be not the test, I can see no escape from the conclusion that under this section every political agitation which can be shown to be apt to create a seditious temper is illegal. I am confident that by such language Congress had no such revolutionary purpose in view.[36]

Judge Hand's eloquent defense of political speech was quickly rejected on appeal. In reinstating the Post Office ban on *The Masses*, Appeals Court Judge Henry Wade Rogers disagreed with each of Hand's interpretations. Rogers reasoned that the Espionage Act was consistent with the free press clause of the First Amendment because it did not constitute a prior restraint on speech: the law did not prevent the publication of *The Masses,* just its mailing. And since Congress gave the postmaster the authority to decide whether something is mailable under the Espionage Act, Postmaster Patten's decision was final.[37]

Learned Hand was correct that Congress did not intend a blanket condemnation of antiwar rhetoric by individuals or by the press. The law only criminalized statements that directly threatened to disrupt the war effort.[38] But most courts agreed instead with Judge Rogers' view that the Espionage Act meant to stifle any criticism of the war. And so *The Masses,* declared nonmailable once more, ceased publication a few months before its editors went on trial for conspiracy. But it was replaced by a new magazine, *The Liberator,* also edited by Eastman and with many of the same staff and contributors. More important, even though it was rejected by the Appeals Court, Learned Hand's reading of the Espionage Act was widely discussed in legal circles. His exhortation to differentiate between incitement and mere criticism did not come into play when Justice Oliver Wendell Holmes wrote his opinion in *Schenck* v. *United States,* the case in which the Supreme Court began shaping free-speech doctrine in 1919. But it may have helped Holmes to re-focus *Schenck* a few months later in his dissent in *Abrams* v. *United States,* another First Amendment case. But along with *Schenck,* but before *Abrams,* the Court heard the appeal of Eugene Debs, also convicted for violating the Espionage Act.

*The Masses* trials generated local interest in New York, but the Debs trial drew national attention.[39] Eugene Debs was a frequent Socialist candidate for president. In his most successful campaign, in 1912, he received 6 percent of the popular vote. In 1918, Debs was arrested after speaking to a crowd of about one thousand at a Socialist Party picnic in Canton, Ohio. In that two-hour speech, Debs attacked the war as an example of capitalist greed, a common antiwar theme echoed by Charles Schenck and by the Abrams defendants. For example, one Art Young cartoon in *The Masses* depicted a group of tycoons studying a document labeled "war plans" while ignoring a member of Congress standing hat in hand at the door. The caption reads:

CONGRESS: "Excuse me, gentlemen, where do I come in?"
BIG BUSINESS: "Run along, now. We got through with you when you declared war for us."[40]

Arthur Young.

CONGRESS: "EXCUSE ME, GENTLEMEN—WHERE DO I COME IN?"
BIG BUSINESS: "RUN ALONG NOW!—WE GOT THROUGH WITH YOU WHEN YOU DECLARED WAR FOR US.

**3.4** Art Young's cartoon in *The Masses* reflects the common critique that America's entry into the First World War was fueled by Wall Street greed, not the need to make the world safe for democracy. *The Masses*, August, 1917, p. 33. Courtesy of the Newberry Library.

Although Debs did not encourage draft dodging, a zealous Ohio prosecutor found enough antiwar sentiment in his words to charge Debs with conveying false statements about the war. At trial, Debs freely admitted that he had said everything he was accused of saying. Instead of answering questions, with the court's permission he delivered a long and eloquent speech outlining his ideals and general political philosophy and pointing out that President Woodrow Wilson had said many of the same things he was saying about free speech and political critique. Debs' courtroom oration had no impact on the jury, who found him guilty. Debs was sentenced to ten years in prison, and he promptly appealed all the way to the Supreme Court. Because Debs was such a prominent figure, the Supreme Court's decision on his appeal drew reporters to Washington on Monday, March 3, 1919, for a big story. But that day the Court issued its opinion in a different Espionage Act case, *Schenck* v. *United States*, making the press wait another week for what would prove to be a brief, anticlimactic ruling in *Debs* v. *United States*.

Most judges and juries did not take kindly to criticism of the war. On top of that, any criticism of government policy magnified already-strong public fears sparked by the Russian Revolution that the American economic system was being attacked by wild-eyed, bomb-throwing radicals. Learned Hand was one of a few judges to argue for restraint in the face of the war fever and the red-baiting. The Supreme Court, perhaps taking its cue from popular opinion and never eager to second-guess juries, affirmed Debs' conviction with little comment, referring to its decision in *Schenck*, announced the week before, for an explanation. A few months after that, Debs began his sentence.

Debs ran one last time for president in 1920, campaigning from prison and getting some 913,000 votes, more than he had gotten in his previous runs. In 1921, President Warren Harding commuted Debs' sentence and invited the Socialist leader to the White House. But *Debs* v. *United States* set no precedent. Instead, it is the Supreme Court's decision in *Schenck* v. *United States* that is now one of the best known in this group of early free-speech prosecutions, because Schenck's conviction prompted the Court to define the scope of the First Amendment's speech clause for the first time.

**WAKE UP, AMERICA! YOUR LIBERTIES ARE IN DANGER!** As general secretary of the Socialist Party of Philadelphia, Charles Schenck took the lead in printing and mailing 15,000 circulars urging men eligible for the draft to resist conscription. Schenck, along with Dr. Elizabeth Baer, who kept the party minutes, were convicted of violating two sections of the Espionage Act: interfering with the draft and mailing circulars declared nonmailable – the same charges leveled unsuccessfully against the editors of *The Masses*. In affirming the convictions of Schenck and Baer, a unanimous Supreme Court found that their speech was not protected by the First Amendment. Schenck spent six months in prison; Baer served ninety days.

The circular that led to Schenck's conviction – a single sheet of paper printed on both sides – equated the military draft with slavery in violation of the Thirteenth Amendment, and it urged those opposed to the First World War to assert their First Amendment rights to protest the Conscription Act.[41] The circular cajoled, "*Wake Up, America! Your Liberties*

**LONG LIVE THE CONSTITUTION OF THE UNITED STATES**
Wake Up, America! Your Liberties Are in Danger!

The 13th Amendment, Section 1, of the Constitution of the United States says: "Neither slavery nor involuntary servitude, except as a punishment for crime whereof the party shall have been duly convicted, shall exist within the United States, or any place subject to their jurisdiction.

The Constitution of the United States is one of the greatest bulwarks of political liberty. It was born after a long, stubborn battle between king-rule and democracy. (We see little or no difference between arbitrary power under the name of a king and under a few misnamed "representatives.") In this battle the people of the United States established the principle that freedom of the individual and personal liberty are the most sacred things in life. Without them we become slaves.

**3.5** Detail from Charles Schenck's anti-conscription leaflet. Courtesy of the National Archives, Washington, DC.

*Are in Danger!"* and it warned readers not to let "the [venal and] mercenary capitalist press wrongfully and untruthfully mould your thoughts." It asked, as well, "Do you want to see unlimited power handed over to Wall Street's chosen few in America?" But with the Espionage Act in mind, in almost every paragraph these inflammatory remarks appeared with multiple reminders that opposition to the draft was protected by the First Amendment:

> Exercise your rights of free speech, peaceful assemblage and petitioning the government for a redress of grievances … sign a petition to congress for the repeal of the Conscription Act. Help us wipe out this stain upon the Constitution … Long live the Constitution of the United States. Long live the Republic![42]

In their appeal to the Supreme Court, attorneys Henry J. Gibbons and Henry John Nelson argued that punishing the leaflet's antiwar speech would cut off the political discussion vital to American democracy and force Americans to watch their words rather than risk punishment. They cited lower court precedents distinguishing illegal acts that actually urged resistance to the draft or interference with the war effort, from speech which, though critical of government policy, did not break the law or incite others to do so. They cited *United States* v. *Hall,* in which a Montana federal judge dismissed the case against a defendant charged with the following offenses under the Espionage Act:

> At divers times in the presence of sundry persons, some of whom had registered for the draft, defendant declared that he would flee to avoid going to war, that Germany would whip the United States, and he hoped so, that the President was a Wall Street tool, using the United States forces in the war because he was a British tool, that the President was the crookedest-ever President, that he was the richest man in the United States, that the President brought us into the war by British dictation, that Germany had [the] right to sink ships and kill Americans without warning, and that the United States was only fighting for Wall Street millionaires and to protect [banker J. P.] Morgan's interest in England.[43]

Although Hall did make the statements in question, Judge George Bourquin found that his words could not interfere with the war effort because they were rash, drunken, ill-considered speech uttered in a small town far from any military base. Hall stopped no one from enlisting and prevented no soldier or sailor from fighting:

> The Espionage Act is not intended to suppress criticism or denunciation, truth or slander, oratory or gossip, argument or loose talk, but only false facts willfully put forward as true and broadly, with the specific intent to interfere with army or navy operations ... To sustain the charge, actual obstruction and injury must be proven, not mere attempts to obstruct.

That was not a popular position to take during the First World War, and it so angered Montana legislators that they immediately passed a bill to ensure that any antiwar comments would be punished. Spurred on by Montana Senator Thomas Walsh, who cited the importance of avoiding more decisions like *Hall*, Congress passed the 1918 anti-sedition amendment to the Espionage Act.[44]

In another case, Judge D. J. Anderson found that speech against the draft would be illegal only if the government could show that it had actually convinced a draftee not to enter the army. Otherwise, criticism of the government and the war effort was constitutional: "Are we, notwithstanding we are at war, not permitted to speak? I still think that a man has a right to speak freely, and that means he has a right to speak foolishly as well as wisely. If we are going to limit the right of free speech to people who talk wisely, there would probably be dead silence all around."[45]

The defense in Schenck's trial had taken a similar line: the leaflet in question constituted words, not deeds. The prosecution called Louis Passarello, a draft-eligible man who testified, after receiving Schenck's circular, "I didn't think such literature as that should be permitted to be sent through the United States mail." On cross-examination, defense attorney Henry Nelson asked Passarello, "Did the reading of the circular cause you to act in an insubordinate way towards your government?" He replied, "No sir."[46] Several witnesses agreed that, if anything, reading the antidraft leaflet strengthened their resolve to comply with Selective Service regulations.

The defense also cited Judge Augustus Hand's jury instructions in the *Masses* trial to emphasize the difference between speech and action:

It is the constitutional right of every citizen to express his opinion about the war or the participation of the United States in it; about the desirability of peace; about the merits or demerits of the system of conscription, and about the moral rights or claims of conscientious objectors to be exempt from conscription. It is the constitutional right of the citizen to express such opinions, even though they are opposed to the opinions or policies of the administration; and even though the expression of such opinion may unintentionally or indirectly discourage recruiting and enlistment.[47]

These arguments did not convince the Supreme Court. Justice Oliver Wendell Holmes rejected them outright and articulated the Court's rationale for separating protected from unprotected speech. Holmes downplayed the words of the antidraft leaflet, which "in form at least confined itself to peaceful measures," and focused instead on the intent to disrupt the draft: "Of course the document would not have been sent unless it had been intended to have some effect, and we do not see what effect it could be expected to have upon persons subject to the draft except to influence them to obstruct the carrying of it out."[48] Observing that wartime provides a context in which other-wise-protected speech may be abridged, Holmes specifically addressed the contingent nature of the First Amendment, illustrating this with what would become the familiar example of crying fire in a crowded theater:

> We admit that in many places and in ordinary times the defendants in saying all that was said in the circular would have been within their constitutional rights. But the character of every act depends upon the circumstances in which it is done. The most stringent protection of free speech would not protect a man in falsely shouting fire in a theatre and causing a panic.

Holmes then articulated a "clear and present danger" test to distinguish between protected and unprotected speech, and he reiterated the distinction between speech in wartime and in times of peace:

> The question in every case is whether the words used are used in such circumstances and are of such a nature as to create *a clear and present danger* that they will bring about the substantive evils that Congress has a right to prevent ... When a nation is at war many things that might be said in time of peace are such a hindrance to its effort that their utterance will not be endured so long as men fight and that no Court could regard them as protected by any constitutional right.[49]

Although Holmes remained convinced that Schenck had violated the Espionage Act, cases like *United States* v. *Hall* may have given him pause. Holmes was certainly aware of Learned Hand's opinion in *Masses* v. *Patten,* and, in 1919, in his dissent in *Abrams* v. *United States,* a case brought under the new Sedition Act, Holmes found that the statements of Abrams and his co-defendants, much like those of Hall, were silly; that they influenced no one; and that they were not likely to cause any disruption of the war effort. Justice Louis Brandeis, who joined the Court in 1916 and had concurred with the unanimous opinions in *Schenck* and *Debs,* signed on to Holmes' dissent in *Abrams,* but the rest of the Supreme Court, clinging to *Schenck,* did not agree.

## SILLY LEAFLET OR CLEAR AND PRESENT DANGER?

*Schenck* turned out to be the first draft of an evolving Supreme Court definition of unprotected speech that began during the First World War and continues to the present. A few months after *Schenck*, the Court took up *Abrams* v. *United States*, another case involving freedom of speech in wartime. This time, however, Holmes believed the defendants' words were protected, and he found himself in the minority.

Jacob Abrams and his six co-defendants, Hyman Lachowsky, Samuel Lipman, Gabriel Prober, Hyman Rosansky, Jacob Schwartz, and Mollie Steimer, were Russian immigrant anarchists and socialists arrested for violating the Sedition Act by distributing leaflets opposing the 1918 American troop intervention in Russia. Schwartz died in custody, allegedly from a police beating. Prober cut a deal and was found not guilty. The others, who were convicted, appealed to the Supreme Court, which affirmed their convictions in a 7:2 vote.

The 1918 Sedition Act amended the earlier Espionage Act to add a ban on saying or printing anything that was unpatriotic or that interfered with the war effort:

> Whoever, when the United States is at war ... shall willfully utter, print, write, or publish any disloyal, profane, scurrilous, or abusive language about the form of government of the United States, or the Constitution of the United States, or the military or naval forces of the United States, or the flag of the United States ... or ... any language intended to incite, provoke, or encourage resistance to the United States, or to promote the cause of its enemies ... [or] shall willfully advocate, teach, defend or suggest the doing of any of the acts or things in this section enumerated ... [or] favor the cause of any country with which the United States is at war ... shall be punished by a fine of not more than $10,000 or imprisonment for not more than twenty years, or both.[50]

Although the Court affirmed the *Abrams* convictions, as it had affirmed those in *Schenck*, this time Holmes felt that the leaflets in question were ineffective, not dangerous.

He was correct in that assessment. Abrams and his co-defendants were part of a loosely connected, reasonably disorganized, predominantly Jewish community of immigrant leftists: socialists, anarchists, and Communists who met informally to discuss the revolution of the proletariat. Toward the end of the First World War, the United States sent troops to Siberia, ostensibly to aid a contingent of Czech troops in Siberia who were returning to Europe to assist the fight against Germany. But supporters of the Russian Revolution saw this incursion as a deliberate act of anti-Soviet aggression. To protest the American presence in Russia, Abrams and his friends bought a used printing press and installed it in a basement apartment in Harlem. There, on this "clandestine" press, they printed about 10,000 leaflets, 5,000 in English, the rest in Yiddish.

Although the Schenck leaflets had been mailed to select young men of draft age, most of the Abrams leaflets were tossed from a fourth-floor window of a hat factory on Manhattan's Lower East Side, to be picked up by pedestrians below. Passers-by generally trampled the flyers underfoot or quickly tossed them aside, but three people took copies of the leaflets to the Military Intelligence Police, who eventually tracked down the cell of young activists behind them.[51]

The English-language leaflet, headed "The Hypocrisy of the United States and her Allies," is a passionate screed against American corporate attacks on the new socialist utopia of Russia. It seems hastily written in a colorful style, apparently by someone new to English, and it reads, in part:

> "Our" president Wilson, with his beautiful phraseology, has hypnotized the people of America to such an extent that they do not see his hypocrisy.
>
> Know you, people of America, that a frank enemy is always preferable to a concealed friend. When we say the people of America, we do not mean the few Kaisers of America, we mean the "People of America." You people of America were deceived by the wonderful speeches of the masked President Wilson. His shameful, cowardly silence about the intervention in Russia reveals the hypocrisy of the plutocratic gang in Washington and vicinity ...
>
> The tyrants of the world fight each other until they see a common enemy – WORKING CLASS – ENLIGHTENMENT as soon as they find a common enemy, they combine to crush it.

**3.6a and b** Abrams and his co-defendants installed a basement printing press and ran off 5,000 copies of each of two flyers, one in English (Exhibit A in their trial (detail shown in Fig. 3.6a)), the other in Yiddish (Exhibit B) (detail shown in Fig. 3.6b). Images of the leaflets in the Harry Weinberger papers at the Yale University Library, photographed by the author and used by permission.

THE RUSSIAN REVOLUTION CALLS TO THE WORKERS OF THE WORLD FOR HELP.

The Russian Revolution cries: "WORKERS OF THE WORLD! AWAKE! RISE! PUT DOWN YOUR ENEMY AND MINE!"

Yes friends, there is only one enemy of the workers of the world and that is CAPITALISM! ...

AWAKE! AWAKE, YOU WORKERS OF THE WORLD!

REVOLUTIONISTS

A postscript asserts that these "Revolutionists" are not pro-German: "We hate and despise German militarism more than do your hypocritical tyrants. We have more reasons for denouncing German militarism than has the coward of the White House."

Here is a translation of a snippet from the Yiddish leaflet, written in a similar style. In contrast to the English flyer, which urges no specific action, the Yiddish one calls for a general strike that would impact munitions factories:

Workers, wake up!! The preparatory work for Russia's "deliverance" is finished, and has been made clear by his Majesty, Mr. Wilson, and his comrades:

dogs of all colors. America together with the Allies will march after Russia, not, God forbid, to intervene in its internal affairs but only to help the Czecho-Slovaks in their fight against the Bolsheviks ...

While working in the ammunition factories you are creating bullets, swords cannons to murder not only Germans, but also your most-beloved, your best ones, who are in Russia and who are fighting for freedom ... Workers, our answer to the barbaric intervention has to be a general strike![52]

At trial, Abrams and his co-defendants were represented by Harry Weinberger, a friend of the revolutionary, Rosa Luxemburg, and well-known champion of left-wing causes. The Abrams defendants could have drawn free-speech advocate Learned Hand for their trial judge, but because the docket of the Southern District of New York, over which Hand presided, was too crowded, they drew Judge Henry D. Clayton, imported from Alabama just for the occasion. Clayton had been an antitrust specialist when he served in Congress and was known as an apologist for slavery who had strong anti-immigrant feelings. He used the *Abrams* trial to display his contempt for radicals, Jews, immigrants, and as a more recent characterization might put it, "New York values."

To put it mildly, Clayton did not possess a judicial temperament. During the trial, he regularly berated the defendants for their un-American attitudes. He interrupted both Weinberger and the prosecutor to cross-examine the defendants himself or to shut down their testimony. When Molly Steimer protested that her indictment was an attempt by the government to "stifle free speech," Clayton told her, "Freedom of speech is one thing, and disloyalty is another. What you term free speech does not protect disloyalty. I am sorry for the people of New York that have to deal with individuals who have no more conception of what free government means than a billy goat has of the gospel."[53]

Clayton asked Steimer for her views on love and marriage, demanded to know where Abrams had studied anarchy, and told Abrams he wished that the defendants were all in Russia instead of in his courtroom. He instructed the jury that throwing the flyers out the window was enough to signal an intent to defame the government and interfere with the war effort:

> If it were a case where the defendant was indicted for homicide, and he was charged with having taken a pistol and put it to the head of another man and fired the pistol and killed the man, you might say that he did not intend to do that. But I would have very little respect for a jury that would come in with a verdict that he didn't have any intent.[54]

With instructions like this from the judge, it is no surprise that the jury took only an hour to convict on all four counts. At sentencing, Clayton barred protesters from the courtroom and took the opportunity to berate the defendants one last time:

> There will be no propaganda started in this court, the purpose of which is to give aid and comfort to soap-box orators and to such as these miserable defendants who stand convicted before the bar of justice … You don't know anything about democracy, and the only thing you understand is the hellishness of anarchy.[55]

Clayton then doled out the sentences, some much stiffer than Charles Schenck's. Rosansky, who had led authorities to the others, got three years in prison and a $1,000 fine. Mollie Steimer, at twenty-one the youngest, was sentenced to fifteen years and a $500 fine. Lipmann, Lachansky, and Abrams received the maximum sentence of twenty years, the same sentence they would have received had they actually shut down every munitions plant in the country. And they were fined $1,000 on each count (about $18,000, or £13,200, today). On hearing the sentence, Abrams thanked Clayton, and Lipman told the judge, "I did not expect anything better." Clayton retorted, "I do not think you deserve anything less."[56]

The Abrams co-defendants appealed their convictions on First Amendment grounds, but they did not fare much better in the Supreme Court than at their trial. Writing for the majority, Justice John Hessin Clarke found that the earlier decision in *Schenck* shot down any free speech defense for the anarchists, and that "the language of these circulars was obviously intended to provoke and to encourage resistance to the United States in the war." Even Oliver Wendell Holmes, in his dissent, took care not to walk back his clear and present danger test: "I do not doubt for a moment that, by the same reasoning that would justify punishing persuasion to murder, the United States constitutionally may punish speech that produces or is intended to produce a clear and imminent danger that it will bring about forthwith certain substantive evils."[57]

But Holmes went on to clarify "clear and present danger" to mean "the present danger of immediate evil or an intent to bring it about," and he stressed that in all other contexts, the First Amendment continues to apply, even in wartime: "Congress certainly cannot forbid all effort to change the mind of the country."[58] Holmes found Charles Schenck's anti-conscription flyer dangerous because Schenck was a Socialist Party official; the flyer was part of an *organized* antiwar effort; and it targeted men who might be persuaded to resist the draft. In contrast, Abrams and his friends were the very definition of *dis*-organized: a ragged bunch of anonymous radicals tossing out of a window handfuls of incoherent flyers likely to be ignored. No one who took the time to read the leaflets would take them seriously. The flyers did not attack the American government in any real sense, and they posed no danger to the war effort – in fact, they weren't even about the war. As Holmes put it:

Nobody can suppose that the surreptitious publishing of a silly leaflet by an unknown man, without more, would present any immediate danger that its opinions would hinder the success of the government arms or have any appreciable tendency to do so ... the only object of the [leaflets] is to help Russia and stop American intervention there against the popular government – not to impede the United States in the war that it was carrying on.[59]

Furthermore, Holmes found that even though the defendants' Yiddish flyer called for a general strike, the two flyers represented little more than hot air – in his more-eloquent words, "opinions and exhortations" – and he declared that the prosecution in the case failed to prove any *intent* "to cripple or hinder the United States in the prosecution of the war," as the Sedition Act required. Holmes also decried the harsh punishment: "In this case, sentences of twenty years' imprisonment have been imposed for the publishing of two leaflets that I believe the defendants had as much right to publish as the Government has to publish the Constitution of the United States now vainly invoked by them."[60]

Holmes, giving voice to some of the less-popular Espionage Act opinions in the lower courts, formulated in his dissent a marketplace of ideas theory that would later gain traction in cases involving political speech. For Holmes, the First Amendment promotes the free and open discussion that is generally inimical to censorship laws like the Sedition Act, which "sweep away all opposition":

> When men have realized that time has upset many fighting faiths, they may come to believe ... that the ultimate good desired is better reached by free trade in ideas – that the best test of truth is the power of the thought to get itself accepted in the competition of the market.[61]

Holmes did not revise his "clear and present danger" formula in *Abrams*. Rather, he and Brandeis found that the formula did not fit the facts of the case.

### RE-INTERPRETING A CLEAR AND PRESENT DANGER

Not only is it necessary to interpret the law, as Learned Hand admonished in *Masses*, it is also necessary to interpret the interpretations. For years, the Supreme Court applied some version of the *Schenck* test to free-speech cases, most of them dealing with the kind of radical political speech that ran afoul of the Sedition Act. But although the Court followed Holmes' "clear and present danger" formula, it did not adopt his stipulation that the danger must be immediate. In his concurrence in *Whitney* v. *California* (1927), Justice Brandeis complained that the clear and present danger standard remained far from clear. In *Whitney*, the Court unanimously affirmed the conviction of Anita Whitney for being a member of the American Communist Labor Party, a group that advocated the overthrow of the US government by force. But Brandeis urged the Court to define "clear danger" more precisely, and he insisted that a "present danger" must be one that is immediate:

> This Court has not yet fixed the standard by which to determine when a danger shall be deemed clear; how remote the danger may be and yet be deemed present; and what degree of evil shall be deemed sufficiently

substantial to justify resort to abridgement of free speech and assembly as the means of protection ... There must be reasonable grounds to believe that the danger apprehended is imminent.[62]

The justices agreed in *Whitney* that the Communist Party posed a clear threat to American democracy. The question, for Brandeis, was whether that danger was also a present one, rather than something more remote and abstract. Although Brandeis articulated this idea in 1927, it was not until forty years later, in *Brandenburg* v. *Ohio* (1969), that the Court interpreted *present danger* to mean that the criminal response to provocative speech must happen right away.[63]

The majority opinion in *Whitney* was written by Justice Edward Terry Sanford, who made it clear that free speech is never absolute, that when national security is on the line, the state may pre-emptively ban speech in order to ensure its own survival:

> The freedom of speech which is secured by the Constitution does not confer an absolute right to speak, without responsibility, whatever one may choose, or an unrestricted and unbridled license giving immunity for every possible use of language and preventing the punishment of those who abuse this freedom, and ... a State in the exercise of its police power may punish those who abuse this freedom by utterances inimical to the public welfare, tending to incite to crime, disturb the public peace, or endanger the foundations of organized government and threaten its overthrow by unlawful means.[64]

In contrast, Brandeis eloquently channeled many of the radical ideas about free speech voiced earlier by Robert La Follette and Eugene Debs:

> Those who won our independence believed that freedom to think as you will and to speak as you think are means indispensable to the discovery and spread of political truth; that without free speech and assembly discussion would be futile; that with them, discussion affords ordinarily adequate protection against the dissemination of noxious doctrine; that the greatest menace to freedom is an inert people; that public discussion is a political duty; and that this should be a fundamental principle of the American

government. They recognized the risks to which all human institutions are subject. But they knew that order cannot be secured merely through fear of punishment for its infraction; that it is hazardous to discourage thought, hope and imagination; that fear breeds repression; that repression breeds hate; that hate menaces stable government; that the path of safety lies in the opportunity to discuss freely supposed grievances and proposed remedies; and that the fitting remedy for evil counsels is good ones. Believing in the power of reason as applied through public discussion, they eschewed silence coerced by law – the argument of force in its worst form. Recognizing the occasional tyrannies of governing majorities, they amended the Constitution so that free speech and assembly should be guaranteed.[65]

For Brandeis, the government may abridge the right to speak only in an emergency and only when the danger posed is significant, not trivial. Holmes had clarified a *present danger* to be an *immediate* one. Brandeis used an even stronger term, *imminent*, arguing that if a danger is not imminent, then the best remedy for bad speech is more speech:

> No danger flowing from speech can be deemed clear and present, unless the incidence of the evil apprehended is so *imminent* that it may befall before there is opportunity for full discussion. If there be time to expose through discussion the falsehood and fallacies, to avert the evil by the processes of education, the remedy to be applied is more speech, not enforced silence.[66]

## I AM NOT NOW, NOR HAVE I EVER BEEN ...

The notion that political speech is protected by a doctrine of free trade in ideas persisted, with one striking exception: the speech of Communists remained steadfastly outside the First Amendment's free speech guarantee for decades. And despite the arguments of Holmes and Brandeis, the courts continued to declare that the danger of radical political speech was something that could occur either immediately or at some unspecified time in the future.

The Alien Registration Act of 1940, known popularly as the Smith Act, reinforced the Espionage and Sedition Acts of the First World War by criminalizing speech that teaches or advocates the overthrow of the American government. Simply joining a group that advocated that goal was sufficient evidence for a conviction.[67] The Smith Act prohibited "any written or printed matter advocating, advising, or teaching the duty, necessity, desirability, or propriety of overthrowing or destroying any government in the United States by force or violence." In practice it targeted Communists, suspected Communists, or Communist sympathizers during the red scares of the 1950s. It lay behind the infamous Hollywood blacklist, which banned suspected leftists from the entertainment industry. It was leveraged to force public employees to sign loyalty oaths swearing that they were not now, nor had they ever been, members of the Communist Party. It saw teachers suspected of left-wing sympathies hounded from their posts. Although some of the loyalty oaths were ultimately overturned and others have fallen into disuse, the key provisions of the Smith Act remain in force as 18 USC § 2385, and its provisions could conceivably apply to rioters arrested on January 6. But its principal targets were Communists.

In 1948, the leaders of the American Communist Party were convicted under the Smith Act for conspiring to teach the overthrow of the government of the United States. A federal appeals court upheld these convictions in *United States* v. *Dennis* (1950).[68] Writing that opinion was Learned Hand, the judge who ruled in 1917 that the antiwar sentiments of *The Masses* did not constitute a clear and present danger. But by 1950, Hand had concluded that the revolution of the proletariat must be stopped even though it was not likely to happen any time soon. Hand, now chief judge of the Second Circuit Court of Appeals – the same court that had overruled his opinion in *Masses* – rejected the imminent danger standard that Brandeis had proposed in *Whitney*. According to Brandeis, even Communist speech was protected if there were no immediate plans to carry out the revolution and there was time to test the Communists' assertions in the marketplace, time to meet bad speech with more speech. But Hand insisted that Brandeis, who had died in 1941, would change his mind about protecting radical speech in the current case, because the Communists had learned to mask their destructive purposes with "fair words," and because world events suggested that the dangers of Communism had become greater after the Second World War.

Hand then reiterated the imperative of interpretation that he had articulated years earlier in *Masses:*

No longer can there be any doubt, if indeed there was before, that the phrase, "clear and present danger," is not a slogan or a shibboleth to be applied as though it carried its own meaning; but that it involves in every case a comparison between interests which are to be appraised qualitatively.

Echoing utilitarian philosopher Jeremy Bentham, Hand then offered a formula for measuring whether a given utterance posed a clear and present danger: "In each case [the courts] must ask whether the gravity of the 'evil,' discounted by its improbability, justifies such invasion of free speech as is necessary to avoid the danger." Hand's formula actually defies quantitative measurement, and he compounded this absurdity by crafting an interpretation of "clear and present" in which *present* can also mean "future." If the courts may stop a bad act that is imminent, he reasoned, then they are bound to stop that same bad act from occurring at some unspecified future date if its occurrence is not altogether improbable: "It would be wholly irrational to condone future evils which we should prevent if they were immediate."

Hand did acknowledge that the Communist Party was not yet in a position to overthrow the American government, but he recited a list of signs that the revolution, if not at hand, was coming closer day by day: the spread of Communism in eastern Europe after the war; the Soviet-backed Berlin blockade of 1948; and the shift of the American Communist Party from a loosely organized collection of supporters unable to formulate a revolutionary plan, to a well-organized and disciplined machine committed to subversion and espionage. For Hand, the Communist conspiracy at home and abroad was working toward the eventual overthrow of democracy, and that was enough to satisfy his formula: "Such a conspiracy creates a danger of the utmost gravity and of enough probability to justify its suppression. We hold that it is a danger 'clear and present.'"

A year later, the Supreme Court affirmed Hand's ruling.[69] The high Court found that although it was legal to discuss Communism – for example, in a politics class – no discussion could *advocate* Communist doctrines.

Furthermore, simply belonging to a group whose philosophy calls for the violent overthrow of the government was evidence of intent to overthrow that government, whether by direct action or through speech. And in any case, a government may always protect itself from armed and violent rebellion, or from words advocating such rebellion. Justices Hugo Black and William O. Douglas separately dissented in *Dennis*, arguing that the defendants had engaged in speech, not action, and that the Court's decision ignored the well-established "clear and present danger" standard for First Amendment prosecutions. Despite this objection, the Supreme Court affirmed the *Dennis* convictions even though the defendants had committed no documented acts of rebellion, because the revolution, though perhaps not imminent, was not improbable. As Justice Fred M. Vinson put it in his opinion, "It is the existence of the conspiracy which creates the danger. If the ingredients of the reaction are present, we cannot bind the Government to wait until the catalyst is added."

## DEFINING PRESENT DANGER

Twenty years after *Dennis*, the Supreme Court revised its interpretation of *clear and present danger*, along with its approach to unprotected political speech, yet again. In *Brandenburg* v. *Ohio* (1969),[70] the Court reversed the conviction of Clarence Brandenburg for violating Ohio's law against "criminal syndicalism" – the act of joining a group that advocated "crime, sabotage, violence, or unlawful methods of terrorism as a means of accomplishing industrial or political reform."[71] Brandenburg was a member of the Ku Klux Klan, and at a Klan "rally" of a dozen men burning a cross in an isolated field, he called for deporting Jews to Israel and Blacks to Africa, and urged "revengeance" against African Americans. Brandenburg's tirade was witnessed only by the participants and a local TV journalist who had been invited to observe. In letting Brandenburg off the hook, the Court also overturned the Ohio criminal syndicalism law, passed in 1919 to target unions and Communists, a law which closely resembled the California statute under which Anita Whitney had been convicted and whose constitutionality the Court had affirmed in 1927. In *Brandenburg*, the Court finally adopted Justice Brandeis' recommendation that to constitute a "present danger," speech must be likely to produce an immediate action that can't be prevented by further speech: "The constitutional guarantees of free speech and free press do not permit a State to forbid or proscribe advocacy of the use of force or of law violation except where such advocacy is directed to inciting or producing *imminent lawless action* and is likely to incite or produce such action."[72] Uttered in an remote field before a few witnesses, Brandenburg's words could have no immediate impact, and so his white supremacist speech came within the protections of the First Amendment.

It may seem significant that it eventually took an instance of extreme right-wing speech to clarify the meaning of "clear and present danger." The *Brandenburg* standard was applied again to defend the speech of then-presidential candidate Donald Trump. On March 1, 2016, Super Tuesday, three protestors unveiled anti-Trump signs as Trump spoke to a rally in Louisville, Kentucky. In response, Trump shouted from the podium, "Get 'em out of here." Interpreting the words as marching orders, several Trump supporters attacked the protesters, striking them, shoving them, and punching them. Security personnel – a mix of Secret Service, police, and private guards – did not intervene, which suggests that they, too, thought Trump's imperative "Get 'em out of here" was an order to his audience of supporters, not to those who, charged with rally security, might be expected to maintain order. The protesters then sued their attackers in federal court for assault and battery, and they sued Trump as well for "incitement to riot."[73] A federal appeals court eventually dismissed the suit because Trump's directive, "Get 'em out of here," did not result in immediate, lawless action on a wide-enough scale, and because Trump also tempered his command by saying, "Don't hurt 'em." The court did not weigh the probability that the audience discounted Trump's "Don't hurt 'em" before it did, in fact, hurt the protestors.[74]

The Supreme Court found Brandenburg's words protected because they were said in a context that all but guaranteed they would be ineffective. The Sixth Circuit Court of Appeals found Trump's words protected as well, even though they were quickly followed by violent acts in much the same way that Trump's words were followed by lawless action on January 6. Presumably the court would protect the same words coming from a speaker on the left. That's because the protections of the First Amendment are neutral with respect to point of view: they apply to speech across the political spectrum. Had the *Brandenburg* standard of "imminent lawless action" been in place in 1918, the "silly" *Abrams* leaflets would surely have come under the heading of protected speech. Even Charles Schenck's serious and coordinated campaign against conscription in the First World War, which may have actually swayed some conscientious objectors to resist the draft, would be protected speech today.

## PROTECTING SPEECH IN SCHOOL

Historically, student speech has not enjoyed the same protections as the speech of adults, and in some cases the speech of teachers is even less secure than that of students. Despite First Amendment guarantees, speech restrictions are baked into the educational process, with states telling teachers what they can and cannot teach, and teachers telling students what they can and cannot say. School authorities routinely prescribe curriculum and methodology, and schoolwork regularly requires students to speak and write both in class and for homework. In addition, teachers may assign speech or writing to students as punishments for infractions.

Although student speech is critical to education, schools often assume that some student speech may disrupt the education process. Anticipating such danger, schools constrain speech with "no talking" rules to maintain discipline. Until the second half of the twentieth century, student political speech enjoyed no special protection. And despite a major victory for student speech in 1969, schools still control much of what a student can and cannot say or write.

For much of American history, courts typically regarded student speech as something for schools to handle internally, and they were reluctant to support students who challenged restrictions on their speech. In an 1859 Vermont case, a teacher named A. B. Seaver whipped his pupil, eleven-year-old Peter Lander, Jr., for calling Seaver a jackass off school grounds but in the presence of other students. The Vermont Supreme Court observed that in general a teacher could not punish a student for acts committed outside the classroom, but it upheld the right of teachers to punish students for words which "heap odium and disgrace upon the master" and which have "a direct and immediate tendency to injure the school and to subvert the master's authority," no matter where they are uttered.[75] In such cases, student speech was not protected speech.

For over a century, US courts assumed that schools could punish student speech and censor student publications. Then, in *Tinker v. Des Moines* (1969), the US Supreme Court upheld students' right to speak out on political issues.[76] John F. Tinker, Christopher Eckhard, and Mary Beth Tinker were suspended from their Iowa schools in December, 1965, after they wore black armbands to class to protest the Vietnam War. Courts had already recognized that wearing an armband at an anti-war protest was a form of protected political speech. Writing the opinion in *Tinker*, Justice Abe Fortas extended the First Amendment right to protest to the classroom: "It can hardly be argued that either students or teachers shed their constitutional rights to freedom of speech or expression at the schoolhouse gate." Although the decision also covered teachers, it focused on the speech of students, warning that the heckler's veto cannot be used to stifle student protests: "[F]ear or apprehension of disturbance is not enough to overcome the right to freedom of expression." But the Court also made clear that disruptive student speech was not protected: "[C]onduct by the student, in class or out of it, which ... materially disrupts classwork or involves substantial disorder or invasion of the rights of others is, of course, not immunized by the constitutional guarantee of freedom of speech." Note that the clear and present danger of student speech has nothing to do with interfering with the war effort (the standard set in *Schenck*), or inciting imminent lawless action (the stricter *Brandenburg* standard). Instead, it covers unspecified disruptions to lessons or to other aspects of the school routine, anything from wisecracks during math class to raised voices in the lunchroom.

Finding that no such disruption had occurred during the students' silent armband protest, the *Tinker* court affirmed the students' right to express their opinions even when those opinions differ from those held by the school:

> In our system, state-operated schools may not be enclaves of totalitarianism. School officials do not possess absolute authority over their students. Students in school as well as out of school are "persons" under our Constitution. They are possessed of fundamental rights which the State must

respect, just as they themselves must respect their obligations to the State. In our system, students may not be regarded as closed-circuit recipients of only that which the State chooses to communicate. They may not be confined to the expression of those sentiments that are officially approved. In the absence of a specific showing of constitutionally valid reasons to regulate their speech, students are entitled to freedom of expression of their views.

Subsequent courts have applied a *Tinker* test to student speech – would the words in question clearly disrupt the educational process, or did they in fact disrupt that process? If the answer is no, then the speech is protected. But other rulings narrowed the *Tinker* protections and broadened schools' authority both to punish students whose speech triggered a disruption, or to affirm the heckler's veto by shutting down potentially disruptive student speech. In some instances that echo the earlier decision in *Lander*, schools were permitted to stifle speech that either embarrassed the school or that had the potential to do so.

Justice Potter Stewart, concurring in *Tinker*, cautioned that children's First Amendment rights are not the same as those of adults. Even the free-speech absolutist Hugo Black supported some restrictions on where and when protests were protected – the permissible time and manner constraints on speech: "I have never believed that everyone with opinions or beliefs to express may address a group at any public place at any time." Justice Black further argued that a school has the right to make rules about appropriate speech not just for students, who are there to learn rather than to teach, but also for teachers, who are hired not to take political stands but to deliver the curriculum chosen for them: "The truth is that a teacher of kindergarten, grammar school, or high school pupils no more carries into a school with him a complete right to freedom of speech and expression than an anti-Catholic or anti-Semite carries with him a complete freedom of speech and religion into a Catholic church or Jewish synagogue." Black's comment echoes that of Oliver Wendell Holmes in his dissent in *Meyer* v. *Nebraska* (1923), a case that we will look at in Chapter 6: "No one would doubt that a teacher might be forbidden to teach many things."[77]

The main impact of *Tinker* was to give students, not teachers, important speech protections. But although general First Amendment protections have continued to expand, subsequent school-related cases narrowed some student speech rights. In the state of Washington in 1983, high school student Matthew N. Fraser delivered a bawdy speech at a school assembly nominating a friend for student government. According to the complaint against him, "During the entire speech, Fraser referred to his candidate in terms of elaborate, graphic, and explicit sexual metaphor."[78] He was suspended for violating a school rule prohibiting "Conduct which materially and substantially interferes with the educational process ... including the use of obscene, profane language or gestures." Responding to Fraser's lawsuit protesting his suspension, a district court ruled that the student's speech was protected under the First Amendment, and that the school's rule was unconstitutionally vague and overbroad.

The appeals court affirmed that decision, but in *Bethel School District v. Fraser* (1983), the Supreme Court reversed. In his opinion, Chief Justice Warren Burger observed that even Thomas Jefferson had drafted a congressional rule prohibiting impertinent and indecent speech in House debates. Burger further explained, "the constitutional rights of students in public schools are not automatically coextensive with the rights of adults in other settings."[79] Concurring in that decision, Justice William Brennan acknowledged that courts "have a First Amendment responsibility to insure that robust rhetoric in student publications is not suppressed by prudish failures to distinguish the vigorous from the vulgar." But Brennan, too, found that in this case, the Bethel School District had acted appropriately to punish a student's disruptive speech. The disruption in question? Students hooted and yelled; some made gestures simulating sexual activity; others "appeared to be bewildered or embarrassed"; and one teacher "found it necessary to forgo a portion of the scheduled class lesson in order to discuss the speech with the class." None of this constitutes the imminent lawless action of a *Brandenburg* test, but it does qualify as a literal disruption of school activities, which satisfies the *Tinker* test. This is not to challenge the school's right to discipline the words of a class clown, but it is striking when we compare what was at stake in *Tinker* and the early political speech cases with what is at stake in *Fraser*: serious war protests versus frivolous off-color remarks. Bethel High punished Fraser for speech that embarrassed the school, and the Supreme Court validated that punishment.

In another case involving student speech that *might* make a school look bad, the Supreme Court further narrowed *Tinker* in 1988 by affirming a school's right to censor student publications. The principal of Hazelwood East High School, in Missouri, removed two pages from the school newspaper that contained stories about students' experiences with pregnancy and with divorce. The principal feared that readers would be able to guess the identities of the students discussed in the articles and that references to sexual activity and birth control were inappropriate for younger students – in effect he was afraid the school would be viewed as endorsing the activities discussed in the articles.[80]

The student editors sued on First Amendment grounds, and the Circuit Court agreed that the newspaper, though it was school-sponsored, was also a "public forum" with constitutional protection. The Court of Appeals reversed that decision, and the Supreme Court agreed that school newspapers are not public forums in the way that streets and parks are, open indiscriminately to all. Instead, Hazelwood High's journalism class and the newspaper it produced functioned as educational laboratories, and as such they came under the ultimate control of the school administration. In his opinion, Justice Byron White noted that as publisher, the school is within its rights to remove newspaper speech that is "ungrammatical, poorly written, inadequately researched, biased or prejudiced, vulgar or profane, or unsuitable for immature audiences." Consequently, although three dissenting justices maintained that the school's censorship ignored the *Tinker* precedent and served no educational purpose, the majority agreed that "educators do not offend the First Amendment by exercising editorial control over the style and content of student speech in school-sponsored expressive activities so long as their actions are reasonably related to legitimate pedagogical concerns." But as with *Hazelwood*, the principal's main goal was more about avoiding controversy than ensuring effective pedagogy.

In another striking case, the Supreme Court upheld a school's right to punish a student for speech that purportedly advocated illegal drug use. Speech promoting criminal behavior is never protected. But applying that doctrine to the words in question in *Morse* v. *Frederick* (2007), popularly known as the "Bong Hits 4 Jesus" case, seems at best a stretch.[81]

When the Olympic Torch Relay reached Juneau, Alaska, in 2002, Deborah Morse, principal of Juneau-Douglas High School, allowed students and staff to go outside to watch the parade. As the torchbearers marched by, Joseph Frederick and his friends unfurled a fourteen-foot banner bearing the hand-lettered words, "Bong hits 4 Jesus." When Morse ordered the students to put away the banner, all complied except Frederick. Morse suspended Frederick for ten days for displaying a banner that encouraged illegal drug use, a violation of school policy. Frederick challenged his suspension, and although the District Court found the punishment to be valid, the Ninth Circuit Court of Appeals ruled that Frederick's First Amendment speech rights had been abridged. Ultimately, though, the Supreme Court supported Principal Morse.

In his opinion in *Morse*, Chief Justice John Roberts conceded that the phrase "Bong hits 4 Jesus" is cryptic: "It is no doubt offensive to some, perhaps amusing to others. To still others, it probably means nothing at all." Frederick himself insisted that the words on the banner had no meaning. The atmosphere among the students lining both sides of the street outside the school was boisterous as they waited for the Olympic torch, and Frederick's banner bore a nonsense message designed to attract the attention of television cameras accompanying the torchbearers, scoring some local air time for him and his friends. But Morse read the banner as advocating the use of illegal substances. The Court majority held that, since the banner's message was ambiguous and Morse's reading was plausible, she was within her rights to suspend Frederick for speech that violated school rules.

Chief Justice Roberts found Frederick's cryptic message to be either an imperative, *take bong hits*, or a declarative statement that *bong hits are a good thing*. Even if Frederick's motive was simply to get on TV, Roberts found that his method of attracting attention "was by unfurling a pro-drug banner at a school event, in the presence of teachers and fellow students." In his concurrence, Justice Clarence Thomas went further, citing the 1859 decision in *Lander* and arguing that *Tinker* should be overruled because students never have speech rights in school. And Justice Samuel Alito argued that since "schools can be places of special danger," they may ban speech like Frederick's because "illegal drug use presents a grave and in many ways unique threat to the physical safety of students." Justice Stephen Breyer cautioned against limiting students' First Amendment rights, but he believed that Morse, acting in her role as principal, was justified in asking a student to remove a huge banner that was likely to prove disruptive no matter what it said. And Justice John Paul Stevens supported the principal's right to punish Frederick for creating a disturbance, even though the banner itself merited First Amendment protection.

For Stevens, who cited Learned Hand's opinion in *Masses*, Frederick's "ridiculous sign" was not about to start an epidemic of student drug use. It was "a nonsense message, not advocacy." Stevens added, "it takes real imagination to read a 'cryptic' message ... with a slanting drug reference as an incitement to drug use." Stevens further described the Roberts' reasoning as "ham-handed" and "deaf to the constitutional imperative to promote unfettered debate." And he accused the Court of "inventing out of whole cloth a special First Amendment rule permitting the censorship of any student speech that mentions drugs, at least so long as someone could perceive that speech to contain a latent pro-drug message."

It is clear that Frederick's banner did not meet the *Tinker* disruption test: the students were already in a relaxed and noisy party mood, and it is not likely that any of them paid much attention to Frederick's prank. But it is also clear that Principal Morse acted as she did not to prevent a wave of drug use, but to keep the school from looking bad. That's one part of the *Lander* test – do the words pose "a direct and immediate tendency to injure the school?" – which *Tinker* never addressed or overruled.

Stevens further characterized the decision in *Morse* as impermissible viewpoint discrimination. The Court generally finds that any attempt to restrict free speech must be neutral: it cannot privilege one opinion over others. Maintaining this neutrality was the basis for a 2011 decision in the US Seventh Circuit Court of Appeals, which ruled that a school district cannot permit student speech on one side of a controversy but censor student speech that takes the opposite position.[82] In that case, Heidi Zamecnik and Alexander Nuxoll sued Neuqua Valley High School, in Naperville, Illinois, for forbidding them to wear t-shirts at school with the message "Be Happy, Not Gay," the day after the annual pro-LGBTQ national Day of Silence. The Day of Silence protests the silencing of gay, lesbian, and nonbinary voices. It is observed by students and teachers in many American high schools and colleges, and it was formally supported by the Neuqua Valley school authorities.

Zamecnik and Nuxoll objected to the Day of Silence by proclaiming the next day to be a "Day of Truth" and wearing t-shirts with hand-lettered anti-gay messages. School authorities, arguing that these t-shirts violated school antiharassment policies, ordered the students to remove the shirts or leave school. In response, the students sued, arguing that the school had violated their First Amendment speech rights. In his opinion supporting the students, Judge Richard Posner found a "very real tension between antiharassment laws and the Constitution's guarantee of freedom of speech." He reasoned that "a school that permits advocacy of the rights of homosexual students cannot be allowed to stifle criticism of homosexuality." Posner added, "people in our society do not have a legal right to prevent criticism of their beliefs or even their way of life." In addition, Posner found the t-shirt messages relatively tame: they did not constitute fighting words, and although some students voiced their displeasure toward Zamecnik and Nuxoll, they did not disrupt the educational process.

In most post-*Tinker* cases, all that the school authorities must show is that some student speech or writing either disrupted a classroom or had the potential to make the school look bad, at least as far as speech in school or during school-sponsored activities is concerned. In its most recent student speech case, however, the Supreme Court finally rejected *Lander* and upheld the constitutional protection for much off-campus student speech, even when that speech is about school.

Brandi Levy, a student at Mahanoy Area High School, in Pennsylvania, had failed to make the varsity cheerleader squad. She gave vent to her frustration in a weekend Snapchat image showing her and a friend who had not made the softball team with their middle fingers raised and the caption, "Fuck school fuck softball fuck cheer fuck everything." Although snaps are designed to vanish after a day, one student screenshot Levy's post and the image made its way to the cheerleading coaches. They suspended Levy from the junior varsity squad for profanity that violated team and school rules.

Levy sued, arguing that the school could not police her off-campus speech. The lower courts agreed, and in *Mahanoy Area School District v. B. L.* (2021), the Supreme Court affirmed that Levy's speech was protected because she was off campus; she was not engaged in a school-sponsored activity at the time she spoke; and her speech did not substantially disrupt the educational process.[83] In a lone dissent, Justice Clarence Thomas invoked *Lander* and the historical practice of censuring students for speech that injures the school. But the Court's majority declined to go that far. They did acknowledge that "public schools may have a special interest in regulating some off-campus students speech," for example, speech that bullies, harasses, or threatens; speech related to school assignments; speech while using school devices; or speech while engaged in school-related online activities. But because Levy's speech was none of those things, it merited constitutional protection.

Free trade in ideas may be fine for political speech, broadly defined as anything to do with matters of public concern. But as the courts have ruled repeatedly, not all ideas qualify for protection. Obscene speech is always unprotected. But as we see in the next chapter, courts have trouble deciding between what is obscene and what is not. It turns out that obscenity, just like "clear and present danger," is a matter of interpretation.

## CHAPTER 4

# Strong Language

I know it when I see it.

Potter Stewart, *Jacobellis* v. *Ohio*, 1964

Over the course of the twentieth century, the test for unprotected political speech shifted from words that present a "clear and present danger"
to those likely to produce "imminent lawless action." The new test is
narrower, but courts must still determine whether the speech in question merits constitutional protection. In contrast, obscenity has always
been unprotected speech. States ratifying the Bill of Rights in 1791 saw
no contradiction between the new First Amendment speech protections
and the anti-obscenity laws that they already enforced.

Just as the line between protected and unprotected political speech has
shifted in the direction of protecting more speech, the tests to help courts
determine what is obscene and what is not have shifted over the course of
time, protecting more and more speech that once was banned. Over time,
courts asked whether the speech in question aroused prurient interest – a
delicate way of asking, did it make you have sexy thoughts? Did it deprave
susceptible audiences? Violate national standards of decency? Or, the test
as it stands now in the United States, does it offend local community sensibilities? The last standard may be as vague as the others, but at least it is not
one-size-fits-all. Although more speech that once was banned as too strong
has become commonplace and acceptable in more contexts, the tests for
determining language that is too strong to warrant protection remain subjective, often leaving speakers unsure whether their words violate the law.
And they leave audiences with little more than the "test" for hard-core
pornography formulated by Justice Potter Stewart in 1964: you may not be
able to define it, but *you'll know it when you see it.*

## READER DISCRETION ADVISED

It turns out there is plenty of strong language to see, plenty to hear, and plenty to ban. Strong language in public is against the law in England, and in 2016, a British court told a homeless man who was prone to shouting abuse when he was drunk that he could no longer swear anywhere in the United Kingdom.[1] On their Frequently Asked Questions site, the British police warn, "You could be arrested for swearing in the street ... However, a person is only likely to be arrested for this offence if the behaviour occurs in the presence of a police officer."[2] And the homeless inebriate in question would do well to stay away from the 200 pubs belonging to the Samuel Smith breweries, whose owner has banned swearing in any of their establishments. A company "secret sipper," who normally goes pubbing to check that the pours are neither skimpy nor excessive, cleared out a bar in Yorkshire because the language of the regulars was just too raw. Smith's doesn't supply a list of banned words – even mentioning the words would violate the company no-swears policy – relying instead on a version of Potter Stewart's formula, "You'll know it when you hear it."[3]

Swearing is a crime in parts of the United States, as well. A Milwaukee woman was arrested in 2016 for language that "unreasonably offends the sense of decency or propriety of the community." Her offense? Swearing at her teenage son when they were alone in their house.[4] In 2014, a South Carolina woman was arrested for swearing in front of her children in a grocery store. She directed an f-bomb at her husband for crushing the bread in the shopping cart.[5] And as I was putting the final touches on this chapter, the McMinn County Board of Education, in Tennessee, banned Art Spiegelman's *Maus,* a graphic novel about the Holocaust that won a Pulitzer Prize in 1992. The reason? Nudity in two pictures of anthropomorphic mice and eight instances of curse words like *damn.*

Even using strong language in front of an audience of consenting adults can be a criminal offence. In the 1960s, the comedian Lenny Bruce was arrested four times for using obscenity in his nightclub act. Like Justice Stewart, we all know obscenity when we see it, but the problem, for the law, is that we don't all agree on what is obscene. Officer James Ryan arrested Lenny Bruce in 1961 for an obscene monologue that the audience at San Francisco's Jazz Workshop thought hilarious. When Bruce was tried on that obscenity charge, the judge had to caution the jury *not to laugh* when they listened to a recording of the comedian's act. Stifling their guffaws, they found Bruce not guilty.[6] But other juries in other venues did convict him of obscenity and, for good measure, drug abuse.

The protections both for political speech and for strong language have narrowed the kinds of words that can't be said or written, with one key difference. Unprotected political speech, for example, picketing inside the Supreme Court building, is still *political* speech; it is just political speech that can't take place in one specific venue, a legitimate time and manner restriction. But for obscene speech to enjoy any protection at all, it must no longer count as obscene. When Paul Robert Cohen was arrested inside the Los Angeles County Courthouse in 1968 for wearing a jacket with the words "Fuck the Draft" written on the back, the Supreme Court found that Cohen's use of a four-letter word was not obscene because it was not erotic in that particular context. According to the Court, Cohen's message did not excite thoughts of sex in those who read it. Rather, it protested the Vietnam War. His words were not obscene speech, which the state may ban; they were political speech, which the state must protect.[7]

The line that separates obscene words from acceptable ones shifts with time and context. It shifts with audience as well: many of the examples we will look at raise the question, *obscene for whom?* Novels that once were banned for obscenity, like James Joyce's *Ulysses* or D. H. Lawrence's *Lady Chatterley's Lover,* have become mainstream literary classics. When it was shown in Ohio, outraged residents condemned Louis Malle's *Les Amants* (1958) as obscene pornography for a fleeting bathtub scene with little visible skin, and an overall theme of marital infidelity. But Justice Stewart disagreed: "I shall not today attempt further to define the kinds of material I understand to be embraced within [hard-core pornography], and perhaps I could never succeed in intelligibly doing so. *But I know it when I see it,* and the motion picture involved in this case is not that."[8] Anyone watching *Les Amants* today would wonder what all the fuss was about.

Even normally uncontroversial texts like dictionaries can fall victim to the over-eager censor. In 1982, Carlsbad, New Mexico, barred *Merriam-Webster's Collegiate Dictionary* from local classrooms because some of its definitions were too racy for young children,[9] and in 2010, the

Menifee, California, Union School District did the same.[10] Both British and American law now require a book or film to be considered as a whole before it can be judged obscene, but none of the school censors had read the offending dictionaries from cover to cover. They went straight to what they considered the dirty bits and set off a hue and cry against obscenity. Banning dictionaries for defining specific words also reminds us that many discussions of obscenity focus on the need to protect *other people* from strong language, further complicating the legal wrangling that surrounds obscenity: we – whoever *we* are – can handle it, because we have taste, maturity, and refinement, but those people – you know who we're talking about – they simply can't.

School boards banning dictionaries seems extreme. Even though bookish children may run to dictionaries to look up sexual terms, as early as 1930 researchers reported that more children learned about sex from the Bible than from any other book.[11] That may be why, in 1833, Noah Webster took time off from his dictionary-making to re-translate the Bible, replacing some of the blunter words in the King James Version with euphemisms to protect the tender sensibilities of women and children. As Webster explained in the introduction to his sanitized scriptures, "Many words and phrases are so offensive, especially to females, as to create a reluctance in young persons to attend Bible classes and schools, in which they are required to read passages which cannot be repeated without a blush; and containing words which, on other occasions, a child could not utter without rebuke."[12]

## LITERACY AND BAD WORDS

Mandatory universal education, introduced in the nineteenth century in England and the United States, produced massive numbers of new readers. Public policy at the time encouraged literacy as essential for economic success and good citizenship. Workers had to read to do their jobs in the increasingly technological environment of the industrial revolution. But the spike in literacy had a downside as well. Government and religious authorities feared that too much education could lead to social unrest, as workers or the faithful, exposed to books and newspapers, might seek to rise above their station or reject current orthodoxies.

To guard against such dangers, selective censorship would steer these new readers to appropriate texts and shield them from bad ones.

We associate censorship with authoritarian states, but two case studies, a debate in the English House of Commons in 1888 on the problem of obscenity, and a similar debate in the US Senate in 1930, show that liberal democracies like Britain and the United States also sought to regulate access to print to protect vulnerable citizens, not just from revolutionary ideas but also from bad words. The goal in both countries was to keep strong language away from the eyes of those easily swayed, on the theory that obscene books led these newly-literate middle-class women and children, as well as all members of the lower classes, directly to drink, crime, and prostitution. Legislators in both countries, all of them well-off, well-educated men, assumed that only other well-off and well-educated men possessed the judgment and sophistication necessary to process anything the least bit racy.

## THE TRIALS OF HENRY VIZETELLY

In 1870, England's Education Act established elementary schools in areas where none had previously existed. Ten years later, elementary education became compulsory nationwide. The adult literacy rate in England in 1770 was no more than 40 percent. By 1880 that had doubled, and by the end of the 1880s, it was assumed that all British children could read.[13] This explosion in readership contributed to an explosion of inexpensive newspapers, magazines, and novels targeting the new audience. In Britain, the novels were called "penny dreadfuls" or "shilling shockers," and in the United States, where mandatory schooling was implemented state by state over several decades, they were known as "dime novels." These labels marked such books as distinct both in content and in price from the more expensive, leather-bound, high-brow literature available to those readers who were considered higher up on both the economic and the moral scales.

Literacy was vital for maintaining Britain's competitive edge in manufacturing, but as literacy rates rose, so did concerns that these new readers, particularly young children and unmarried women, might be exposed to literature that could damage their moral fiber. The MP Samuel Smith (no relation to the brewery) was a member of the National

Vigilance Association (NVA), a group devoted to protecting women and minors from sexual exploitation. In a speech to the House of Commons in 1888, Smith argued that cheap books, like cheap liquor, promoted crime, and he blamed the 1870 Education Act for failing to protect the new readers it had created from the scandalous books that led children directly into prostitution. Smith charged that booksellers specializing in shilling shockers were no better than pimps and brothel keepers:

> It had become the rule with a class of low booksellers in London to provide indecent literature for young girls ... to provide them with private rooms stocked with the vilest class of literature ... In many cases these shops were in league with houses of the worst class, to which the girls when their minds were sufficiently polluted and depraved were consigned.[14]

Smith's puritanical diatribe – that books were the gateway drug to prostitution – didn't target actual pornography – a genre that has been around for thousands of years. Instead, he focused on a new publishing phenomenon, the mass-produced, 2-shilling English translations of the scandalous French novels of Emile Zola being published in England by Henry Vizetelly. Smith's attack led directly to Vizetelly's conviction and imprisonment for obscenity. Though Smith opposed Zola in any language and at any price, in prosecuting Vizetelly, the government's concern was to keep these steamy French novels out of the hands of workers, a group incapable of understanding whatever literary merit they might have, and too easily corrupted by the sexual themes that permeated the tales. The authorities took no action against booksellers who imported Zola's works in the original French, or against the English publishers of finely-bound, limited-edition Zola translations that were too expensive for the masses.[15]

Novelists themselves, all of them members of the privileged classes they wrote for, tended to agree that their books were dangerous in the wrong hands. Although the characters in their novels might be members of the lower orders, many writers wanted "modern" literature kept away from those not able to understand and appreciate it because of their low social position, and even Zola agreed that people like his characters should never read his novels. Zola's puritanical English critics conceded that Chaucer and Shakespeare could also be bawdy, but their works had other redeeming qualities, and besides, new readers went straight for the new French novels, not these hoary English classics.

The two obscenity trials of Henry Vizetelly focused on the issue of who should be allowed to read what. In 1888, Vizetelly was charged with producing obscene translations of three Zola novels, *Nana* (1884), *Pot-Bouille* (published in England as *Piping Hot* in 1887), and *La Terre* (*The Soil*, 1888). The title page of Vizetelly's edition of *The Soil* calls the novel "realistic," a code word that warned – or promised – that the book contained what we might today call "strong language," "adult themes," and "sexual content." At Vizetelly's trial, Solicitor General Edward Clarke relied on the obscenity test set earlier in the case of *Regina* v. *Hicklin* (1868), a decision that set the standard for literary censorship in England and America for almost seventy years.

In *Hicklin,* a prosecution under the Obscene Publications Act of 1857, the Lord Chief Justice, Sir Alexander Cockburn, found the publication of an anti-Catholic pamphlet obscene because, in order to expose "the practices and errors ... in the Roman Catholic Church" it contained too many accounts "involving practices and propensities of a certain description." That was Cockburn's chaste way of referring to the work's frank discussion of adultery, sexual stimulation, and copulation. For Cockburn, the rehearsal of such questions, even to criticize them, suggested "thoughts and desires which otherwise would not have occurred to [readers'] minds." And he confirmed that even if only part of a book is obscene, then all of it must be condemned. This view did not change until the mid-twentieth century, when courts began assessing the impact of the entire work, not just a few of its words.

England's Obscene Publications Act had not defined obscenity, the assumption being, "you'll know it when you read it." *Hicklin* established an obscenity test that courts would use for decades: "Whether the tendency of the matter charged as obscenity is to deprave and corrupt those *whose minds are open to such immoral influences,* and into whose hands a publication of this sort may fall."[16] There are two essential elements to the *Hicklin* test: the context of the work and its audience. *Hicklin* found that some readers are able to handle without a blush material that would provoke others to lust and abandon. But the concern of the law must be the actual or potential audience, not the intended one. Even placing a book on the wrong shelf can render it obscene. As Cockburn put it, a medical text with anatomically correct illustrations is not obscene in the hands of doctors. But the moment that book is placed in a shop window, where it can be viewed by those "whose minds are open to … immoral influences," it becomes obscene: "It can never be that these prints may be exhibited for any one, boys and girls, to see as they pass." Obscenity laws are meant to protect these vulnerable readers, and if there is a chance such readers can see a problematic book, then moving it to a secure location is not enough. That book must be destroyed.

For the prosecutors going after Henry Vizetelly, the groups likely to be corrupted weren't children, who didn't read Zola, but the poor and women of all classes, although there was no evidence that they read Zola either. With a pint of beer or a measure of gin selling for a couple of pence, it is not likely that coal miners and factory workers were lining up to shell out 2 shillings – about £7 or $10 today – for the latest import from across the Channel. Instead, Vizetelly's customers were more likely to be the men and women working in shops and offices who had begun accumulating both disposable income and leisure time and were seeking refinement, not cheap thrills.

The Solicitor General warned the Vizetelly jurors that Zola's novels were not high-class literary works with two or three offensive passages, but rather books "filthy from beginning to end." As he began to read offensive snippets from *The Soil* into the record, the scandalized all-male jury asked the prosecutor to stop, which he agreed to do if they would agree that what he was reading was obscene. At that point Vizetelly, realizing that he could not possibly be acquitted, changed his plea to guilty, reminding the judge, in mitigation, that the works in question were written by a great French author. But the judge refused to see any literary merit in Zola and found that Vizetelly deliberately published the novels "in order to deprave the minds of persons who might read the books." On October 31, 1888, the court fined Henry Vizetelly £100 for breach of the peace (about £6,500 or $8,900 today) and required him to post a £200 bond to keep the peace for one year. Vizetelly promised to withdraw the books from circulation and not to publish any more Zola.

The press almost universally praised the verdict, though some commentators thought it didn't go far enough. The *St. James Gazette* called for the regulation of true crime books as well as novels: "If dirty fiction is to be suppressed, why should we not take one step further and check the sensational histories of actual crimes?"[17] The *Whitehall Review* blamed increased literacy for the increase in "impure literature," which in turn had "an evil and contagious effect upon the morals of the nation." It noted as well that, in another trial involving an unexpurgated edition of Boccaccio's *Decameron,* the judge found it necessary to clear all the women from the courtroom. The real problem, according to the *Review,* was making European books available in an inexpensive format aimed specifically at those not mature enough to resist its depravity:

> It is no use to say that these books are literature. It may be right that they should remain in our libraries in the original languages, or perhaps in English, accessible to students of literature or of manners. That is no reason why they should be distributed broadcast in cheap issues, unexpurgated, or in careful selections of the most indecent parts, specially for the corruption of young people.

The *Methodist Times* echoed the call to leave such literature untranslated: "Let those who have a liking for the 'scrofulous French novel' read it if they will, but let it at least be in the original." And the *Western Morning News* observed, "[Zola] is more unclean, and realistically so, than any other writer, not an Oriental, whose name we can record."

The British, then at their height as a colonial power, had no problem locating the source of sexual depravity across the Channel or further to the East. But the moralists charged that bad books were being promoted at home as well by greedy publishers profiting from the new literacy. Writing to *The Standard,* Samuel Smith repeated what he had already told the House of Commons, that advances in education and the spread of literacy to the masses had led directly to the present crisis in morality: "Compulsory education has developed a capability for reading among classes who formerly took little interest in books, and the cheapness of sensational publications makes easy the gratification of this taste." Smith warned that publishers remain eager to profit from their new market, putting out "foul sensational publications, which stimulate the animal passions, and enable fleshly impulses to domineer over conscience and duty."[18]

Perhaps the public was indeed eager to buy cheap versions of the latest French novels, or perhaps Vizetelly simply need the money, but in any case he went back on his promise and cranked out more Zola translations. In a second trial a year later, he was sentenced to three months' imprisonment and forfeiture of his £200 bond.

## THE SENATE DEBATES OBSCENITY

America, too, responded to obscene books by emphasizing the need to protect women and children from strong language, blaming immoral foreigners for dirty books, and warning that such trash would spur the lower classes to commit more, and more horrendous, acts of depravity.

The first American laws against obscenity focused on imported art, not writing. An 1842 statute banned "the importation of all indecent and obscene prints, paintings, lithographs, engravings, and transparencies." But the 1865 Post Office law made it a misdemeanor to mail any "obscene book, pamphlet, picture, print, or other publication of a vulgar and indecent character."[19] And a few years later, at about the same time that Parliament debated obscenity, Congress passed the Comstock Act, banning any "Trade in, and Circulation of, obscene Literature."[20] That law was named after its chief proponent, Anthony Comstock, founder of the New York Society for the Prevention of Vice. In a particularly puritanical American twist, the Comstock law targeted not just obscene books but also "articles of immoral use," a category that included contraceptives and instruments for abortion, along with any written material advocating birth control, and it punished infractions with imprisonment "at hard labor" up to five years, or a fine up to $2,000 (about $43,000 or £31,200 today). Comstock was a postal inspector, and his law provided even stiffer penalties for sending such banned words through the mails: up to ten years in jail. It prohibited imports of any form of strong language as well. Customs clerks were directed to seize and destroy obscene books being brought into the country from abroad, and Comstock, as chief enforcer of the law, boasted that he had destroyed some 160 tons of obscene literature.[21]

Customs inspectors were given no definition of obscenity, but they knew it when they saw it. And they saw it in abundance. Each year, agents in New York – the major port of entry at the time – lit a festive bonfire of the books and magazines they had taken from passengers debarking at the West Side piers. But in 1929, the ability of untrained customs inspectors to distinguish dirty books from classic literature became the focus of a showdown in the Senate over a new anti-obscenity measure. Section 305 of a massive revision of the tariff law declared, "All persons are prohibited from importing into the United States from any foreign country any ... obscene book, pamphlet, paper, writing, advertisement, circular, print, picture, drawing, or other representation, figure, or image on or of paper or other material."[22]

The Smoot–Hawley tariff, as the omnibus bill was called, was co-sponsored by Senator Reed Smoot, of Utah, and Representative Willis Hawley, of Oregon. It significantly increased protective duties on a large number of imported goods, which prompted America's trading partners to raise their own tariffs on American products. As a result, US exports declined by half at the peak of the Depression. However, what got the nation's attention was not the complex economics of the tariff bill, but the Senate debate on its obscenity clause, which proved catnip for reporters. Lawmakers' heated discussions of how to identify and control obscene literature revealed the fault lines separating an isolationist and puritanical America from a progressive, worldly one.

Reed Smoot, a graduate of Brigham Young University and leader in the Mormon church, was the champion of the anti-obscenity campaign. To counteract widespread anti-Mormon prejudice in America, Smoot presented himself as thoroughly conventional and unbendably moral.[23] In keeping with that image, he added a section to his tariff bill that echoed the Comstock law. On the other side of the aisle, arguing that free speech was more important than collecting import duties, was Senator Bronson Cutting, an urbane New Yorker who had gone to Groton and Harvard but later moved to New Mexico for his asthma. Cutting led a liberal faction that sought to drop the obscenity clause from the tariff bill.

Over several days in October, 1929, shortly before the Wall Street crash, and again in March, 1930, some months after it, Cutting and his supporters argued strongly, rationally, and sometimes sarcastically, against Smoot's obscenity ban.[24] They questioned the ability of customs agents to identify offensive books and railed at the folly of letting the federal government dictate literary taste. Smoot and his supporters replied with passion, warning that bad literature corrupted America's women and its youth, blaming immigrants for bringing obscene literature into the country, and insisting that such books in the hands of the young invariably led them to crime and prostitution. Unlike the parliamentary discussion surrounding the Vizetelly case, the Senate obscenity debate was long and rambling. It was far-ranging, too, straying into racism, xenophobia, red-baiting, and personal attack. And it included show-and-tell: in March, 1930, Reed Smoot brought to the Senate floor copies of obscene books seized at the border, and Cutting countered with a display of similar books printed in America that he had purchased at a newsstand at Chicago's Union Station.

Cutting insisted that the average customs clerk might have no difficulty distinguishing dirty pictures from the old masters, but these civil servants lacked the training or refinement to identify literary obscenity. In addition, since clerks didn't have time to read an entire text before judging it, their decisions were often based on one objectionable word or phrase. Cutting warned, "Many books of highly moral tendency would be excluded if a man's attention were confined to one page, or one paragraph, or one sentence, or one word."[25] He cited an incident where overeager post office clerks declared the city of Chicago's annual vice report too dangerous to be sent through the mails, and he reported that customs inspectors were confiscating serious books about sex, including works by Havelock Ellis and Krafft-Ebbing, even when such books had been ordered by doctors and scientists.

Cutting cited a Customs Bureau report that explained its anti-obscenity focus:

[I]n passing upon such literature the Bureau of Customs has considered, primarily, its evil influence upon the impressionable minds of those persons the statutes, according to the courts, aim to protect – i.e., the young and inexperienced. In examining the text it is sought to determine if the psychological effect of the language would be to create in the mind of the individual libidinous thoughts, and unduly excite the sexual functions or arouse the animal passions.

The report separated the classics from obscene books masquerading as classics: "A 'classic' should be defined … on the one hand, wherein the obscene passages are incidental to the voluminous text of the superb literature, and the alleged 'classics,' cleverly conceived in an ancient medieval atmosphere, wherein obscenity is the motif."[26]

To this Cutting objected that censorship should be exercised not by the state, but by parents, adding that America's extensive education system should be enough to counteract the influence of any bad book. He reminded senators that bans on imported books were ineffective because many of the banned books were already being sold domestically and could be read in any library, including the Library of Congress.[27]

In addition to targeting obscenity, Smoot's tariff revision also banned the import of seditious publications, for example, the works of Karl Marx or other Russian political writers. Alabama Senator Thomas Heflin, who had helped shut down immigration to the United States with the 1924 "reform" bill, supported the sedition ban, expressing his contempt for anarchist literature: "I am going to vote today to keep America from becoming the dumping ground of the obscene, treasonable, and murderous literature of the anarchistic foreigners."[28] In the ensuing debate, the senators opposed to book bans stressed First Amendment concerns, while supporters emphasized the government's need to protect both the morals of Americans and the nation's political structure from pernicious outside influence. In the end, the Senate narrowly approved an amendment banning obscene art along with writing that advocated forcible resistance to American laws, but it dropped the ban on obscene literature.

Cutting's success in stopping the obscene books ban proved only temporary. Smoot reintroduced §305 when the Senate resumed its discussion of the tariff on March 17, 1930. In a concession to his critics, Smoot's revised amendment required that a book be judged as a whole, not on a few bawdy passages. It also told agents to seize "any book, which ... offends the moral sense of the average person." A number of senators pointed out that many of the books in question were not intended for the average reader. Acknowledging the concerns of scholars and physicians, the revised law would allow the Secretary of the Treasury to admit otherwise obscene books into the country if they had literary or scientific merit as long as they were being imported for personal use by an acknowledged expert and not for commercial purposes.[29]

Cutting renewed his objections to censorship, but Smoot, setting himself up as the defender of the nation's youth, was ready for a fight: "This question is one that strikes at the morals of every young boy and girl in the United States." He then presented for the senators' inspection an assortment of seized books – the Treasury Department had conveniently marked the offensive passages to make them easier for Smoot to spot – and he promised to read obscenities from *Lady Chatterley's Lover* and Casanova's *Memoirs* into the record. When word of Smoot's plan leaked to the press, reporters gathered to watch the spectacle. Although the highly-anticipated reading never took place, Smoot was clearly playing to the press gallery when he began his remarks:

> I have here books the reading of which would ... disgust Senators of the United States ... I did not believe there were such books printed in the world – books that the Senator from New Mexico referred to and said ought to be in the libraries of the people of the United States. They are lower than the beasts![30]

Smoot insisted that keeping the occasional classic out of the country was a small price to pay:

> It were better, to my mind, that a few classics suffer the application of the expurgating shears than that this country be flooded with the books, pamphlets, pictures, and other articles that are wholly indecent both in purpose and tendency, and that we know all too well would follow the repeal of this provision, and that even if in one of these old and rare books there is any obscene matter it ought to be kept out and never permitted to go to the youth of the land.[31]

He argued that there are vulnerable groups – notably, the young – who must be protected, particularly when smut is dressed up as fine literature and taught in the schools:

> Mature, well-regulated minds may not be subverted by such matter. But such legislation is enacted to prevent such matter from coming into the hands of those whose minds are open to influence, whose morals are

likely to be corrupted, and I am thinking particularly of the youth of our country, and proof that such matter would get into the hands of the young is offered by the statement made in the debate regarding the customs' rejection of such a book brought by a professor of literature in a great university to teach to his class.[32]

Concluding his oration, Smoot pointed dramatically to his stack of books and said, "No father of a child would ever want the child to see this obscene matter ... They are disgusting. They are beastly, beastly."[33]

Senator Hugo Black, who would become a free speech absolutist staunchly opposed to censorship when he was appointed to the Supreme Court in 1937, added an amen, comparing bad books to opium, a theme that Smoot immediately echoed, assuring the senators – and the gallery – that bad books were worse than drugs:

> I would rather have a child of mine use opium than read these books ... I'd rather keep out a thousand than have one mistake made ... Here are the books imported into the US – How to Seduce Young Girls. Another one, How Young Girls Can Seduce Boys. I do not want to read the others, they are so rotten![34]

Senator Coleman Livingston Blease, an openly racist xenophobe from South Carolina, based his support for the obscenity ban specifically on the need to protect women as well as children. To Blease, keeping books clean was even more important than preserving the republic:

> It is a horrible thought that in some libraries ... [children] can get the dirtiest, filthiest kind of trash ... So far as I am concerned, I had rather see both the democratic form of government and the republican form of government forever destroyed if that should be necessary in order to protect the virtue of the womanhood of America.[35]

Blease blamed children's access to such books on negligent mothers "out somewhere playing bridge and taking tea" instead of tending to their families, and he concluded that filthy books turned the nation's youth to prostitution:

If you will look around the jails, if you will look around some of our houses of detention, if you will look around some other kind of houses, you will find boys and girls there to-night who were put there by some scoundrel slipping dirty literature into their possession ... one could trace their road to the penitentiary, their road to the chain gang, and some of the girls could be traced into bawdy houses, through the dissemination of just such vile literature.[36]

Blease then charged that immigrants were the source of obscene books, and by implication, sexual depravity: "The virtue of one little 16-year-old girl is worth more to America than every book that has ever come into it from any other country ... I want to protect them from this devilish literature that foreigners are bringing in and trafficking away amongst our people."[37]

But Cutting challenged this connection between reading bad books and a life of depravity:

This is not a question of indecent literature; it is a question of freedom of speech and freedom of thought ... The first page of *King Lear* is grossly indecent; the love-making of Hamlet and Ophelia is coarse and obscene; in Romeo and Juliet the remarks of Mercutio and the nurse are extremely improper ... There may be people whose downfall and degeneration in life have been due to reading Boccaccio but I do not know who they are.[38]

When Cutting suggested that Smoot had spent the Christmas recess reading *Lady Chatterley,* along with the rest of the obscene books he brought into the Senate chamber, Smoot rose and indignantly denied the charge:

I have not read it. It was so disgusting, so dirty and vile that the reading of one page was enough for me ... I've not taken ten minutes on *Lady Chatterley's Lover,* outside of looking at its opening pages ... It is most damnable to undertake to read such stuff ... It is written by a man with a diseased mind and a soul so black that he would obscure even the darkness of hell![39]

Smoot's protestation surely met with some smirks: it was widely reported that Smoot not only relished the seized works given to him by the Customs

Bureau, he also couldn't resist quoting the raciest bits to friends and colleagues.[40]

Cutting argued that banning obscene imports would have no impact on public morality, since similarly questionable domestic imprints could be found anywhere books were sold, and he poked fun at Smoot's threat to read aloud from his collection of obscenity:

> I do not think foreign countries have very much on us in the way of indecent literature. From a railway bookstall in Chicago I purchased these important works which I now exhibit: *Joy Stories, Paris Nights, Hot Dog, Hot Lines for Flaming Youth, Jim Jam Jems, Whiz Bang*. I'm not going to circulate these books. I don't think any risk should be run of corruption of the morals of the members of this honorable body.[41]

Cutting also showed the senators a copy of a Zola novel, published by Henry Vizetelly and banned in Britain, that he had borrowed from the Library of Congress. The senator went on to cite a survey by a leading criminologist which confirmed that literature was not the gateway to sex for children. Twelve hundred adults from "all occupations and all classes of life" were asked where they first learned about sex when they were children. Of the seventy-two who named a book at all, their top source of information was the Bible, followed by the dictionary and the encyclopedia, and only then, by Dickens and Shakespeare.[42]

The Senate was debating books, not movies, but Cutting predicted that the proposed federal censorship of the movies would have a chilling effect on the newly-popular talking pictures (we will look at censoring movies in the next section). And he cited letters supporting his repeal of the obscenity ban from prominent educators and clergy, including Nicholas Murray Butler, the president of Columbia University, James Russell Lowell, president of Harvard, and the distinguished religious philosopher Reinhold Niebuhr.

As the debate wound down, Senator Blease could not resist a final plug for his home state of South Carolina, "the mother of secession," a state which defended womanhood, banned divorce, and executed rapists. Blease declared himself equally proud to support a ban on importing immoral, filthy literature. And Senator Heflin, a white supremacist from

Alabama who warned the senators against the dangers of miscegenation as well as imported books, likened the obscenity ban to building a border wall along the eastern seaboard. We stop foreigners at the border, he reasoned, so why not stop foreign books as well? – "Let us build the dike on the border line between us and foreign countries so compact and strong that none of this filthy literature can come in here."[43]

Smoot's bill passed the Senate on March 18, 1930. Thanks to the protracted debate, which occasionally took on the characteristics of a side show, the new tariff law offered a compromise: customs agents could seize suspect books, but only the courts could determine if they were obscene. Cutting was satisfied that agents would be more careful about confiscating books with judges looking over their shoulders. And Smoot, in turn, was content that the virtue of the nation would be preserved. As for the Customs Bureau, it soon relaxed its literary surveillance. In 1933, a federal court ruled against the Bureau's attempt under §305 of the 1930 Tariff Act to bar the import of James Joyce's *Ulysses*. In his opinion in that case, Judge John M. Woolsey acknowledged that *Ulysses* may be hard to read, but it is not obscene:

> Reading "Ulysses" in its entirety ... did not tend to excite sexual impulses or lustful thoughts, but ... its net effect ... was only that of a somewhat tragic and very powerful commentary on the inner lives of men and women ... I am quite aware that owing to some of its scenes "Ulysses" is a rather strong draught to ask some sensitive, though normal, persons to take. But my considered opinion, after long reflection, is that, whilst in many places the effect of "Ulysses" on the reader undoubtedly is somewhat emetic, nowhere does it tend to be an aphrodisiac. "Ulysses" may, therefore, be admitted into the United States.[44]

## YOU'LL KNOW IT WHEN YOU READ IT

Although *Ulysses* passed the obscenity test, *Lady Chatterley's Lover* did not. Universally condemned as obscene, D. H. Lawrence's novel was banned in the United States until 1958, and in England until a year later. Under the precedent established in *Hicklin,* a book could be banned in Britain if any passages from it were proved obscene. Because *Lady Chatterley* was full of explicit sex and four-letter words, Lawrence, already a well-established English novelist, had to publish his new novel in Italy in 1928. Lawrence wrote an expurgated version for consumption at home, but any copies of the full-on *Lady C* that managed to make their way to England were destroyed.

Britain's revision of the Obscene Publications Act in 1959 changed all that.[45] The new obscenity law distinguished literature from pornography. In doing so, it revised the *Hicklin* test, freeing the police to go after criminal vice rather than writers, artists, and filmmakers. Under *Hicklin*, a single word or phrase could damn an entire book. The new Act required the authorities to consider the whole work, not just any occasional strong language that it might contain: "[A]n article shall be deemed to be obscene if its effect ... is, *if taken as a whole*, such as to tend to deprave and corrupt persons who are likely, having regard to all relevant circumstances, to read, see or hear the matter contained or embodied in it."[46] Even an obscene work could not be banned if it served the public good through its literary, artistic, or scientific merit:

A person shall not be convicted ... if it is proved that publication of the article in question is justified as being for the public good on the ground that it is in the interests of science, literature, art or learning, or of other objects of general concern ... The opinion of experts as to the literary, artistic, scientific or other merits of an article may be admitted in any proceedings under this Act.

Penguin Books decided to test the new obscenity law by adding an unexpurgated *Lady Chatterley's Lover* to its popular and inexpensive catalogue of D. H. Lawrence novels, which included the highly acclaimed *Sons and Lovers, The Rainbow,* and *Women in Love.* Penguin printed 200,000 copies of *Lady Chatterley,* but before releasing it they arranged for a dozen to be picked up by Scotland Yard. Police then cited Penguin for violating the revised Obscene Publications Act, and at the order of the Director of Public Prosecutions, the six-day trial known as *Regina* v. *Penguin Books Ltd.* began at London's Central Criminal Court – the Old Bailey.[47]

At the start of the trial, the jurors were ordered to read the book, a process that took them about three days. But first they listened to opening statements. Prosecutor Mervyn Griffith-Jones hammered at the book's obscenity, hoping to shock the jury by telling them that Lawrence portrayed Lady Chatterley having sex not once, but thirteen times, "leaving nothing to the imagination." He then ticked off these blunt statistics: "The word 'fuck' or 'fucking' occurs no less than thirty times … 'Cunt' fourteen times; 'balls' thirteen times; 'shit' and 'arse' six times apiece; 'cock' four times; 'piss' three times, and so on."[48]

Griffith-Jones also suggested that by selling copies at 3s. 6d. (about £3.67, or $5, today), Penguin made a dangerous book accessible to the classes of reader who needed to be shielded from it the most: women, young people, and the lower orders. Peddling cheap fiction was the same "crime" that led to Henry Vizetelly's obscenity conviction more than seventy years earlier, the same one that roiled the US Senate during its tariff discussion in 1930. But two world wars had shaken up England's class structure – the theme of war-related social leveling resonates throughout *Lady Chatterley,* though Mervyn Griffith-Jones seemed blithely unaware of it – and by 1960 not everyone was shocked by Lady Chatterley's affair with her aristocratic husband's low-born gamekeeper. Still fewer felt the need to censor art and literature. That may be why some of the jurors, of a more modern cast than the stodgy prosecutor, laughed out loud in the courtroom when Griffith-Jones told them in his opening statement,

> One of the ways in which you can test this book … is to ask yourselves the question, when you have read it through, would you approve of your young sons, young daughters – because girls can read as well as boys – reading this book. Is it a book that you would have lying around in your own house? Is it a book that you would even wish your wife or your servants to read?[49]

Unlike the all-male jury in the Vizetelly trial, which begged the prosecutor to stop reading racy passages from Zola, the *Chatterley* jury of nine men and three women patiently listened to the strong language and the sex scenes without exhibiting fear or revulsion, or expressing concern that their wives or servants might get their hands on the book, not to mention how Lawrence's explicit words might affect any husbands, civil partners, or employees who might encounter them, because they can read as well.

Griffith-Jones called only one witness for the prosecution, the officer who had received copies of the book from Penguin. The Director of Public Prosecutions had suggested that the prosecution call Rudyard Kipling to testify, but unfortunately Kipling had died more than two decades earlier, and despite Griffith-Jones' later boast that he could have matched the thirty-five defense witnesses don for don and bishop for bishop, no one else seemed available.[50] In contrast, Gerald Gardiner Q.C. easily found experts for the defense who were eager to testify that *Lady Chatterley*, though perhaps not Lawrence's best work, was an important novel with clear literary merit. In the days that followed, Gardiner called such well-known writers as E. M. Forster, Dame Rebecca West, and C. Day Lewis (he would become the poet laureate in just a few years); eminent academics like Helen Gardner, Kenneth Muir, and Raymond Williams; members of the clergy, including the Bishop of Woolwich; and some big-name journalists, publishers, and newspaper editors.

The defense also called two legal experts intimately involved in the creation and passage of the revised Obscene Publications Act. Norman St John-Stevas, author of the textbook *Obscenity and the Law*, who drafted an early version of the bill, testified that *Lady Chatterley* was "a book of high literary merit." The jury heard as well from Roy Jenkins, the bill's chief sponsor in Parliament. A month before the trial, Jenkins had written to the *Spectator* expressing his surprise and distress at the *Chatterley* prosecution: "The Act ... was a compromise designed to give the police the stronger powers for which they had asked in dealing with the trade in pornography, while affording a greater security to works with any claim to literary merit."[51] In exchange for backing the war against pornographers, the Obscene Publications Act would not be used to prosecute serious novelists, even novelists like Lawrence who pushed the boundaries of taste with thirteen explicit love scenes and one hundred or more four-letter words. At the trial, Jenkins reaffirmed the understanding that Parliament intended to protect literature, not prosecute it, and he testified that *Lady Chatterley* "most certainly" was literature.

After the defense rested, the jury took only three hours to reach a verdict of not guilty, and Penguin rushed *Lady Chatterley* into bookshops. The first printing sold out immediately, and over the next three months 3 million copies of the book flew off the shelves. For those who preferred to listen to strong language instead of reading it, Caedmon Records offered an LP of *Lady Chatterley's* choicest passages. Although he received many complaints about that recording, presumably from people who hadn't actually listened to it, the Director of Public Prosecutions ruled on December 22, 1960, that the recording was not obscene – just in time for Christmas (that recording is still available on lastfm and Spotify).

## REDEEMING SOCIAL VALUE

After the *Lady Chatterley* verdict was delivered, Gerald Gardiner announced that an American court had already allowed the sale of the unexpurgated *Lady Chatterley*.[52] Some of the jurors in the Penguin trial may have known this – everyone else in the courtroom certainly did – but it was the first time anyone had referred to it in court. That American ruling was based on *Roth* v. *United States,* a landmark 1957 Supreme Court decision that introduced a new test: to be obscene, a work of literature must be utterly without redeeming social value.[53] Now all the American publisher had to do was prove that *Lady Chatterley* had the least bit of literary merit and it was no longer unprotected speech.

*Roth* did not legalize obscene speech. Instead, it sought to clarify the boundary between obscenity and protected speech. In his opinion in *Roth,* Justice William Brennan affirmed the common judicial belief that obscenity does not contribute anything vital to communication:

> All ideas having even the slightest redeeming social importance – unorthodox ideas, controversial ideas, even ideas hateful to the prevailing climate of opinion – have the full protection of the [First Amendment's] guaranties ... But implicit in the history of the First Amendment is the rejection of obscenity as utterly without redeeming social importance.

Obscene speech still exists in the post-*Roth* world – but it is now much harder to prosecute: how do you prove that words, or books, have no redeeming social value?

*Roth* didn't specify why obscene speech lay outside the bounds of the First Amendment, but it did provide a legal test for obscenity to supplant the overly broad *Hicklin* test. *Hicklin* measured the influence of a text on the most-vulnerable readers, the young, the innocent, or the depraved (though it did not define those terms), but the *Roth* test asked, "whether, to the average person, applying contemporary community standards, the dominant theme of the material, taken as a whole, appeals to prurient interest."

In 1973, *Miller v. California* added two more prongs to the *Roth* obscenity test:

(a) whether "the average person, applying contemporary community standards" would find that the work, taken as a whole, appeals to the prurient interest ... (b) whether the work depicts or describes, in a patently offensive way, sexual conduct specifically defined by the applicable state law; and (c) whether the work, taken as a whole, lacks serious literary, artistic, political, or scientific value.[54]

*Miller* rejected a single standard for obscenity, offering instead a test that defers to state law; provides an exception for art, opinion, and science; and allows local communities to decide what is acceptable to them. According to *Miller*, "It is neither realistic nor constitutionally sound to read the First Amendment as requiring that the people of Maine or Mississippi accept public depiction of conduct found tolerable in Las Vegas, or New York City." This assumes that the average person in Maine or Mississippi is a prude and it perpetuates the canard that New York and Las Vegas epitomize sin cities.

In his opinion in *Miller*, Chief Justice Warren Burger echoed the refrain in *Roth* that anti-obscenity laws do not limit the expression of important ideas, even unpopular ones:

There is no evidence, empirical or historical, that the stern 19th century American censorship of public distribution and display of material relating to sex ... in any way limited or affected expression of serious literary, artistic, political, or scientific ideas. On the contrary, it is beyond any question that the era following Thomas Jefferson to Theodore Roosevelt was an "extraordinarily vigorous period," not just in economics and politics, but in *belles lettres* and in "the outlying fields of social and political philosophies." We do not see the harsh hand of censorship of ideas – good or bad, sound or unsound – and "repression" of political liberty lurking in every state regulation of commercial exploitation of human interest in sex.

The *Roth* and *Miller* decisions weren't about literary fiction labeled as obscene. Roth sold pornographic books and magazines through the mail, and Miller mailed "adult" advertising to people who hadn't asked for it. If American courts ultimately declared such stuff to have a modicum of redeeming social value, then the law certainly protected novels full of strong language like *Lady Chatterley*, John Cleland's eighteenth-century novel, *Fanny Hill*, William Burroughs' *Naked Lunch* (1959), Henry Miller's *Tropic of Cancer* (1961), and, of course, James Joyce's *Ulysses* (1933), all books that had to have their day in court before they could be sold freely. Even *Jim Jam Jems* – a twenty-five cent "men's magazine" that Senator Bronson Cutting bought at Union Station – counts as protected speech, assuming you can still find a copy of *Jim Jam Jems* anywhere.[55] But for most of the twentieth century, as strong language in print was gaining increased legal protection, the movies, cheap entertainment with the potential to reach a far-wider audience than print, struggled to win any First Amendment protection at all.

## LOSING IT AT THE MOVIES

The Senate's obscenity debate reflected a fear that twentieth-century urban culture corrupted women and children and incited the lower classes to crime. But while the Senate focused on the harms wrought by imported literature, the rest of the nation's reformers targeted the home-grown Hollywood movie. Despite Reed Smoot's rantings, puritanical American censors probably didn't worry that foreign books would actually corrupt the vulnerable poor, who weren't going to pay serious money to sneak *Lady Chatterley* across the border. But it seemed that everyone was willing to buy a ticket for a picture show, and that made movies public enemy number one in the eyes of the social watchdogs.

Censors considered films to have a greater reach than books. A book affected one reader at a time. In contrast, by 1930, movies were being watched simultaneously by millions of people in thousands of theaters all over the country. That year, the US population was close to 123 million, and more than 65 percent of them went to see a double bill once a week.[56] Add to that the fact that crowds are more volatile than solitary readers – Justice Holmes didn't need to explain why falsely shouting fire in a theater was unprotected speech – and crowds in multiple theaters could be more volatile still. Although films were popular with all elements of society, they were thought to attract the working classes most of all. Children, too, formed a significant part of the movie-going audience. Children didn't go to plays much, or read French fiction in translation, but they often went to the movies with their siblings and friends, unaccompanied by an adult. One legislator keen on movie censorship warned that in 1930, the typical American child spent two hours a week at the movies. Too much screen time, even then, seemed a recipe for ill-health, moral decay, and antisocial behavior.

By the early 1900s, watchdogs complained that the seductive realism of silent films could turn innocent, poor, uneducated, and impressionable Americans toward lives of crime and depravity simply by showing too much skin or glamorizing adultery or robbery. With the advent of the talkies in 1927, the guardians of morality warned that films had become more dangerous than ever, as children and adults who could not read the titles of the silents would now be corrupted by spoken dialogue.

The potential for movies to do harm made it imperative to keep them clean. Concerned reformers, educators, and psychologists joined with church groups and prohibitionists to rein in Hollywood's dream factory. In 1907, Chicago gave its police chief the authority to censor the movies in that city. The next year, New York City's mayor, George McClellan, held a hearing on December 23 to address the evils of motion pictures. When Christian religious leaders testified that Sunday screenings were luring people away from church and corrupting children's minds, McClellan took immediate action, shutting the city's movie houses the very next day, Christmas Eve, and promising not to reopen any theater showing films "that degrade or injure the morals of the community."[57] Theater owners obtained an injunction against the mayor's order, and the cinemas reopened in time for Sunday screenings of that year's holiday pics, "A Christmas Carol" and "The Night Before Christmas." But the task of policing the movies continued unabated: New York City established a film censorship board in 1913, and for years both New York and Chicago, two of the largest markets for film, served as national movie watchdogs.

Even though film's harshest critics acknowledged the positive educational and entertainment value of the new technology, by 1915 many more municipalities, and a number of states, had set up film censorship boards. Censors banned movies outright or they required producers to cut scenes highlighting crime, illicit romance, or other behaviors seen to violate community standards. For example, Chicago censors would not let children watch *The Scarlet Letter* because of the adultery. Ohio's board demanded that the tempestuous Carmen act more ladylike in the film version of Bizet's opera. And Pennsylvania banned a movie with a pregnant character because "thousands of children ... believe that babies are brought by the stork."[58] When newsreels began accompanying feature presentations, they too were censored if they treated sensitive subjects or slanted the news in ways that didn't match the censors' politics.[59]

## MOVING PICTURES ARE NOT PROTECTED SPEECH

Responding to one distributor's objection that Ohio's film censorship board was an unconstitutional abridgment of First Amendment rights, in 1915 the US Supreme Court ruled that motion pictures were not protected speech for the simple reason that they weren't speech at all, they were entertainment. There was no actual speech, to be sure, as this was still the era of silent film, but the silents did have title cards with dialogue and narrative. In *Mutual Film Corporation* v. *Industrial Commission of Ohio*, the Court found that movies were not like books or magazines. Rather, they resembled the circus – a business, not a vehicle for discussing matters of public concern – and so they fell outside the protection of the First Amendment.

In an opinion muddied by convoluted language, Justice Joseph McKenna stated that the suggestive imagery of motion pictures posed a threat to adults and children alike. According to McKenna:

Their power of amusement, and, it may be, education, the audiences they assemble, not of women alone nor of men alone, but together, not of adults only, but of children, make them the more insidious in corruption by a pretense of worthy purpose or if they should degenerate from worthy purpose. Indeed, we may go beyond that possibility. They take their attraction from the general interest, eager and wholesome it may be, in their subjects, but a prurient interest may be excited and appealed to. Besides, there are some things which should not have pictorial representation in public places and to all audiences.[60]

The *Mutual Film* decision stood until 1952, when in *Burstyn* v. *Wilson*, the Supreme Court finally recognized movies as a major medium for the "communication of ideas" and acknowledged films to have First Amendment protection.[61] But even though the *Burstyn* court found that films did not warrant the prior restraint imposed by censorship or licensing, and obscene movies had no constitutional protection at all, it recognized that the potential of the medium to do harm could be taken into account by communities setting appropriate local controls on what could be shown.

For much of their history, movies were seen to need some kind of regulation. Even today, the rating system put in place by the industry is a measure designed to keep government from controlling cinema content. But the 1915 decision declaring movies unprotected speech tempted Congress to impose a national standard for movie censorship to replace the jumble of local regulations. In 1916, the House Education Committee held hearings on a bill by Senator Hoke Smith and Representative Dudley Hughes, both of Georgia, to create a federal motion picture commission to bar any film exposing children and vulnerable adults to obscenity, sexual content, or glamorized portrayals of crime.[62]

Movie censorship wasn't only about sex. H. F. Worley, of the group Christian Endeavor, testified at the Congressional hearings that many movies "show the details of safe breaking and other criminal acts [that] make the show a school in crime."[63] Worley also complained that movies depicted the races too liberally, in ways that "do not have a decent regard for the sentiments of the people of the Southern States." And as late as 1934, the chair of the National Parent–Teacher Association's

Motion Picture Committee testified before the House that movies are "teaching young people how to commit crime": an analysis of 115 movies presented children with "18 murder techniques … methods that were quite successful" (it is not clear how the PTA chair determined that these methods actually worked).[64]

Besides sex and guns, the movies featured smoking and drinking. Dr. Wilbur Crafts, a Methodist clergyman who supported Prohibition and frowned on any Sunday activity except church, introduced data to demonstrate the pernicious influence on children of films containing scenes with cigarettes, alcohol, guns, and "deceit, intrigue, jealousy, or treachery."[65] Crafts was not the only moralist who wanted the movies to quit smoking. In 1915, the Ohio film board cut a scene from a movie version of Bizet's *Carmen* that showed Carmen, who works in a cigarette factory, smoking a cigarette.[66]

Crafts also cited data that half the films screened featured drink, half featured "gun play and murder," but only 25 percent of films showed activities that were "good," or at least, "not bad." The numbers proved to him that the evil of film far exceeded any good that it might contain. And Crafts introduced a report by a group of school principals and teachers complaining that unaccompanied children were being allowed into movie theaters to watch vulgar and immoral films containing, "such scenes as silly love affairs; highly sensational scenes – fights, drinking scenes, robberies, hairbreadth escapes from fires, etc., accidents, scenes of violence, western hold-up, etc.; incidents making light of crime – ridiculing the officers of the law, sympathizing with the culprit, etc.; conjugal infidelity; and social impurity."[67]

Crafts quoted Carl Laemmle, the head of Universal Studios, who said that theater owners preferred risqué offerings – Laemmle explained that *risqué* was French for "smutty" – because that is the kind of film that moviegoers would pay to see. And Crafts endorsed the opinion of prominent child psychiatrist William Healy that juvenile delinquency could be prevented through "rigorous censorship of perverting pictures and … radical prosecution of those who produce and deal in obscene and other demoralizing pictorial representations."[68]

In contrast, many opponents of censorship argued for preserving the artistic independence of movies. Others protested the cost to studios of making changes demanded by censorship boards, or the inadvisability of appointing a small board to make moral decisions for an entire nation. A few appealed to the similarity between film and literature, or, despite the ruling in *Mutual Film,* they likened movies to the free press. One or two even dared to suggest that movies benefited the nation's morals, since in many cities the growth of the movie audience meant fewer people in saloons.

## ANYTHING OBSCENE, INDECENT, IMMORAL, INHUMAN ...

Congress never voted on the Smith–Hughes Act. But like many large markets, the city of Chicago had its own movie regulator. From November, 1917, to November, 1918, the city's censor cut more than 55,000 feet of film from movies before they could be screened, in order to remove scenes that were unlawful, immoral, indecent, nude, or obscene, or that had problems in the depiction of race or creed.[69] Despite these cuts, one prominent Chicago physician told the city's Motion Picture Censorship Commission that movie attendance "produce[d] neurosis or St. Vitus dance" in children (it later turned out that St. Vitus Dance is caused by strep, not celluloid). Professor Ernest W. Burgess, a respected sociologist at the University of Chicago, confirmed that most school teachers and principals thought motion pictures gave children an unrealistic view of the world, disrupted home life, encouraged resistance to authority, stimulated sexual precocity, reduced attention spans, interfered with school work, and led the child away from reading good books.[70]

In order to minimize interference from state and local censorship boards like Chicago's, and to fend off the threat of federal monitoring, in 1922 the major studios, through their trade association, the Motion Picture Producers and Distributors of America (MPPDA), began to formulate a code of acceptable moral practices to guide films past the censors. Led by former Postmaster General Will Hays, the Hays Office, as it was known, shaped American film for decades, and between 1934 and 1968, years after the Supreme Court acknowledged that movies were protected speech, its Production Code kept Hollywood pretty much on the straight and narrow. As the Code evolved, it became increasingly detailed, ultimately covering many aspects of plot, dialogue, costume, and movement. Broadly speaking, Hays required villains never to be sympathetic; dance never to be suggestive; religion never to be criticized;

romance always to be heterosexual and racially segregated. Sex must always be implied, always within marriage. Violence was to be portrayed only obliquely, unless absolutely necessary to demonstrate that bad guys always lose. And actors could never swear. Still, critics insisted that the industry had failed to police itself effectively, and once again some members of Congress tried to set up a federal board to clean up Hollywood.

Initially, compliance with the Hays Code was voluntary. But in 1924, Representative William D. Upshaw, of Georgia, a religious fundamentalist who supported temperance, proposed legislation that would give the rigid set of moral standards developed by the Hays Office the force of law. The Upshaw Bill targeted movies depicting a broad range of behaviors designated as improper by Hays, including:

A. anything obscene, indecent, immoral, inhuman, salacious, unpatriotic, sacrilegious, or offensive to the sentiment of religious reverence;
B. anything of such character that its exhibition would tend to impair the health, debase or corrupt morals of children or adults, incite to crime, produce depraved moral ideas, debase moral standards, cause moral laxity in adults or minors, disturb public peace, or impair friendly relations with any foreign power;
C. anything which holds up to scorn any race, nation, sect, or religion;
D. the reproduction of an actual cock fight, bull fight, or prize fight;
E. anything that exploits or depicts persons notorious for some crime or public scandal; and
F. anything that aims to or does assist the election or defeat of any political candidate.[71]

In addition, Upshaw's Federal Motion Picture Commission would refuse to license any motion pictures:

(a) that emphasize and exaggerate sex appeal or depict scenes therein exploiting interest in sex in an improper or suggestive form or manner;
(b) are based upon white slavery or commercialized vice, or scenes showing the procurement of women or any of the activities attendant upon this traffic;

(c) that thematically make prominent an illicit love affair that tends to make virtue odious and vice attractive;

(d) with scenes that exhibit nakedness or persons scantily dressed, particularly suggestive bedroom and bathroom scenes and scenes of inciting dances;

(e) with scenes that unnecessarily prolong expressions or demonstrations of passionate love;

(f) that are predominantly concerned with the underworld or vice and crime and like scenes, unless the scenes are part of an essential conflict between good and evil;

(g) of stories that make drunkenness and gambling attractive, or with scenes that show the use of narcotics and other unnatural practices dangerous to social morality;

(h) of stories and scenes that may instruct the morally feeble in methods of committing crimes or by cumulative processes emphasize crime and the commission of crime;

(i) of stories or scenes that ridicule or deprecate public officials, officers of the law, the United States Army, the United States Navy, or other governmental authority, or that tend to weaken the authority of the law;

(j) of stories or scenes or incidents that offend the religious belief of any person, creed, or sect, or ridicule ministers, priests, rabbis, or recognized leaders of any religious sect, and that are also disrespectful to objects or symbols used in connection with any religion;

(k) of stories or with scenes that unduly emphasize bloodshed and violence without justification in the structure of the story;

(l) of stories or with scenes that are vulgar and portray improper gestures, posturing, and attitudes; and

(m) with salacious titles and subtitles in connection with their presentation or exhibition, and the use of salacious advertising matter, photographs, and lithographs in connection therewith.[72]

The commission would have the power to reject a film outright or to suggest modifications. For an additional fee, the censors would send a consultant to the movie set to work directly with the studio to ensure that the production conformed to the law.

That same year, Representative William Swoope, of Pennsylvania, introduced his own bill to regulate film. During debate on the issue, Swoope quoted Professor Horace Heckman, of the City College of New York, who wrote that the children who made up the bulk of the movie audience were unable to contextualize what they saw on the big screen and were apt to imitate movie depictions of violence:

> A film story which may contain some picture of lawlessness or murder may be accepted by the intelligent adult as a justifiable moral picture, because in the end justice prevails, and the criminal ... is punished. But what impressed the child during that picture was the bravado, the kind of activity which the individual engaged in while performing that particular act, and that is what influences his life; he doesn't carry it through to the end to get the justification of the act in its whole setting.[73]

The following July, Upshaw read into the *Congressional Record* a far-ranging diatribe, "The Child and the Motion Picture," that decried the teaching of evolution, supported Prohibition, and charged that moving pictures deposit "insidious poison ... in mind and soul." He insisted that his bill called not for censorship of motion pictures, but for their "purification at the source." He warned that a few frames of film, just "one liquor-drinking scene which defies the majesty of our constitutional law – one lecherous climax of sex appeal which tramples every sacred law of God and man" can turn children toward a life of crime (drinking scenes defied "our constitutional law" because Prohibition was then in effect).[74] But, as with previous attempts at setting up a federal censorship board, Congress adjourned without acting on Upshaw's bill.

### FOR FAMILY USE

Finally, in 1930, Representative Grant M. Hudson, of Michigan, re-introduced Upshaw's proposal retitled, unironically, as "A Bill to Protect the Motion-picture Industry," setting up a federal commission to enforce the Hays Code, since Hays couldn't get studios to comply with his rules.[75] Like Upshaw before him, Hudson insisted that his bill was not censorship, but "social control," and he asked Congress to declare the movie industry a public utility, like the gas company. Hudson told the House that regulating every aspect of movie-making from the initial screenplay, through day-to-day filming, to the advertising posters, was critical, because every school-age child in America was exposed to two hours of movies a week, producing these harmful effects: "false and distorted views of life, mental development retarded, nervousness and excitability increased, sensitiveness to crime diminished, standards of modesty and social conduct demoralized."[76]

In 1914, Chicago had instituted a two-category rating scheme for its movie licenses: general permits allowed anyone to see a film, while "pink permits" meant "adults-only."[77] Unfortunately, the pink permits backfired when some theaters found that advertising these films as "over-21 only" actually boosted attendance. In a similar vein, Upshaw's proposed motion picture commission, reintroduced by Hudson, would encourage the production of films suitable for viewing by the entire family: "[The Commission] shall have power to give a special mark of approval of such films as are especially beneficial for children and young people both in their amusement, educational and character building values and shall place upon the label … the words "for family use."[78] The Catholic Legion of Decency, formed in 1933, took movie labeling a step further. Instead of awarding a seal of approval to movies aimed at a general audience, the church stamped its own scarlet letter, a glaring C for "condemned," on movies that no one should be allowed to see.

While senators in the Smoot–Cutting obscenity debate were blaming foreigners for corrupting American morals, Swoope and Hudson argued just the opposite: it was Hollywood that was peddling American-made filth abroad. Exported Hollywood movies gave the nation's trading partners the false impression that life in the United States was dominated by sexuality and crime. As Swoope put it, "The children in foreign lands are being injured by American-made films."[79]

Even though liberal social activists and conservative religious zealots backed the federal censorship of motion pictures, Hudson's bill, like its predecessors, never made it to a vote. Neither did a similar bill introduced in 1934 by Representative Wright Patman, of Texas. Patman went even farther than Hays, proposing a Federal Censorship Commission that could ban any movie that:

harmfully portrays the life, manners, or customs of this or any other nation or which holds up to ridicule or contempt or disparagement any race, nationality, or religion, or which fosters ill will among or toward the people of this or any other nation, or tends to debase or corrupt morals or to incite to crime or to disrespect for law or religion, *or which promotes or encourages war against the peace of the world,* or which is harmful to the public or any part thereof in any respect.[80]

Patman's proved to be the last in a string of unsuccessful film censorship bills proposed before the Second World War, and it was the most extreme. He not only thought that moving pictures were being made by immoral profiteers who didn't give a damn about the young and vulnerable, but he was also convinced that movies – presumably those prewar films with anti-fascist themes – threatened world peace. Patman's bill extended the notion of indecency to include pretty much anything that a movie could portray. Even though the studios defended their products against these charges point-by-point, they were surely dismayed by the unusual combination of progressive and conservative do-gooders bent on controlling not just access to films, but their very production. It was not surprising, then, that the loud and relentless condemnation of the offerings of the movie industry led Hollywood to revisit its self-censorship efforts.

In order to head off further federal attempts at licensing and censorship, in 1934 the Hollywood studios finally agreed to require that all films adhere to the Hays Code before they could be shown in theaters. The Code's philosophy, which shaped American movies for over thirty years, stressed that unlike highbrow art and literature, movies were art for the modern, classless society:

> Most arts appeal to the mature. This art appeals at once to every class, mature, immature, developed, underdeveloped, law abiding, criminal. Music has its grades for different classes; so has literature and drama. This art of the motion picture, combining as it does the two fundamental appeals of looking at a picture and listening to a story, at once reached every class of society.[81]

Because of the medium's mass appeal, industry censors argued that film must do no harm. From the 1930s to the 1960s, the Production Code

Administration (PCA) scrutinized pre-production scripts and previewed final cuts to root out references to sex, crime, and general depravity before they hit the big screen. The PCA boasted that in its first four years, it had forced producers to make more than 100,000 cuts and script changes to clean up their films.[82]

## ZERO DAMNS

Although some suggestive bits of plot and dialogue got past the censors from time to time, the decision of the Hays Office was always final, and no film could be shown to the public without the PCA's official seal. But in one high-profile case, a studio managed to get the Hays Office to relent. In October, 1939, the producer David O. Selznick wrote directly to Will Hays for permission to use one banned word, one time only, in his soon-to-be-released movie of the best-selling Margaret Mitchell novel, *Gone with the Wind*:

> As you probably know, the punch line of *Gone With the Wind*, the one bit of dialogue which forever establishes the future relationship between Scarlett and Rhett, is, "Frankly, my dear, I don't give a damn." Naturally, I am most desirous of keeping this line and, to judge from the reactions of two preview audiences, this line is remembered, loved, and looked forward to by millions who have read this new American classic.[83]

Selznick, whose scriptwriters tried out a list of alternatives in anticipation of a negative response from Hays, including the unlikely "I don't give a hoot" and "I am completely indifferent," cited the *Oxford English Dictionary* to demonstrate that *damn* as used in *GWTW* is not an oath or curse. As further proof of *damn*'s acceptability, Selznick noted its regular appearance in such "moral publications" as *Woman's Home Companion, The Saturday Evening Post, Collier's,* and *The Atlantic Monthly:*

> I understand the difference, as outlined in the code, between the written word and the word spoken from the screen, but at the same time I think the attitude of these magazines toward "damn" gives an indication that the word itself is not considered abhorrent or shocking to audiences.

The Production Code treated the spoken word as more damaging than its written equivalent because readers are likely to put down a text that they find offensive, while people went to the movies no matter what was playing (the practice may seem odd to today's more selective movie-goers, but for decades that was indeed what happened), and they would more likely be shocked by any bad language that came at them without warning. But Selznick stressed that allowing a single "damn" in this one movie would not "open up the floodgates and allow every gangster picture to be peppered with 'damns' from end to end." Instead, it would simply give the Code's censor the flexibility to permit "certain harmless oaths and ejaculations whenever, in his opinion, they are not prejudicial to public morals."

Perhaps Hays found Selznick's arguments convincing, or maybe he thought that *Gone with the Wind* was in a class by itself, but he promptly amended the rules on *hell* and *damn*, which could now be used only when their use, "shall be essential and required for portrayal, in proper historical context, of any scene or dialogue based upon historical fact or folklore ... or a quotation from a literary work, provided that no such use shall be permitted which is intrinsically objectionable or offends good taste."[84]

With Clark Gable's *damn* intact, *Gone with the Wind* went on to win the 1939 Oscar for best picture over the other major contenders, *Mr. Smith Goes to Washington, Dark Victory, Goodbye, Mr. Chips,* and *The Wizard of Oz.* In what turned out to be a very good year for films, Selznick's blockbuster received Hays's approval certificate No. 5729, sandwiched between licenses for two extremely forgettable films, *Man from Montreal,* No. 5728, and *Day-Time Wife,* No. 5730.

The Hays Code was finally abandoned in 1967. Even so, children are still singled out in movie ratings as needing protection from strong language. That protection also forms the basis of the Federal Communications Commission's continuing ban on indecent language on radio and television when children are likely to be in the audience.

## SEVEN DIRTY WORDS

Film was a new phenomenon when the Supreme Court decided in 1915 that movies did not merit constitutional protection, so new that in his

*Mutual Film* opinion, Justice McKenna felt the need to describe exactly how movies used still pictures to create the illusion of motion: "The film consists of a series of instantaneous photographs or positive prints of action upon the stage or in the open. By being projected upon a screen with great rapidity there appears to the eye an illusion of motion." McKenna himself may have never seen a film, since he drew this technical description almost verbatim from Mutual's brief in the case.[85]

Eventually America got used to movies, and by the time of *Jacobellis* v. *Ohio* (1964), the Supreme Court was content to let local communities, and ultimately, individual movie-goers, decide when a movie was obscene: they would know it when they saw it. At the same time, concerns about protecting the nation's moral and psychological fiber transferred to the new medium of radio, and in the 1950s, to the even-newer technology of television. The 1927 Radio Act, whose provisions are still part of US broadcast law, did three things for these emerging media that the federal government had not done for film: it gave radio First Amendment protection and barred any pre-broadcast censorship. But the law also banned obscene, indecent, and profane language from the airwaves, and it created a federal agency, the precursor of today's Federal Communications Commission (FCC), to license broadcasting and enforce standards:

> Nothing in this Act shall be understood or construed to give the licensing authority the power of censorship over the radio communications or signals transmitted by any radio station, and no regulation or condition shall be promulgated or fixed by the licensing authority which shall interfere with the right of free speech by means of radio communications. No person within the jurisdiction of the United States shall utter any obscene, indecent, or profane language by means of radio communication.[86]

The apparent contradiction between free speech and a ban on broadcasting strong language was not resolved until the 1978 Supreme Court decision in *Pacifica* v. *FCC* (1978), and the need to protect children from such language proved to be the deciding factor in that case.

In 1973, the New York City radio station WBAI aired a recording of comedian George Carlin's nightclub routine, "Seven Dirty Words You Can't Say on the Air," a monologue satirizing taboo words and American prudery. A few weeks later, a man complained to the FCC that he and his young son heard Carlin's dirty words monologue while the two were out driving in the afternoon. The FCC found the complaint justified, and though it did not punish WBAI for airing Carlin's monologue, it reserved the right to impose sanctions should the offense be repeated. This prompted WBAI's owners, the Pacifica Foundation, to mount a First Amendment challenge to the FCC's rule against broadcasting indecent speech. The case made its way to the Supreme Court, which affirmed the FCC's indecency rule.

In his opinion in *Pacifica*, Justice John Paul Stevens recognized the satiric value of Carlin's monologue, but he found as well that the indisputably "vulgar, offensive, and shocking" language in the sketch merited limited rather than absolute protection: "Although these words ordinarily lack literary, political, or scientific value, they are not entirely outside the protection of the First Amendment."[87] Stevens backed up this context-dependent protection by citing *Schenck*, along with *Cohen v. California*: "Words that are commonplace in one setting are shocking in another ... one occasion's lyric is another's vulgarity." And in a move reminiscent of the Court's earlier dismissal of film as unprotected speech, Stevens declared that compared with political speech, radio communications were relatively unimportant: "Of all forms of communication, it is broadcasting that has received the most limited First Amendment protection." Citing *Webster's Third* (1961), Stevens found that Carlin's words met the normal definition of indecent language, "nonconformance with accepted standards of morality," and in keeping with the legal philosophy that strong language does not contribute anything of value when discussing matters of public concern, Stevens located such speech at the "periphery of First Amendment concern," even though Carlin was using strong language to discuss public concerns about strong language.

Given this limited protection for radio speech, and the still-more-limited protection for indecent speech, the *Pacifica* court ruled that the FCC could legally prohibit the broadcast of indecent material during times when children were likely to be in the audience. The Court emphasized one argument in *Pacifica* that was often made earlier in the twentieth century about the movies: "Broadcasting is uniquely accessible to children, even those too young to read." And it used this rationale to justify banning such speech from daytime and early-evening broadcasts. Such family viewing time now typically ends in the United States at 9 p.m.

It is important to note that *Pacifica* was not about obscene speech – the right to ban obscenity was never in doubt. Instead, Carlin's monologue met the lesser threshold of "indecent speech." And even that was banned only when uttered in the wrong place, at the wrong time. The ban did not, for example, cover two-way radio transmissions between a cab driver and a dispatcher – transmissions where strong language might be acceptable. But in suggesting that inappropriate language "may be merely a right thing in the wrong place – like a pig in the parlor instead of the barnyard," Stevens again yoked Carlin's indecency with obscenity: "These words offend for the same reasons that obscenity offends." He also found that fine distinctions between obscenity and indecency are not necessary in this case. The law simply requires that Carlin's words be out of place, and Stevens agreed that they were definitely out of place on the air, at two o'clock in the afternoon: "When the [Federal Communications] Commission finds that a pig has entered the parlor, the exercise of its regulatory power does not depend on proof that the pig is obscene."

The Supreme Court reaffirmed its *Pacifica* decision most recently in *FCC* v. *Fox* (2012). In that case, a coalition of broadcasters protested an FCC ban on "fleeting expletives" such as the unscripted, spontaneous use of *shit* and *fuck* on a television reality show and an award ceremony that aired during prime time, when children might be watching. In oral arguments in *Fox*, Justice Ruth Bader Ginsburg wondered whether the FCC ban on expletives might no longer be necessary, since children in 2012 were less likely to be shocked by strong language than they would have been when *Pacifica* was decided in 1978.[88]

Ginsburg observed as well that attitudes toward strong language have relaxed, and that it is used regularly on cable broadcasts, which are not covered by FCC rules. But Chief Justice John Roberts countered that banning such words when children are likely to hear them had become even more important, since it gave parents who wanted one a safe harbor for their children. The *Pacifica* court printed an unexpurgated transcript of George Carlin's "Seven Dirty Words" monologue in an appendix to its opinion. But in oral arguments in *Fox*, Roberts refrained from uttering the words in question:

People who want to watch broadcasts ... or expose their children to broadcasts where these words are used, where there is nudity, there are 800 channels where they can go for that. All we are asking for, what the government is asking for, is a few channels where you can say I'm not going to – they are not going to hear the S word, the F word.[89]

That safe harbor line of reasoning prevailed, as the Court's majority agreed that the FCC could continue to restrict times when indecent words, whether scripted or accidental, could be used on the air.

Although the *Pacifica* decision still stands, in some ways it has become increasingly irrelevant, as broadcasting has been dramatically overtaken not just by cable, but also by online streaming. Children may have a safe harbor on broadcast radio and television, but they do not have one on the Internet. Cyberspace has become the place where anyone can say anything, and where the kind of language used online has made the Internet a target for anti-obscenity legislation. But none of the digital decency laws, not the Communications Decency Act of 1996, nor the Child Online Protection Act of 1998, both designed to shield children from the web's dark matter, survived First Amendment challenges. Instead of censoring words and images at the source, which courts now see as an overbroad and content-based speech prohibition, it is more acceptable, legally, to filter content at the receiving end. Thus, the Children's Internet Protection Act (CIPA) of 2000 instructs all K–12 schools and libraries receiving federal aid to install filters that prevent children from accessing any online "visual depiction" that is obscene or may be otherwise harmful to them. The law does not specifically ban strong language, but since software filters work by searching keywords as well as images, in practice, CIPA blocks words as well as JPEGs, even though some of that material is medical, scientific, artistic, or literary, rather than indecent. If Senator Smoot were still around, he would certainly approve of such context-free censorship.

The Internet has generally become a home for saying whatever you want, but it has also become a place where what you say can have serious consequences. In the next chapter, we will look at threats, another form of speech that lies outside the bounds of the First Amendment, but one that, like obscenity, resists a clear definition.

## CHAPTER 5

# Threat Level: Orange

What is a threat must be distinguished from what is constitutionally protected speech.

*Watts* v. *United States,* 1969

Can a Facebook post land you in jail? The answer is yes, if it is a threat. Will you stay there? That depends on how you define *threat.*

Threats, like obscenity, are always unprotected speech. Anthony Elonis served three years in federal prison for a series of Facebook threats against his ex-wife, an FBI agent, and a local kindergarten, because the jury didn't buy his three-pronged defense: I didn't mean it; I'm an artist; I was just kidding. Instead, they believed that anyone reading his posts would know they were threats. Elonis appealed his conviction to the US Supreme Court because the jury at his trial was told his intention didn't matter.[1] But the Supreme Court's job is to review cases, not to re-try them. So instead of second-guessing Elonis' intentions, it sent the matter back to the lower court to determine, not whether Elonis' audience read his posts as threats – it was clear that they did – but whether he *meant* to threaten them. As Chief Justice John Roberts put it in his opinion, there can be no guilt without intent.

Anthony Elonis is not the first person to tangle with the law for posting threats online, and he will not be the last. For example, after the Brussels terror bombings in March, 2016, in which thirty-two people were killed and over 300 injured by ISIS-inspired terrorists, Matthew Doyle, a London communications specialist, tweeted, "I confronted a Muslim woman yesterday in Croydon. I asked her to explain Brussels. She said 'Nothing to do with me.' A mealy mouthed reply."[2] The tweet went viral, and for a brief time "a mealy mouthed reply" became an internet meme. Worse still, for Doyle, he was arrested for inciting racial hatred on social media.[3] The guidelines for handling online threats advise British prosecutors to determine whether "the … offence involves proof of an intention that the message should be of a menacing character or, alternatively, proof of awareness or recognition of a risk at the time of sending the message that it may create fear or apprehension in any reasonable member of the public who reads or sees it."[4] Doyle's communication skills did not keep him out of trouble, but he did manage to use the "just kidding" defense more successfully than Anthony Elonis had. The charges against him were dropped a few days later.

Here is another example: after five police officers were killed in a 2016 Dallas shooting, there was an increase in US arrests for online threats. Four men in Detroit and a Chicago woman were among those charged in separate incidents, along with a Connecticut man accused of inciting injuries to persons or property for posting that the Dallas shooter was a hero and police officers should be killed.[5] These are not isolated incidents. Earlier that year, a Virginia twelve-year-old being bullied by students at her middle school was arrested for threatening the school after she posted an Instagram with an implied threat: emojis of a gun, a knife, and a bomb.[6] And after January 6, the police investigated online threats of violence in Washington to identify and arrest posters who had stormed the Capitol.

Despite the many prosecutions for online bullying and direct threats to individuals, social media providers tend to avoid taking action against offenders, even though threats violate their terms of service. When Twitter banned a controversial right-wing blogger for threatening an actor, the company explained that although it supported free expression, "our rules prohibit inciting or engaging in the targeted abuse or harassment of others," and CEO Jack Dorsey reassured investors, "Freedom of expression means little if we allow voices to be silenced because of fear of harassment if they speak up. No one deserves to be the target of abuse online, and it has no place on Twitter."[7] "The Twitter Rules" do ban "violent threats, harassment, and hateful conduct."[8] But those rules are merely suggestions. In contrast, Twitter's binding Terms of Service (TOS) agreement protects the company from liability for users' posts, even those that violate the Twitter Rules, and although Twitter says it may remove improper content, harassment comes last in the hierarchy of Twitter don'ts, after copyright and trademark violations and other unlawful conduct. Nor is it reassuring when Twitter warns, "By using the Services, you may be exposed to Content that might be offensive, harmful, inaccurate or otherwise inappropriate ... Under no circumstances will Twitter be liable in any way for any Content."[9] It is a clear Catch-22: if you want to use Twitter, you must agree not to abuse anyone, but you also have to accept the risk that you will be abused.

A recent study revealed that 72 percent of internet users have witnessed online harassment and abuse, and 47 percent have experienced it personally. In addition to the emotional damage of such abuse, threatening words have the potential to chill speech: "The threat of harassment can suppress the voices of many of our citizens ... 27% of all American internet users [and 40 percent of young women] self-censor their online postings out of fear of online harassment."[10] The study added that, although men and women are equally likely to be targets of online threats, women experience more kinds of threatening behavior, and that behavior is likely to be more severe. In addition, both the young and those who are nonbinary or gender nonconforming are more likely to experience online abuse, and they are more likely to be harmed by it. Even so, social media platforms, as they speed communications from sender to audience, are slow to address threats. Private companies like Twitter, Facebook, and Instagram can suspend anyone who violates their terms of service, but their response to complaints often finds that no violation has occurred. The upshot is that, to avoid harassment, users must avert their eyes.

Online threats violate social media terms of service, but in the United States it is not clear exactly what law is broken when someone says, "I'm mad as hell about this," or, "These people deserve to die," or "Secretary of State X should be shot for treason," or even this, "If the police stops and request me to get out of the car I'm shooting instantly," the Facebook post which got Jenesis Reynolds charged with disorderly conduct by Chicago police.[11] The legal scholar Larry Dubin said about such online rants, "Having a bad thought isn't necessarily a crime."[12] But having a bad thought online *can* be a crime when that thought becomes a threat, and having a bad thought about a president can be a very big crime indeed.

## THREATS AGAINST THE PRESIDENT

To repeat: threats, like obscenity, are always unprotected speech, always illegal. New Jersey, Illinois, and Florida were among the states that had no problem reconciling antithreat laws with the free speech provisions in their own constitutions in the late eighteenth and early nineteenth centuries.[13] On the other hand, the federal government didn't pass an antithreat law until 1917, when in a much-delayed response to the assassinations of presidents Abraham Lincoln (1865), James Garfield (1881), and William McKinley (1901), Congress finally made threats against the president a crime. That law resurfaced in the news when, during the 2016 presidential campaign, then-candidate Donald Trump suggested at a campaign rally that "Second Amendment people" might respond if his opponent, Hillary Clinton, won the election and tried to stiffen gun controls. *Was that a threat?* people asked. *Did Trump just break the law?* We will revisit that question later in this chapter.

There are several other federal threat laws besides the one protecting presidents, including a ban on threats in interstate commerce. That is the law that got Anthony Elonis in trouble for posting on Facebook. These statutes raise two important questions: When do words constitute a threat? and, What does it take to be convicted for threatening someone? Like obscenity, an accurate definition of a threat would help. But after a century of legislation and many convictions for making threats, we are still waiting for a satisfactory legal interpretation of what makes words threatening, not just to the recipient, but also in the eyes of the law. The Supreme Court has never defined threats, but it did go so far as to affirm, in *Watts* v. *United States* (1969), that threatening speech lies outside the scope of the First Amendment.[14] *Watts* involved a threat against President Lyndon Johnson. Looking at how the courts have handled presidential threats will help us to understand their approach to online threats made by people like Elonis.

The earliest prosecution for threatening a president involved an incident in the summer of 1798. As John Adams traveled from the nation's capital in Philadelphia to his home in Massachusetts to escape an outbreak of yellow fever, the president's carriage passed through Newark, where the local militia greeted him with an artillery salute. Not everyone among the onlookers outside a pub along the way was an Adams fan, and when one of them joked, "They are firing at his arse," an inebriated Luther Baldwin declared, "I don't care if they fire through his arse." To which the innkeeper, John Burnet, replied, "That is sedition."[15] Baldwin was arrested the following November, charged by US Attorney Lucius Horatio Stockton under the provisions of the 1798 Sedition Act with threatening the president's life – even though the cannon saluting the presidential posterior contained only powder and wadding but no cannonballs. Here is an excerpt from Baldwin's indictment:

> Luther Baldwin ... being a pernicious and a seditious man and contriving & maliciously intending the faithful citizens of the United States to encite and move to hatred and dislike of the person of the President of the United States; on the twenty seventh day of July ... the President of the United States being then and there passing on the high way thro' the township ... and divers faithful citizens of the United States in testimony of their respect and affection for & towards the said President of the United States being then and there firing a cannon, unlawfully, maliciously and wickedly did publish, utter and declare with a loud voice, three english words, the President ... "is a *damned rascal* and ought to have his (meaning the President of the United States) arse kicked." "I wish one of the charges (meaning the charges then and there firing and discharging aforesaid from the cannon as aforesaid) "would pass thro' his (meaning the President of the United States) arse ... to the great scandal and contempt of the President of the United States and government thereof, to the evil example of all others in the like case offending, and against the peace of the United States the government and dignity of the same.[16]

The odds stacked against him, a now-sober Baldwin pled guilty to sedition – there was no antithreat law at the time – and paid the $150 fine (about $3,200 or £2,350 today).

Luther Baldwin, drunk and unarmed, posed no threat to President Adams, who only learned about the incident in retrospect, if he learned of it at all. Lincoln, Garfield, and McKinley were not so lucky, but Congress didn't act on presidential threats until the twentieth century. To accompany the 1917 Espionage Act, Congress passed a law criminalizing threats against the president. That law reads, in part, "Any person who *knowingly* and *willfully* ... [makes or conveys] any threat to take the life of or to inflict bodily harm upon the President of the United States ... shall upon conviction be fined not exceeding $1,000 or imprisoned not exceeding five years, or both" (about $20,000 or £14,700 now).[17] Prosecutions under that law began soon after, and federal courts found themselves trying to answer the question, *What makes a threat a threat?* The presidential threat law doesn't tell us, though it specifies that a threat must be uttered both *knowingly* and *willfully*.

In one of the first presidential threat cases, Pemberton W. Stickrath, a veterinarian from Marietta, Ohio, was arrested for saying, "President Wilson ought to be killed. It is a wonder some one has not done it already. If I had an opportunity, I would do it myself."[18] Ignoring Stickrath's "just kidding" defense, it took a jury just five minutes to convict him.[19] In upholding that conviction, Judge John Elbert Sater found that for threats against the president, "the motive ... is immaterial." Sater, who shared the national dislike of antiwar protests, stressed that the presidential threats law was put in place at a time of great national challenge in part to criminalize words that could harm not just the president, but the nation as a whole:

> To threaten to kill him ... incites the hostile and evilminded to take the President's life, adds to the expense of his safeguarding, is an affront to all loyal and right-thinking persons, inflames their minds, provokes resentment, disorder, and violence, is akin to treason, and is rightly denounced as a crime against the people as a sovereign power.

Sater cited *Webster's Dictionary* to show that Stickrath's use of *ought* "denotes an obligation of duty" – someone *should* kill Wilson – and he noted that when Stickrath said "If I had an opportunity," he expressed both the "intention and expectation of fulfillment." Finally, Sater found that a presidential threat is always a crime, regardless of any political justification: "The prohibited crime is not the less odious because it is sanctioned by what some person or class of persons may conceive to be a correct national policy, or adopt as a political faith, or designate as a religion." Sater fined Stickrath $1,000 (about $22,000 or £17,000 today) and sentenced him to thirteen months in prison.

*Stickrath* served as a model for other convictions under the new presidential threat law. Sater read the law as unambiguous. Once the words are uttered, the damage is done, the threat can't be taken back: "The subsequent abandonment of the bad intent with which it was made does not obliterate the crime." But in another decision, a Montana federal judge found the presidential threats law was indeed ambiguous. William Metzdorf was indicted for saying, "If I got hold of President Wilson, I would shoot him," a statement that would count as a presidential threat under *Stickrath*. But Judge George M. Bourquin, one of the few jurists to oppose the wartime sedition laws, insisted that a conviction must show explicitly that the words were directed at Wilson as an officer of the federal government, not at Wilson, the man. That reasoning seems a stretch, since Metzdorf explicitly referred to *President* Wilson. But Bourquin also found Metzdorf's words ambiguous. They could either mean, "If I *had gotten* hold of President Wilson I would have shot him," referring to the past, or "If I *get* hold of President Wilson I will shoot him," pointing toward the future. According to Bourquin, to be a threat, the statement must anticipate a future act, not simply comment on a missed opportunity.[20] Bourquin's active defense of war protestors led to a failed attempt by the Montana legislators to impeach him, but the views he expressed in *Metzdorf* remained in the minority.

## CRIMINAL INTENT

*Metzdorf* was an isolated case that set no precedents, but in *Ragansky* v. *United States* (1918), the Seventh Circuit Court of Appeals established a formula for defining threats that courts would follow for the next fifty years.[21]

Walter Ragansky was convicted for making three threats against Woodrow Wilson. He said the following, in the presence of others who reported him:

- I can make bombs and I will make bombs and blow up the President;
- we ought to make the biggest bomb in the world and take it down to the White House and put it on the dome and blow up President Wilson and all the rest of the crooks, and get President Wilson and all of the rest of the crooks and blow it up;
- I would like to make a bomb big enough to blow up the Capitol and President and all the Senators and everybody in it.

In his defense, Ragansky insisted that his words were just a joke. Although we do not know the context, the "threats" sound more like the hyperbolic rants in *Abrams* than the more reasoned antiwar arguments in *Schenck*. It is also reasonable to assume that Ragansky himself was not preparing to blow anybody up, nor was he actively recruiting volunteers to do the work. But the court rejected Ragansky's "just kidding" defense because a joking threat is still a threat. Ragansky knew the meaning of his words – their dictionary definitions – and he said those words of his own accord – no one forced him to speak. Therefore, he uttered them both knowingly and willfully within the meaning of the Act. As the court defined these terms:

> A threat is *knowingly* made, if the maker of it comprehends the meaning of the words uttered by him; a foreigner, ignorant of the English language, repeating these same words without knowledge of their meaning, may not knowingly have made a threat.
>
> A threat is *willfully* made, if in addition to comprehending the meaning of his words, the maker voluntarily and intentionally utters them as the declaration of an apparent determination to carry them into execution.[22]

These explanations of *knowingly* and *willfully* became known as the Ragansky test, and furnished proof of intent in subsequent threat cases. The *Ragansky* court noted that the presidential threat law does not require the "evil or malicious intent" that is necessary in other criminal convictions – also called "criminal intent" or *mens rea*. Instead, the presidential threat law simply requires that Ragansky's words "would naturally be understood by the hearers as being a threat: that is, the expression of a determination, whether actual or only pretended, to menace the President's safety."

To answer the sticky question, *How do we know what anyone intends?*, the court sidestepped mind-reading in favor finding "an apparent determination to carry [the words] into execution." Subsequent convictions for threatening the president applied the *Ragansky* standard, proof that the speaker knew the meaning of the words and spoke voluntarily, not under duress, or while asleep, or in a trance. All that a prosecutor needed to prove for a conviction was the speaker's apparent intent: an observer, hearing the words, understood their meaning. It was not necessary to meet the standard of criminal intent, assessing the speaker's state of mind, which is necessary for a conviction in any other crime. The "apparent intent" standard prevailed until 1969, when the Supreme Court revisited the meaning of *willfully* in the presidential threats law.

**"THE FIRST MAN I WANT TO GET IN MY SIGHTS IS LBJ"** In 1966, Robert Watts, an eighteen-year-old New York City high-school senior and Harlem civil-rights worker, was arrested for threatening the life of President Lyndon Baines Johnson, often referred to as LBJ. The incident occurred during a rally organized by the W. E. B. Du Bois Club at the Washington Monument. At one point, the thirty to forty people present broke up into discussion groups, and Watts, who had joined a group focusing on police brutality, announced that he wasn't going to go to Vietnam: "I have already received my draft classification as 1-A and I have got to report for my physical this Monday coming. I am not going. If they ever make me carry a rifle the first man I want to get in my sights is LBJ … They are not going to make me kill my black brothers."[23] Even though the event was small, more of a teach-in than a full-on antiwar protest, law enforcement was there to listen and take names. The next day, one of those observers, Park Police Sergeant Harold Shoemaker, told the Secret Service what Watts had said. Secret Service agents then located Watts, who was still at the Washington Monument, and arrested him.

Did Robert Watts threaten the president? A grand jury agreed with the prosecutor that he had. But like Stickrath and Ragansky before him, Watts claimed he wasn't serious. Sergeant Shoemaker confirmed that many in the group laughed when Watts illustrated his words by aiming an imaginary rifle, and Watts' attorney, Joseph Forer, insisted that Shoemaker didn't take the words seriously either. He didn't report Watts till the next day. As Forer put it, "If he really thought the young man really threatened the President, it would have been unforgivable for him to wait a day to report it."[24] Even so, Watts was indicted. At his trial, an Army Counter Intelligence Corps investigator named Freeburger testified that he also heard Watts threaten the president. And a reporter for the *Milwaukee Sentinel* confirmed this, adding that Watts said, "rather than looking down the barrel of a rifle to kill Vietnamese people he would rather look down a rifle aimed at the President."[25]

Watts was convicted and sentenced to four years probation. That sentence was upheld by a panel of the District of Columbia Court of Appeals. Writing for that court, Judge Warren Burger, who three years later became Chief Justice of the United States, rejected both of the defense's key arguments: that Watts didn't intend to carry out his threat, and that his hyperbolic statement was protected by the First Amendment. Citing the 1916 congressional debate over the presidential threats law, Burger found that the statute's goal was to deter attacks both by the speaker making such threats and by anyone who might hear or read them, "including those less stable than the speaker and perhaps more suggestible."[26]

Watts' attorney interpreted that law's legislative history differently, and because the Supreme Court also considered the early debates over the statute, that history is worth reviewing here. The presidential threats bill was introduced in 1916 by Representative Edwin Webb, of North Carolina. Webb was motivated not only by the assassinations of three earlier presidents, but also by a wave of more recent European assassinations that plunged the continent into war. Webb's bill would "decrease the possibility of an actual assault by punishing threats to commit an assault." It would also prevent such threats from inciting others to do so:

> A bad man can make a public threat, and put somebody else up to committing a crime against the Chief Executive, and that is where the harm comes. The man who makes the threat is not himself very dangerous, but he is liable to put devilment in the mind of some poor fellow who does try to harm him.[27]

Even so, Webb insisted that the speaker's intent is crucial and idle threats should be discounted: "I think it must be a willful intent to do serious injury to the President ... I do not think we ought to be too anxious to convict a man who does a thing thoughtlessly. I think it ought to be a willful expression of an intent to carry out a threat against the Executive."[28]

Webb clearly considered a *willful* threat to be a serious one. Even if the speaker "is not himself very dangerous" – in other words, if the speaker is not likely to carry out the threat – that threat must be intentional, not "just kidding." That reasoning might have let Robert Watts off the hook, but Burger, echoing *Stickrath*, dismissed intent as a non-issue: any threat against the president, even a joking one, must be taken seriously by the security services, and any threat, serious or frivolous, limits the ability of presidents to do their job. Burger noted examples like *Ragansky* where hyperbolic speech was punished under the presidential threat statute, including this clearly hyperbolic statement by a Texas man shortly after the presidential threat law went into effect: "Wilson is a wooden-headed son of a bitch. I wish Wilson was in hell, and if I had the power I would put him there."[29] For Burger, Watts' statements clearly passed the relatively light burden of the *Ragansky* test: Watts knew the meaning of the individual words. He wasn't compelled to speak. And observers like Sergeant Shoemaker and Agent Freeburger thought that Watts could act on his words.

Citing the chilling example of the Holocaust, Burger also dismissed Watts' defense that the audience greeted his words with laughter and applause: "It has not been unknown for laughter and applause to have sinister implications for the safety of others. History records that applause and laughter frequently greeted Hitler's predictions of the future of the German Jews." Burger also rejected any First Amendment defense because the importance of keeping the president safe outweighs an individual's right to speak.

But one judge on the DC Circuit's panel disagreed. James Skelly Wright, who had a strong commitment to social justice, observed in his dissent that the first convictions under the presidential threat law came during the First World War, a time when, as we saw in *Schenck* and *Abrams*, restrictions on civil liberties were challenged with little success.

Judge Wright argued that since Watts was engaging in political speech, that context must be considered before classifying his words as threats: "Where an utterance does convey an idea, particularly an idea about how public affairs should be conducted, the label 'threat' does not preclude First Amendment protection any more than do the labels 'obscenity' … or 'libel.'" Wright dismissed Burger's example of sinister audience laughter: Watts' words "were taken in context by their hearers to be hyperbolic emphasis of a political view which they supported." Instead of abridging Watts' First Amendment guarantees, Wright would apply the stricter standard of criminal intent, as well as a clear and present danger test to show that Watts' "words, taken in their context, are most readily susceptible to the interpretation that they were a crude, even offensive, rhetorical device. They cannot be read unambiguously as a serious threat against the President."

After the DC Circuit denied his appeal, Watts turned to the Supreme Court, and in a *per curiam* opinion, the Court agreed in large part with Judge Wright that the trial judge should have dismissed the case for lack of evidence, and it reversed Watts' conviction.[30] The justices characterized Watts' words as a "very crude offensive method of stating a political opposition to the President." In a concurrence, Justice William O. Douglas took Judge Wright's reasoning further, comparing the presidential threats statute with the now-reviled Alien and Sedition laws of the early republic. Douglas also observed that the first convictions under the presidential threat statute emphasized not actual threats to a president, but wartime political dissent treated as treason.

The *Watts* court did affirm the constitutionality of the presidential threats law, and it placed verbal threats outside the protection of the First Amendment. But it also stressed the need to examine both the context and the words in order to distinguish true threats from protected speech: "A statute such as this one, which makes criminal a form of pure speech, must be interpreted with the commands of the First Amendment clearly in mind. What is a threat must be distinguished from what is constitutionally protected speech."** In short, Watts' words never posed a threat. Rather, they were hyperbolic political speech. Citing its protection of "uninhibited, robust and wide-open" speech when no actual malice had been proved, the *Watts* court observed that, like true threats, protected speech can get nasty, but nastiness in and of itself doesn't turn words into threats:

> The language of the political arena … is often vituperative, abusive, and inexact. We agree with petitioner that his only offense here was "a kind of very crude offensive method of stating a political opposition to the President." Taken in context, and regarding the expressly conditional nature of the statement and the reaction of the listeners, we do not see how it could be interpreted otherwise.

---

** Pure speech consists of words alone, unaccompanied by action.

In reversing Watts' conviction the Supreme Court questioned, without ruling on it, the appropriateness of the *Ragansky* standard that the Appeals Court had accepted: "The willfulness requirement [is] met if the speaker voluntarily uttered the charged words with 'an apparent determination to carry them into execution.'" But the Supreme Court wasn't so sure: "Perhaps this interpretation is correct, although we have grave doubts about it." The Court was certain, however, that in Watts' trial, the prosecution failed to prove even a minimal *Ragansky* standard of intent.

The *Watts* court did not define what constitutes a threat. But in declaring Robert Watts' comments to be crude political hyperbole and not a threat against the president, the Court's concluding assessment, "we do not see how it could be interpreted otherwise," is not so different from Potter Stewart's earlier subjective assessment of pornography in *Jacobellis* v. *Ohio*: we know threats when we see them, and Watts' words are not threats. The important takeaway from *Watts* is the confirmation that threats are never protected speech and the requirement that words must be considered in context in order to determine whether they are, in fact, intended to threaten someone.

## HE POSTED ON FACEBOOK; HE WENT DIRECTLY TO JAIL

You may not be president of the United States, but you may be on Facebook, Twitter, Instagram, or some other social media, the kind of online spaces where threats are common. Some threats are empty words, but what happens if things do get scary? If you've been threatened online, do you have legal recourse? After all, threats are never protected speech. And what if someone accuses you of making an online threat, and that is not what you meant at all, they just took your words the wrong way? And what if your posts walk a fine line between threat and not-a-threat? Unfortunately, whether it is threats against the president or threats against private individuals, the legal boundary between threats and protected online speech remains murky. First Amendment absolutists resist any attempt to regulate internet speech, while victims' rights advocates call for restrictions and protections that go beyond the various internet terms of service to protections that actually work.

When is a threat a threat, and when is it just good, clean fun, or a therapeutic venting of emotion, or even art? If you rap online about killing your ex, or your co-workers, or an FBI agent, or some random school children, but you haven't killed them, at least not yet, will the First Amendment shield you from prosecution? These are some of the questions that the Supreme Court considered in *Elonis* v. *United States* (2015), a case about social media threats.[31]

In 2010, a Pennsylvania federal court convicted twenty-seven-year-old Anthony Douglas Elonis of posting threats on Facebook against a number of people: his estranged wife, after she took out an order of protection against him; an FBI agent who had attempted to question him about his menacing Facebook posts; unnamed police officers who had yet to do anything to annoy Elonis but might do so one day; and an unspecified kindergarten class somewhere near Elonis' home.

Elonis was charged with violating the Interstate Communications Act, which makes it illegal to threaten someone across state lines.[32] Even if Elonis' Facebook friends were all in Pennsylvania, where he lived, and even if he restricted access to his posts only to those friends, Facebook's servers are located in multiple states, and a post may be routed through a number of servers around the country as it makes its way from a writer's keyboard to someone else's screen. That makes any online post an interstate communication governed by federal law.

Convicted of making a series of online threats, Elonis served three years of a forty-four month sentence, followed by three years of court supervision. After his release, Elonis appealed his conviction, arguing that the trial judge wrongfully instructed the jury to ask whether a reasonable person would interpret his posts as threats, but not whether Elonis *intended* to carry them out. When the Court of Appeals rejected that argument, Elonis appealed to the Supreme Court, claiming that his Facebook posts were just him messing around. He didn't *intend* to threaten anyone. His status updates were a combination of therapeutic venting and art. Elonis claimed to be an aspiring rapper, and so his speech should be protected by the First Amendment. Basically, he said, it was all a misunderstanding. He was an artist. He was just kidding.

Free-speech advocates supported Elonis not because they approved of his words, but because users of internet forums and social media would be reluctant to post for fear that their words, if misconstrued, might get them arrested. The *New York Times* editorial board insisted that giving Elonis a free pass would be a small price to pay to protect free speech, that affirming Elonis' conviction "would make it easier to criminalize all sorts of violent speech that flies around the Internet every day, much of it not intended to threaten anyone."[33] In contrast, advocates for the victims of domestic violence wanted the Court to signal that online threats can't hide behind the First Amendment. Justice Samuel Alito agreed that it was time to put an end to online threats, that protecting Elonis' menacing Facebook speech by labeling it art, "sounds like a roadmap for threatening a spouse and getting away with it."[34] In his dissent, Alito added, "A fig leaf of artistic expression cannot convert such hurtful, valueless threats into protected speech."

In opposing Elonis' appeal, the government contended that his words inspired fear in those who read them, citing testimony from Elonis' ex-wife, who had to get an order of protection because she feared for her life. But Elonis insisted that because he didn't mean to threaten anyone, he should not be judged by how readers perceived his posts. He claimed that he was just letting off steam after a bad breakup when he posted, "If I only knew then what I know now ... I would have smothered your ass with a pillow. Dumped your body in the back seat. Dropped you off in Toad Creek and made it look like a rape and murder."[35] And even though one of his posts put local schools on alert, Elonis claimed that he was just channeling the violent lyrics of the rapper Eminem when he wrote:

That's it, I've had about enough
I'm checking out and making a name for myself
Enough elementary schools in a ten mile radius to initiate the most
heinous school shooting ever imagined
And hell hath no fury like a crazy man in a Kindergarten class
The only question is ... which one?[36]

Elonis linked some of his rants to the Wikipedia entry on freedom of speech, and he marked some of his posts as "fictitious" or "for entertainment purposes," insisting that those disclaimers gave his posts constitutional protection.[37] Citing *Cohen* v. *California*, his attorneys argued that bad art qualifies for protection as much as good art: "Wholly neutral futilities ... come under the protection of free speech as fully as do Keats' poems or Donne's sermons."[38] But Justice Antonin Scalia was skeptical. Normally a free speech champion, though one who preferred opera to rap, Scalia suggested in oral arguments that Elonis was no artist, so any judgment against him would not chill artistic expression: "And this is valuable First Amendment language that you think has to be protected, right? ... It doesn't eliminate a lot of valuable speech at all."[39]

Other justices worried about the impact of a negative decision. Justice Elena Kagan said, "We typically say that the First Amendment requires kind of a buffer zone to ensure that even stuff that is wrongful maybe is permitted because we don't want to chill innocent behavior."[40] And Justice Sonia Sotomayor similarly observed, "We've been loath to create more exceptions to the First Amendment."[41] In the end, the Court created no exceptions and added no protections. Rather, it sent the case back to the Appeals Court with instructions to consider whether Elonis intended his words to be threats.

Like the appellants in *Mutual Film* (1915), who explained to the Court how motion pictures created the illusion of movement, Elonis' attorneys offered the Court a detailed description of how Facebook works, on the assumption that the justices would be clueless about the new technology. They reminded the Court that because online messages lack the nuance that facilitates face-to-face communication, asking a reasonable person to look at the words and say, "Yes, that's a threat," would increase the risk of convicting someone for words that look like threats to an outsider – a neutral, objective, reasonable person – but are not threats in the context in which they were uttered.[42] However, that is true whether the writing in question is online or off, whether the words alleged to be threatening are conveyed onscreen or on a piece of paper stuck on a windshield or slipped under a door. The larger concern that the *Elonis* court did not decide is, What standard should a jury use to evaluate a speaker's or writer's intent? Or, as Justice Ginsburg asked rhetorically, "How does one prove what's in somebody else's mind?"[43]

The *Ragansky* test – that the speaker knew the definitions of the words in question and spoke them voluntarily – led to convictions in cases that would be dismissed today. But *Ragansky*'s usefulness as a measure of intent was questioned as soon as it was articulated. Justice Oliver Wendell Holmes lamented in his dissent in *Abrams* (1919) that such a standard could easily result in misunderstandings with serious consequences for the speaker:

> The word intent as vaguely used in ordinary legal discussion means no more than knowledge at the time of the act that the consequences said to be intended will ensue … A man … may be sent to prison, at common law might be hanged, if at the time of his act he knew facts from which common experience showed that the consequences would follow, whether he individually could foresee them or not.[44]

But even after *Watts*, which stressed the need to assess a potential threat in context, exactly what constitutes intent to threaten remains unresolved. The Supreme Court sent *Elonis* back to the Third Circuit Court of Appeals for a rehearing, without additional guidance on how to identify a threat. In that re-hearing, Elonis' attorney argued that a jury must "have an opportunity to … decide whether they believe [the defendant] or not; but that's not what happened in this case."[45] The government countered that Elonis' actions show he was well aware that his words were threats. When his employer fired him for a post threatening a co-worker, Elonis followed up with another post threatening workplace violence. When his ex-wife got an order of protection because Elonis threatened her on Facebook, he responded with further threatening posts. When the FBI questioned him about a post threatening a school, Elonis threatened the FBI agent online. According to the government:

> He knows that these are going to be perceived as threats … [he testified that he] was trying to be shocking … A threat doesn't need the desire or the ability to carry it out … Each time he got a reaction, which he enjoyed, he just kept going farther … Every one of these is a threat to murder people … There's no question that the risk he was taking was unjustifiable … Elonis said, "I knew what people were saying, and I didn't care" … He's posting a disclaimer because he knows people are going to see it as a threat … He admits that he knew it would be perceived as a threat.[46]

The appeals court agreed, and in October, 2016, it reaffirmed Elonis' conviction. In his opinion, Judge Anthony Scirica sidestepped First Amendment issues, ruling narrowly that "it is not for the defendant to determine whether a communication is objectively threatening – that is the jury's role."[47] The court did acknowledge that the trial judge erred when he told the jury that intent didn't matter, but that wasn't a reversible error, a mistake that could alter the outcome of the trial:

> The record contains overwhelming evidence demonstrating beyond a reasonable doubt that Elonis knew the threatening nature of his communications, and therefore would have been convicted absent the error ... Even if Elonis had contested the knowledge element in his testimony, no rational juror would have believed him ... It is not at all credible that Elonis did not know his ex-wife would interpret [his Facebook posts about her] as threats.[48]

The appeals court handily rejected Elonis' "my posts are art" defense because a poetic threat is still a threat. It found that Elonis met either of two standards of intent: the stricter "knowledge" standard, that Elonis knew he was threatening his ex; or the less-strict "recklessness" standard, that he knew she might interpret his messages as threats but he posted them anyway. However, the court declined to specify which standard should be required for a conviction, leaving the test for assessing intent both online and off pretty much like the standard for obscenity: you'll know it when you see it.

There's one final note in the *Elonis* case, to be filed under "some people never learn." Just one day after oral arguments in Elonis' Supreme Court appeal, the US Attorney's office for the Eastern District of Pennsylvania announced that before his release from prison, Elonis mailed this apparent threat to a prosecutor in their office: "I am rapidly approaching the date of my release. Accordingly, I would like to begin researching the ordinances of the municipality in which you reside. I simply do not wish to run afoul of any of them when I set fire to a cross in your yard.:-p"[49] That message, a pencil-and-paper one since Elonis could not use Facebook in prison, was followed by a hand-drawn wink emoticon, :-p, purporting to say, "just kidding."

The reference in Elonis's note to cross burning, generally perceived by reasonable people to be a severe form of threat, alludes to *Virginia* v. *Black* (2003), a case in which the Supreme Court ruled that even though cross burning may be outlawed when it is intended to intimidate, states may not ban any and all cross burnings because some of them may be protected political speech. The example of protected speech cited by the Court occurs in a context sure to produce hate speech: "It is a ritual used at [Ku Klux] Klan gatherings, and it is used to represent the Klan itself."[50] Elonis' note to the prosecutor came too late for the Supreme Court to consider as it reviewed his appeal, but Chief Justice Roberts did not append a winking emoji 😉 to his opinion, assuming he even knew what it meant or how to find it on his keyboard, because the Court was not kidding.[††]

After *Elonis*, Congress briefly considered clarifying the Interstate Communications Act by adding, "the Government shall prove that the defendant intended, had knowledge, or recklessly disregarded the risk, that the communication would be reasonably interpreted as a threat."[51] In the end, the legislators took no action, but trolls have no reason to relax. One strong lesson from *Elonis* is that when the right case comes along, the courts could rule on the appropriate level of intent required for a conviction, making online threats a lot easier to prosecute.

Unfortunately, no ruling will make it easier to decide which online threats to take seriously. Some Facebook rants are just hot air but others result in violence. After a man shot up the Dallas police headquarters in 2015, police chief David Brown said they had been aware of his social media posts threatening to kill police officers, but officials didn't investigate because, "there had been no indication that he was planning to carry out an attack."[52] That was a single threat by one person, but multiple law enforcement agencies also failed to act on the large number of online threats of violence that preceded the January 6 attack by Trump supporters on the Capitol. Many later explained that they did not investigate further because they considered the online threats to be protected by the First Amendment.[53]

---

[††] Emoticons, along with italics, boldface, and punctuation, are some of the many tools that writing systems online and off deploy to replicate the nuances of speech.

## DID CANDIDATE DONALD TRUMP THREATEN THE PRESIDENT?

Now we return to a question raised at the beginning of this chapter. In a campaign speech on August 9, 2016, in Wilmington, North Carolina, Republican presidential candidate Donald Trump seemed to threaten his Democratic opponent, Hillary Clinton: "Hillary wants to abolish – essentially abolish – the Second Amendment. By the way, and if she gets to pick – if she gets to pick her [Supreme Court] judges, nothing you can do, folks. Although the Second Amendment people, maybe there is, I don't know."[54]

Video of Trump's remarks went viral, and the press widely reported this unprecedented potential threat against a presidential candidate. Was Trump, with a track record of violent and reckless rhetoric, calling on the radical fringe of the gun-rights community – "the Second Amendment people" – to shoot Clinton if she won the election, or perhaps to assassinate her judicial nominees? After all, in previous rallies Trump had been videotaped encouraging his supporters to beat up protesters; he threatened to "knock the crap out of" them himself; and he said of one protester in Las Vegas, "I'd like to punch him in the face."[55] Trump also seemed to encourage audiences in loud chants of "Lock her up" and "Kill the bitch," aimed at his opponent – or at least he did nothing to discourage such behavior. But suggesting what could be construed as potentially lethal violence against a presidential opponent seemed a clear-cut case of incitement, and, quite possibly, a violation of federal threat laws.[56]

Many critics on both sides of the aisle found Trump's words to be at best inappropriate for a candidate for such high office. But would they actually violate the presidential threats act? A few hours after his speech, Trump tried to repair the damage, tweeting that he merely meant that Second Amendment supporters would flex their political muscle and rally the vote: "I said pro-2A citizens must organize and get out vote to save our Constitution!"[57] Still, many people read his words as clearly referring to action that could be taken *after* a Clinton victory, long after votes had been counted. What Trump said about Second Amendment people taking aim at Clinton would get a slam-dunk conviction under the *Ragansky* standard: he knew what each word meant, more or less, and he spoke voluntarily. But not today. Given the political context of then-candidate Trump's Second Amendment solutions innuendo, it would be easy to compare his words with those of young Robert Watts more than fifty years ago: crude political hyperbole protected by the First Amendment. In the post-*Watts* era, what Trump said would not trigger an automatic "Go directly to jail" card without first considering the speaker's criminal intent. Political speech has more protection now than it did in 1918, or even in 1966, as long as a speaker isn't calling for an immediate riot or assassination. If there is "room to breathe" between the troubling statement and any action that might follow – the standard for protected speech suggested by Brandeis in 1927 and adopted by the Supreme Court in *Brandenburg* in 1969 – it would be difficult to call candidate Trump's words threats. A century after *Ragansky*, Trump's apparent threat to Hillary Clinton proved just a temporary diversion in a political season in which candidate Trump, and later President Trump, seemed to charge blindly ahead from outrage to outrage.

But there is an earlier case of an implied political threat by an English king that might be apt, particularly in the context of January 6. In 1170, Henry II said of his arch-rival Thomas à Beckett, "Will no one rid me of this meddlesome priest?" – or words to that effect. Hearing this, a group of the king's supporters rushed to Canterbury and murdered the archbishop in the cathedral. Even though Henry, cloaking himself with plausible deniability, claimed he never ordered an assassination, the archbishop was indeed murdered by a loyal band of monarchists. The king wound up doing public penance for Becket's murder, and the martyred priest became a saint.

Warren Burger's warning in the *Watts* appeal about the potential of violent speech to rouse to action "those less stable than the speaker and perhaps more suggestible," seems germane to another incident from the 2016 presidential campaign. Incited by the widely repeated online lie that Hillary Clinton was running a child-abuse ring out of a small Washington pizza parlor, a North Carolina man burst into the restaurant firing an assault rifle in order to liberate the children being kept there. He surrendered to police when he discovered that story was fake news.

Remembering, too, that protestors were roughed up by Trump supporters with some degree of regularity, it is hard to dismiss the technically legal but certainly intemperate potential for incitement of Trump's ominous talk of Second Amendment solutions, or his insistence on January 6 that his followers must "fight like hell" to take back their country. In the end, Trump's words about Second Amendment people became moot when he, not Clinton, became the president. And although Trump's culpability for inciting the January 6 insurrection was ultimately not proved in his second impeachment trial, even some of his long-time supporters, like Senator Mitch McConnell, found that he his words led to the Capitol invasion. And even though Anthony Elonis is back on Facebook, Trump was banned from Twitter, Facebook, and Instagram for intemperate posts which violated their terms of service and a whole lot more.

### TWEET LEVEL: RED

To sum up: First Amendment protections do not apply to threats, and after *Watts*, a threat must demonstrate some degree of criminal intent. Perhaps, as we see from *Elonis*, reckless disregard of a statement's impact is an appropriate legal standard for discerning intent. But the impact of *Ragansky*, *Watts*, and *Elonis* stops at the border, as does the First Amendment. There, defining threats is left to the discretion of border agents, not the courts. As such, it becomes subjective, and occasionally, absurd. That is what happened in 2012, when two tourists were denied entry to the United States because of harmless tweets that were perceived as threats.

The office of Customs and Border Protection (CBP), an agency under the supervision of the US Department of Homeland Security (DHS), "is charged with keeping terrorists and their weapons out of the US while facilitating lawful international travel and trade." As one of its "core values," the agency is "continuously watchful and alert to deter, detect, and prevent threats to our nation."[58] CBP is a vital part of the international war on terror. But its rules – for security reasons they are secret – allow it to deny entry to a visitor if an agent suspects they made a threat online. DHS regularly monitors internet traffic looking for threats. To find potential threats on social media, for example, an algorithm matches the words of a post to a watch list of words supposedly popular with terrorists, words like *assassination, attack, cops, mitigation, recovery, dirty bomb, first responder, militia, shooting, police, gangs, breach, looting, riot,* and *incident.*[59] Typing the word *threat* in a tweet could flag that post. So could using words clearly associated with terrorism, like *white powder, Ricin, Al Qaeda,*

*Hamas,* and *jihad* – though all of these words have descriptive, non-threatening uses as well. Also on the list are ordinary words like *team, interstate, ice, dock, smart, subway, electric, vaccine, wave,* and *cloud.* Facebook founder Mark Zuckerberg might be surprised to learn that the phrase *social media* itself is on the social media watch list.

In effect, tweeting a word on the DHS list could jump the threat level up from green to red in 280 characters or less. That is what happened to two British holidaymakers, Leigh Bryan and Emily Banting, who were denied entry to the United States in 2012 for tweeting threats.[60] When Bryan and Banting arrived at Los Angeles International Airport on a flight from Paris, the would-be tourists were interrogated by Customs and Border Protection agents for five hours. Bryan was handcuffed and locked up overnight with tattooed drug dealers, though they did nothing worse to him than take his food. Banting spent the night in another cell, where "a poster gave advice on what to do if an inmate raped you."[61] The pair were deported in the morning because, before their visit, Bryan tweeted to a friend using words that attracted the attention of federal threat watchers. The offending tweets read, "3 weeks today, we're totally in LA pissing people off on Hollywood Blvd and diggin' Marilyn Monroe up!" and "free this week for a quick gossip/prep before I go and destroy America?" According to the Denial of Entry form, "Mr. BRYAN confirmed that he had posted on his Tweeter website account that he was coming to the United States to dig up the grave of Marilyn Monroe. Also on his tweeter account Mr. BRYAN posted that he was coming to destroy America."[62]

Bryan explained to his interrogators that he meant none of that literally, that *destroy* was British slang for partying and getting drunk, and "digging Marilyn Monroe up" was a joke from the American TV show *Family Guy.* The humorless border agents actually searched the suspects' luggage looking for the shovels they were going to use to exhume Monroe from the Los Angeles area cemetery where she is buried. According to Bryan, "The Homeland Security agents were treating me like some kind of terrorist. I kept saying they had got the wrong meaning from my tweet but they just told me 'You've really f***ed up with that tweet, boy'."[63]

Bryan was detained, interrogated, and stamped "return to sender" for online threats that no reasonable person would perceive as threats, and that he surely did not intend to be taken literally. Banting was detained because the feds suspected she would act as lookout while Bryan did the shoveling. But some Twitter-reading algorithm, or possibly a snitch, tipped off the agents to the couple's nefarious vacation plans, and before the two could do any serious damage, they were intercepted at LAX – according to Bryan, their visas had been canceled while they were in the air. Needless to say, Bryan didn't get to do any serious partying on his seriously truncated vacation, and for a while, he took his Twitter account private.[64]

Certainly the Department of Homeland Security must do its best to keep America safe, and it invades no one's privacy when it scans the web, because anyone posting to a public site has no reasonable expectation of privacy. No one doubts that online posters who make demonstrable threats or otherwise harass victims online, or who conspire on the internet to commit crimes, should be stopped and punished if they're found guilty. And no one doubts that terrorists' behavior is difficult to predict. But now ordinary web users, who aren't terrorists or cybercriminals, must not only worry how many words they can fit into Twitter's 280-character straitjacket, they must also consider whether their words will stop them at the border.

There are some practical problems with watch lists like those used by the security services. They are over-inclusive, catching far more innocent posts than ones meriting serious concern. They make no allowance for hyperbole or jokes that mean nothing to third-party observers. There is no effective sarcasm-detection software. And the government may not be scanning the right posts: although English is still the most common language on the internet and it is the lingua franca of international commerce, it is not yet the official language of international terrorism.

But even well-designed detection algorithms go only so far. Interpreting the nuance of a tweet remains the province of the human analyst and, if necessary, the agent interviewing visitors at the border. And such interpretations, as we saw earlier in the 1930 Senate debate on obscenity, may be made by officials not trained to assess the threat level of a text, or not willing to do so. Bronson Cutting argued in 1930 that customs agents were not able to sort dirty books from great literature. Similarly, CBP agents today, especially those not used to the snark that pervades online speech, may not bother to sort criminal language from "Tweeter" language that is, indeed, "just kidding."

Perhaps the DHS thinks that it is best to accept the literal meaning of a tweet to bar the door to terrorists, even if that means keeping out partiers like Leigh Bryan who do not literally mean what they say. "It's a small price to pay" is a standard defense for an over-broad rule. That is what many senators debating obscenity back in 1930 argued as well: better to keep out one literary classic than to admit hundreds of books harmful to the nation's moral fiber. But Bryan wasn't in an airport or anywhere near LA when he tweeted his vacation plans in terms that alarmed American border guards. There was plenty of time – three weeks should be plenty of breathing room – for security analysts to figure out whether he posed a credible threat to the Hollywood hills. Plus the absence of shovels in the travelers' luggage might have furnished a clue.

Leigh Bryan's is only one of many joking posts that were taken seriously by readers who were not their intended audience. Just google "fired for tweeting" and "the internet ruined my life" and you will find lots of examples where internet communication backfires. But there is also plenty of online speech that merits consequences. As a bartender, Bryan had the authority to ban patrons from the pub in Coventry where he worked if he judged their conduct inappropriate. In the United Kingdom, banned patrons generally have no legal recourse. Now he and Banting are banned from the United States, also with no right to appeal. But the point about what happened to them is that the law offers no clear definition of a threat. Determining a threat, like determining what is obscene, is always an act of interpretation. In criminal cases, that interpretation must include a measurement of intent, which gives mis-tweeters and others accused of uttering threats a chance to argue that their words should be construed as innocent. But when it comes to visitors entering the United States, the definition of a threat is left to the discretion of border agents. What we learn from Leigh Bryan and Emily Banting's brush with the L.A. law is that, if an agent says, "This tweet sure looks like a threat to me," then it is, indeed, a threat.

In the next chapter, we will look at some instances where the law banned not just a type of speech, like a racy novel, a salacious monologue, a hyperbolic anti-war remark, or an off-hand tweet, but an entire language.

## CHAPTER 6

# America's War on Language

Freedom of Speech is guaranteed by federal and state Constitutions, but this is not a guaranty of the right to use a language other than the language of this country – the English language.

William L. Harding, Governor of Iowa, 1918

When the United States declared war on Germany in April, 1917, it declared war on language as well, passing sweeping language legislation at both the federal and local levels to require the use of English and limit that of other tongues. The goal was to suppress German, the language of the enemy, but the effect was to discourage or ban outright all languages except English. Groups of American superpatriots stirred up anti-German sentiment, which in turn led to assaults on people speaking anything that sounded the least bit foreign. If this sounds familiar, that is because the war on language continues today, only the enemy has switched from German to Spanish or one of the many Asian languages common in the United States, but more on this later.

The fear of spies was widespread in the United States in 1917, and spies presumably spoke German. Fake news spread anti-German stories, like the rumor that teachers in German-language Lutheran schools in Nebraska whipped pupils who switched to English during recess.[1] Such unverified atrocities fueled calls for revenge against German as well as Germany. That revenge was swift. The Trading with the Enemy Act of 1917 banned the mailing of any foreign-language book, magazine, or newspaper unless it was accompanied by "a true and complete translation" that had been filed with the postmaster.[2] Taking linguistic chauvinism one step further, in 1918, Representative John M. C. Smith, of Michigan, introduced a bill to change all American place names containing *Germany* or *Berlin* to *Liberty* or *Victory*, and to ban any mail addressed to the old, German name.[3] Vienna, Ohio, considered becoming Peaceton, and residents of Bismarck, Missouri, proposed changing the name to Loyal. But New Berlin, Ohio, did re-name itself North Canton and East Germantown, Indiana, became Pershing. Businesses and people sought name changes as well. The German Mutual Insurance Company, in Traer County, Iowa, became the *American* Mutual Insurance Company.[4] And George Michaelis, of Long Island, changed his family name to Woodbridge, "as a protest against the infamy that calls itself German."[5] Producers of *sauerkraut* showed their patriotism by marketing their product as *liberty* cabbage. An ad for Iffert's Meat Market in Hazelton, PA, reassured customers that they were getting the same great product under a brand-new name: "Liberty Cabbage (Formerly Sauer Kraut) … 8 Cents a Pound."[6] Even diseases turned patriotic, as West Point reported an outbreak of *liberty* measles among the cadets.[7] This sort of chauvinistic rebranding continues to pop up at times when national unity seems threatened. In 2003, when France declined to join the United States in the Gulf War, the House of Representatives ordered its cafeterias to serve *freedom fries* instead of French fries.[8]

## IOWA DECLARES WAR ON GERMAN

Local moves to regulate language went well beyond renaming places, diseases, and things to eat. Prior to the First World War, German was the second most widely spoken language in the United States, after English, and 25 percent of American high schoolers took German. But with the United States at war, Iowa became one of several states where the Superintendent of Schools ordered that German be dropped from the curriculum, and many German teachers abruptly lost their jobs.[9] In addition, German-language publications were boycotted or even banned. In March, 1918, students at Davenport High School publicly burned more than five hundred German books.[10] The next month, employees of the Des Moines school board ripped up two tons of German books and sold them for scrap.[11] But the state went further still. In May, 1918, Iowa Governor William L. Harding issued a proclamation banning foreign languages in public: in the schools, on the streets, on trains, and over the telephone, a more public instrument then than it is now. Harding, whose proclamation had the force of law, believed that speaking English was an affirmation of patriotism, but he also argued that it would protect the state's immigrants from harassment.

The "Babel Proclamation," as Harding's order came to be known, had four provisions: "First. English should and must be the only medium of instruction in public, private, denominational or other similar schools. Second. Conversation in public places, on trains and over the telephone should be in the English language. Third. All public addresses should and must be in the English language. Fourth. Let those who cannot speak or understand the English language conduct their religious worship in their homes."[12] This last rule targeted churches in the state holding German-language services for older residents, though it also impacted Iowa's Dutch-, Czech-, and Danish-language congregations. Even a Welsh church in Williamsburg was forced to suspend services rather than preach in English to older congregants who spoke only Welsh.[13] Responding to critics of his blanket ban on foreign-language worship, Harding told the Des Moines Chamber of Commerce that God is monolingual: "I am telling those who insist upon praying in some other language that they are wasting their time, for the good Lord up above is now listening for the voice in English."[14]

In his proclamation, Harding incorrectly asserted that "the official language of the United States and the State of Iowa is the English language," and he insisted that the First Amendment does not protect "the right to use a language other than the language of this country – the English language." Harding explained that he couldn't just ban German, because Germany had learned to spy on Iowa in other languages as well.[15] Apparently no one asked Harding, "If German spies speak English, shouldn't you ban English too?" Furthermore, Harding, whose anti-German bias was well known, insisted that immigrants who used their native tongues "in time of national peril" had no one but themselves to blame when their outraged neighbors roughed them up. Speaking English, the governor insisted, would restore calm to the streets. But instead of calm, as Nancy Derr put it, Harding's language ban "gave prejudice the force of law," prompting Iowa nativists to harass speakers of German and Dutch and attack them physically.[16] Dutch Reformed churches and a parochial school were set on fire in Pella and Peoria. There were even arrests for speaking German on the phone. In June, 1918, four rural women were

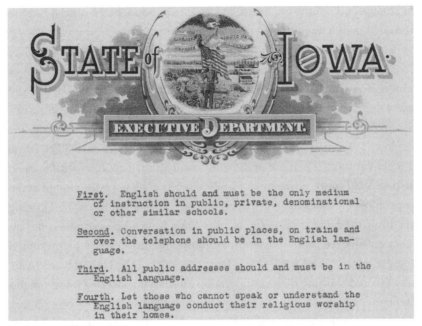

First. English should and must be the only medium
    of instruction in public, private, denominational
    or other similar schools.

Second. Conversation in public places, on trains and
    over the telephone should be in the English lan-
    guage.

Third. All public addresses should and must be in the
    English language.

Fourth. Let those who cannot speak or understand the
    English language conduct their religious worship
    in their homes.

**6.1** Detail from Governor William Harding's "Babel Proclamation," showing the four areas of public discourse where English would now be the only language permitted. Babel Proclamation, May 23, 1918, State Archives of Iowa, RG 43 Iowa Governors', William Harding, 1917–1921, Council of Defense, State Historical Society of Iowa, Des Moines. Used with permission.

hauled before the Le Claire Community Council of Defense and fined $225 (more than $3,800 or £2,784 today) for speaking German on a party-line telephone. One of those convicted told the hearing that she'd pay her fine but never use the phone again, because after thirty-six years in America, English was still too hard for her.[17]

Despite scattered opposition and occasional ridicule, Harding's English-only law had strong support. In its post-Independence Day edition, the Marshalltown *Times-Republican*, a newspaper generally antagonistic to Harding, advised its readers, "Quit arguing with the governor over the foreign language proposition. Law or no law he has four-fifths of all Iowa behind it."[18] Harding's English-only rants drew some national praise as well. Former President Theodore Roosevelt, visiting Des Moines five days after the governor issued his proclamation, endorsed the foreign-language ban, insisting that there was only room in the United States for one flag and one language, and adding the line still quoted by proponents of official English today, "This is a nation, not a polyglot boarding house."[19]

The Babel Proclamation suppressed the use of immigrant languages in Iowa, at least during the war years, and especially among the children of immigrants. German was not taught again in Iowa schools until 1930 – and even then, relatively few students elected to study it. Today, Iowa remains an anglophone state. Even so, when the US Census showed a doubling of Iowa's Spanish-speaking population between 1990 and 2000, from 1.5 per cent to 2.9 percent of the total population, legislators felt the need to defend English by making it Iowa's official language, even though at the time, most of Iowa's 80,000 Spanish speakers spoke English as well, posing no threat to English or to national unity. Steve King, who sponsored that law, went on to serve in the US House of Representatives, where he promoted legislation to make English the official language of the United States. King also favored shutting down immigration, despite the fact that Iowa remains dependent on immigrant labor for its agriculture and meat-packing industries. At one point King even offered to have his construction company build a wall between the United States and Mexico.[20] Over the years, King's extremism grew more strident, but it wasn't until 2020 that his constituents decided he had gone too far, and he was voted out of office.

Harding's English-only restriction expired at the end of the war. That was not the case in Nebraska, which continued to mandate English in public meetings. When Marshal Foch, the French war hero, embarked on a victory tour of the United States in 1921, the *New York Times* warned that, since Foch knew little English, he risked a fine of up to $100 ($1,500 or £1,100 now) if he addressed adoring crowds in French. Instead, the newspaper suggested that Foch "scrape up enough English to tell the Nebraskans what he thinks of their silly law." Whether or not Foch was aware of the English-only restriction, he visited the nearby states of South Dakota and Minnesota but skipped Nebraska.[21]

## SPEAK AMERICAN: IT'S THE LAW

Americanism continued to surge in the postwar nativist boom that promoted the ideal of one nation, one language. Some patriots even took to calling the national language *American*, not *English*. In 1918, a number of prominent St. Louis Jews argued that the use of Yiddish among Jewish Americans was unpatriotic because it sounded too German.[22] An article in the *American Israelite* took linguistic assimilation one step further: "This is, was and always will be an English speaking country and ... it is a great pity that we could not abolish the imported title of our language and call it American."[23]

The push for *American* persisted even after the war. In 1919, H. L. Mencken published the first edition of his celebration of the nation's speech, *The American Language,* though unlike Governor Harding, the pro-German Mencken enthusiastically recorded the words that Americans were borrowing from a variety of native and immigrant languages, including Yiddish. On the legal front, in 1923, Montana Representative Washington Jay McCormick introduced a bill in Congress to make *American* "the national and official language of the Government and people of the United States of America." Hoping to "supplement the political emancipation of '76 by the mental emancipation of '23," McCormick's bill would require American, not English:

All Acts ... including regulations of the departments of Government, wherein the speaking, reading, writing, or knowledge of the English language is set forth as a requirement for purposes of naturalization, official, legal, or other like use, shall be deemed amended to the extent of substituting in the text for the word "English" the word "American."[24]

The bill languished in Congress, but in that same year, Illinois did manage to declare *American* the state's official language. Illinois State Senator Frank Ryan sponsored the measure, with the twin goals of promoting the United States while at the same time punishing England for failing to grant independence to Ireland or to establish a Jewish state in the Middle East. Ryan's bill framed America as a cultural melting pot with the American language as its great unifier: "The name of the language of a country has a powerful psychological influence in stimulating and preserving the national ideal." It seemed only right to Ryan that, if French is spoken in France, and English in England, then the language of America should be *American.* Here is the text of Ryan's bill:

*Whereas,* Since the creation of the American Republic there have been certain Tory elements in our country who have never become reconciled to our republican institutions and have ever clung to the tradition of King and Empire; and

*Whereas,* America has been a haven of liberty and place of opportunity for the common people of all nations; and

*Whereas,* These strangers within our gates who seek economic betterment, political freedom, larger opportunities for their children and citizenship for themselves, come to think of our institutions as American and our language as the American language; and

*Whereas,* The name of the language of a country has a powerful psychological influence in stimulating and preserving the national ideal; and

*Whereas,* The languages of other countries bear the names of the countries to which they belong ... now therefore

*Sec. 1. Be it enacted by the People of the State of Illinois, represented in the General Assembly:* The official language of the State of Illinois shall be known hereafter as the "American" language and not as the "English" language.[25]

Ryan's bill passed with support from Chicago's political machine, always mindful of the city's ethnic voters, but English continued to be taught in Illinois schools, in quiet defiance of the law. In 1969, the Illinois legislature finally conceded "that there was no such language" as American and made English the state's official language instead.[26]

## GIVE US YOUR TIRED, YOUR POOR, YOUR ANGLOPHONES ...

If Americans were being told to speak English or American, it made sense to require immigrants to speak it as well. A century after independence, in his final State of the Union message in 1876, President Ulysses S. Grant asked Congress to require English for citizenship:

Foreigners ... who are educated in their own language, should acquire the requisite knowledge of ours during the necessary residence to obtain naturalization. If they did not take interest enough in our language to acquire sufficient knowledge of it to enable them to study the institutions and laws of the country intelligently, I would not confer upon them the right to make such laws nor to select those who do.[27]

But Congress did not act on Grant's initiative until the 1906 revision of the Naturalization Act, which provided that "no alien shall hereafter be naturalized or admitted as a citizen of the United States who can not speak the English language."[28] Applicants for naturalization now not only had to swear that they were not anarchists or polygamists, they also had to attest, "I am able to speak the English language," as if not speaking English was a crime of similar magnitude.[29]

The nativism stirred up by the First World War culminated in the Johnson–Reed Act of 1924, which reduced immigration to a trickle, effectively walling off the country from immigrants and their languages for the next forty years. During the Congressional debate over that "reform," legislators argued that immigrants were mentally deficient, ineducable, disposed to criminality, and taking jobs away from "real" Americans. Oregon Senator Charles McNary complained that in his state, "there are more than 17,000 who are unable to speak the English language or write their own name."[30] Tennessee Senator Kenneth McKellar insisted he knew a town in Pennsylvania where over 90 percent of the 23,000 residents spoke no English and the rest spoke only "broken English."[31] And Senator John Shields, also of Tennessee, framed the language problem in national terms: "There are more than 3,000,000 who can not read or write English and perhaps 2,000,000 who can not speak our tongue ... There are whole wards in New York and Chicago where the English language is seldom heard."[32]

There was no documentation for any of these claims, but even though other lawmakers objected that English was doing very well in the immigrant neighborhoods in their own districts, that did little to dispel the prevailing anti-immigrant sentiment in Congress. Adding to the growing number of proposals to restrict immigration, in 1923 California Representative Walter F. Lineberger introduced a bill to "regulate immigration and insure the use of the English language by those admitted to the United States." Lineberger, concerned with his state's "oriental" problem, would allow immigrants up to eight years to acquire enough

English to pass an oral interview, demonstrate written fluency, and "read a daily paper printed in English on current topics" to the satisfaction of examiners not familiar with the applicant's native tongue. Anyone failing the English test would get six months to get their affairs in order, after which they would be deported at their own expense.[33]

Congress never did require immigrants to speak English on arrival, but limiting immigration after 1924 sharply reduced the number of non-English speakers coming to the United States, and so between 1924 and 1965, the United States became an "English-mostly" zone. Reduced immigration meant less grumbling about neighborhoods where English was never heard and fewer stores with non-English signage. The issue of what to do about the language problems of newcomers, along with the need to enforce English by legal means, became less pressing. For example, the Naturalization Act of 1940 simply stated, "No person ... shall hereafter be naturalized as a citizen of the United States ... who cannot speak the English language."[34]

The language situation in the United States changed once again after the 1965 revision of the immigration law, shepherded through Congress by Senator Gary Hart, of Colorado, and Representative Emmanuel Celler, of New York.[35] Celler had been elected to the House of Representatives in 1923, and he was one of the few legislators to oppose the 1924 immigration restrictions that he was finally able to reverse forty years later. The 1965 reform opened up American borders to immigrants and their languages, immigrants not just from traditional areas like Europe, but also from Asia, Africa, Mexico, Central and South America, and the Caribbean. With this geographical shift, Spanish, which already had a strong presence in the southwest, overtook German as the second most-spoken language in the United States, and Chinese has become America's third language. The current linguistic landscape also comprises French and Russian, European languages that came to North America with colonization, as well as languages newer to the New World: Hindi, Urdu, Punjabi, Tagalog, Korean, Vietnamese, Arabic, Hmong, and more. Despite the sudden surge of non-English speakers, these post-'65 immigrants transitioned to English at a rate equal to or surpassing that of the pre-1924 immigrants, with many becoming monolingual English speakers by the second generation. But that didn't prevent a new wave of nativists from complaining about renewed threats to English in America. Because learning English does take time, the influx of nonanglophone children after 1965 did pose problems for the schools, which soon found themselves dealing with non-English-speaking students once again.

## THE ENGLISH-ONLY CLASSROOM

There is a long tradition of American schools controlling students' language, a tradition that aims both to get nonanglophones to adopt English and to perfect the English of native speakers. This has often been paired with a policy of replacing the students' first language or dialect. In the nineteenth century, schools that were operated by the Bureau of Indian Affairs (BIA) actively sought to eliminate native languages in order to "civilize" Native Americans. That policy, often brutal in its enforcement, was reversed in the 1970s, when the BIA embraced the need to preserve and revitalize endangered native languages. But throughout American history, most public schools have treated immigrant languages in the same way as they treated pre-colonial local languages, as impediments to be removed, not as a valuable heritage to be preserved and celebrated.

During periods of active immigration, the schools framed their English-only mission as a patriotic effort to Americanize the newcomers. Individual states began designating English as the language of instruction in the nineteenth century. The Illinois School Law of 1845 required English in textbooks and as "the common medium of communication," specifically exempting foreign-language classes. A few urban school districts with heavily German populations, like St. Louis and Cincinnati, set up bilingual public schools, not to preserve the language of immigrants, but to speed the process of assimilation by coaxing parents to enroll their children in public schools instead of the popular German-language parochial schools. But most states chose an English-only approach that simply dismissed other languages as irrelevant. To back up that policy, they insisted that speaking English was necessary to maintain discipline, often repeating the now-discredited psychological claim that using a foreign language caused low intelligence and criminality among the children of immigrants.[36]

Nebraska's Siman Law (1919) banned foreign-language instruction before the ninth grade in part to support students' "right" to be
educated in English, on the false assumption that students voluntarily
attending private schools were being denied that right. Ohio went
further, specifically banning German in its schools. Such bans were
overturned by the Supreme Court in *Meyer* v. *Nebraska* (1923), not
on First Amendment grounds, but because they violated the constitutional right of teachers to pursue their profession, as guaranteed
under the Fourteenth Amendment. But Oliver Wendell Holmes,
Jr., dissented. Justice Holmes, who had become more progressive
about protecting political speech, remained conservative on school
speech. He championed English-only education as an essential tool
for Americanization, and in the matter of free speech for teachers, he
observed, "No one would doubt that a teacher might be forbidden to
teach many things."[37]

Although restrictive school language laws did not survive judicial
review, restrictive language policies continued unchecked. In the early
1900s, an "Americanization" movement, spurred on by an alliance of
progressive social activists and local officials, sought to persuade the
waves of immigrants coming to the United States to cut all cultural ties
with the countries they had left and become red, white, and blue Americans. To this end, in April, 1916, the Cleveland Public Schools began
a campaign focusing on English for immigrant adults, with the theme,
"Many peoples, one language." After the United States entered the First
World War the following year, the nativist National Americanization
Committee warned that some 30,000 draftees did not know enough English to understand their commanding officers. Nevertheless, although
some schools set up evening classes for adult English learners, and large
cities like New York offered children a few specialized daytime classes in
English as a foreign language, when it came to acquiring English, most
schools offered no instruction tailored to the linguistic needs of nonanglophone children, letting them sink or swim instead. Certainly, many
children picked up English by interacting with their English-speaking
peers, but large numbers of them did not master enough "teacher" English to succeed academically, a factor that contributed to high drop-out
rates in areas with large foreign-born populations.

## THE CLASSROOM MELTING POT

Even with these high failure rates, politicians and educators saw school as the primary vehicle for instilling English in newcomers, actively promoting the idea that the classroom should be the melting pot transforming foreign-born children into English speakers. That metaphor for assimilating immigrants was first popularized by Israel Zangwill's 1909 play, *The Melting-Pot*. The melting-pot image conjures up a hearty stew gently simmering on a stove, blending the flavors of its various ingredients. Preserving the food theme, this language melting pot is often contrasted today to a salad bowl, where individual elements – the languages that immigrants bring with them – mix together with English but retain their individual flavors as well. But Zangwill's melting pot is not culinary. It comes instead from medieval metallurgy, where it referred to a vessel in which different elements were forcibly fused together in the searing heat of the furnace to create an alloy superior to the original ingredients. One of Zangwill's characters called America, "God's Crucible, the great Melting-Pot where all the races of Europe are melting and re-forming!"[38] – a fiery transformation which Zangwill and his contemporaries approved.

Turning immigrants into Americans was thought to require stripping away past customs, languages, and ideas, and replacing them with American ideals expressible only through English. Speaking at a naturalization ceremony in Philadelphia in 1915, President Woodrow Wilson told his audience of new citizens, "You cannot dedicate yourself to America unless you become in every respect and with every purpose of your will thorough Americans. You cannot become thorough Americans if you think of yourselves in groups. America does not consist of groups."[39] And at a Convention on Citizenship, Wilson hinted at the crucible, or melting pot, perhaps with a touch of morality thrown in, when he called Americanization a process of "purification."[40] Certainly speaking a language other than English could mark you as both morally impure and politically suspect.

Such talk was commonplace in the Americanization movement. In 1919, Secretary of the Interior Franklin K. Lane advised immigrants, "bring all your soulfulness, your ancient experience to the melting pot and let it enrich our mettle."[41] He wrote these words in his department's *Americanization Bulletin*. But the editor of that journal warned in the very same issue that the phrase "melting pot" was as insulting as the common ethnic slurs of the day, or the geographical designations like "Little Italy," "Ghetto," and "Jewry" that were popularly applied to immigrant neighborhoods. He reminded readers that newcomers did not want to forget their native culture and character in the process of becoming American:

> To the native-born American [melting pot] has no unpleasant meaning, but to the foreign-born ... it suggests the kind of melting down which means to them the sacrifice of their native culture and character. ... It would be better to drop the term and substitute one which conveys the idea not of the destruction of what is rich and desirable in European culture, not a process of burning down, but rather the building up of a new civilization which, being a blend of all the cultures of the earth, will be the higher Americanism of the future.[42]

But no one offered an alternative to *melting pot*, and despite complaints that the term does not characterize assimilation effectively, *melting pot* continues to be used today to describe the process of Americanization.

## SPEAK THE LANGUAGE OF YOUR FLAG

In 1918, the Chicago Woman's Club, a group of prominent do-gooders active in the Americanization movement, established Better American Speech Week in schools around the country, both to encourage immigrants to learn English, and to prod native English speakers to speak it better. Katherine Knowles Robbins, leader of the organization's language committee, articulated the movement's goals:

> We believe in a democracy of which every member uses the same language. We believe in unifying and solidifying the people of the United States by using American Speech as a national language; and by conducting both public and private schools in the American Language. We believe in a democracy of which every member uses a clear, pleasant, and accurate speech. We believe in increasing American efficiency in all walks of life, industrial, civic, and social, by improving American voices, articulation, and enunciation.[43]

**6.2 and 6.3** *Above:* An anonymous winner of the "Speak the Language of Your Flag" poster contest; the children's posters were exhibited at the Art Institute of Chicago, *Chicago Daily News*, December 15, 1918. *Overleaf*: The "Watch Your Speech" Pledge. Photographs by the author, from the archives of the Chicago Woman's Club, used courtesy of the Chicago History Museum.

BETTER AMERICAN SPEECH
WEEK
OCT. 27, to NOV. 2, 1918
ONE LANGUAGE FOR A
UNITED PEOPLE

SPEAK THE LANGUAGE OF
YOUR FLAG.
SLOVENLY SPEECH BESPEAKS
A SLOVENLY MIND
WATCH YOUR SPEECH
PLEDGE:
I love the
UNITED STATES
OF
AMERICA.
I love my country's LANGUAGE.
I PROMISE:
(1) that I will not dishonor my country's speech by leaving off the last syllables of words;
(2) that I will say a good American "yes" and "no" in place of an Indian grunt "um-hum" and "nup-um" or a foreign "ya" or "yeh" and "nope";
(3) that I will do my best to improve American speech by avoiding loud harsh tones, by enunciating distinctly and speaking pleasantly, clearly and sincerely;
(4) that I will try to make my country's language beautiful for the many boys and girls of foreign nations who come here to live;
(5) that I will learn to articulate correctly one word a day for one year.

Better American Speech Committee
Chicago Woman's Club
410 S. Michigan Ave.
Chairman
Katherine Knowles Robbins

Scanlan School Press

**6.2 and 6.3** (*continued*)

Chicago's schools observed the first Better American Speech week from October 27 to November 2, 1918, with the theme, "Speak the language of your flag." Teachers told schoolchildren that their language expressed their patriotism and asked them to take the "Watch Your Speech" pledge, which expressed both love for their country and a desire to improve their English.

The pledge, which stigmatizes the supposed foreign and Native American influence on English, reads:

I love my country's LANGUAGE.

I PROMISE:

that I will not dishonor my country's speech by leaving off the last syllables of words;

that I will say a good American "yes" and "no" in place of an Indian grunt "um-hum" and "nup-um" or a foreign "ya" or "yeh" and "nope";

that I will do my best to improve American speech by avoiding loud harsh tones, by enunciating distinctly and speaking pleasantly, clearly and sincerely;

that I try to make my country's language beautiful for the many boys and girls who come here to live;

that I will learn to articulate correctly one word a day for one year.

The club's American Speech Committee produced lists of slogans for students to learn. Some of these focused on correct grammar and pronunciation, but most stressed patriotism and the war effort. Here are a few:

• Speak the language of your flag.
• American Speech means American Loyalty.
• American Speech means American Unity.
• American Speech for American People.
• The American Flag, the American Home, the American Language.
• One language for a United People.
• Better Speech for Better Americans.
• Be a Patriot in thought, in deed, in speech.

- Better Speech for Better Americans.
- Three Americans: Our Flag, Our Uniform, Our Speech.

During the war years, adults were asked to report suspicious behavior, a precursor to today's "see something – say something." It seemed only natural to recruit children to do their bit in America's war on language by reporting the language errors of their friends. One activity, conducted in conjunction with the first Better American Speech Week at the Carter Practice School on Chicago's South Side, imagines "Bad-English" as the work of enemy spies. Such espionage, carried out at a time when even political speech had little constitutional protection, proved a lesson in rough justice. After taking a pledge "to protect the language of my country, to capture all *spies of Bad-English* and to keep my position secret," the undercover patriots fanned out to monitor their classmates' words. They nabbed offenders, tried them in a court martial before the class, and with no provision for appeal, herded those convicted of offenses against the language into internment camps. Convicts became the objects of public ridicule, forced to wear a sign around their necks displaying their "error." Repeat offenders paid the ultimate price: "If any of these spies escape and again try to harm our speech, they will be shot at sunrise."[44]

The Chicago-based National Council of Teachers of English, with the support of the National Federation of Women's Clubs, the American Academy of Arts and Letters, and the Society of Pure English, promoted Better American Speech Week nationally. By the second year, some 200 Chicago-area schools were celebrating Better Speech Week, with another 150 around the country doing so as well. After the war, Speech Week focused less on Americanization and more on improving speech in general. But when Kansas Governor Henry Allen proclaimed American Speech Week in 1920, he alluded to the recent war and reiterated the dangers posed by nonanglophones:

> The present unrest and the uncertainty concerning the allegiance of some who have for years, if not for a lifetime, enjoyed the benefits of our American institutions, give peculiar reason why we should exalt the importance and dignity of our speech. Each man has tools peculiar to his vocation – the carpenter his plane, the miner his pick, the tradesman his

price list, the student his textbook; but every true citizen, whatever his occupation, should use his American Language.[45]

Better American Speech Week is little remembered today, but the campaign for English in the schools went on. Public schools in New York City and California required applicants for teaching licenses to pass a speech test, ostensibly to show that they could model proper English for their students. In practice, though, such tests kept teachers with an "ethnic" name, accent, or appearance out of the classroom.[46] Schools also continued to ignore the needs of nonanglophone children, assuming that they would pick up English by osmosis rather than through instruction geared specifically to English-language learners.

### BILINGUAL EDUCATION OR IMMERSION?

Responding to the post-1965 wave of immigration, some schools did develop both English as a Second Language (ESL) and bilingual education programs to deal with the new nonanglophones. But like schools in the early twentieth century, they failed to meet demand, and, as before, many children were left behind. That led a group of Chinese American parents to sue the San Francisco schools for ignoring their non-English-speaking children. The parents argued that the inability of these children to speak English presented an insurmountable barrier. San Francisco did provide English learning programs for about 1,000 Chinese students, but another 2,800 had no language services and were effectively denied the opportunity to learn. The suit, *Lau* v. *Nichols* (1974), eventually reached the Supreme Court, which unanimously ruled for the parents because "students who do not understand English are effectively foreclosed from any meaningful education."[47] The Court found that the schools had violated the Civil Rights Act of 1964 by failing to follow the language rules for minority-language children that had been set out by the Department of Health, Education, and Welfare:

Where inability to speak and understand the English language excludes national origin-minority group children from effective participation in the educational program offered by a school district, the district must take affirmative steps to rectify the language deficiency in order to open its instructional program to these students.[48]

The *Lau* court ordered the San Francisco schools to correct this situation, without specifying how they were to do so. The *Lau* remedies, created by San Francisco in response to the decision, affected language education nationwide, as schools implemented programs of transitional bilingual education calculated to move non-English speakers to English. The theory behind bilingual education was both elegant and appealing. In addition to English lessons, these programs taught basics like reading and math in the child's first language so they would not fall behind their English-speaking peers. In the early twentieth century, the last time there had been a significant number of nonanglophones attending school, children frequently lagged in core subjects as they picked up English, with dropout rates in some cities that exceeded 50 percent. Bilingual education promised a way around the language barrier that would ensure that English learners, once their language skills were up to speed, entered mainstream classes with the appropriate level of subject-matter skills.

Unfortunately, the ideal didn't always play out in practice. It proved difficult to find staff trained to deliver instruction in the many languages that immigrant children brought to school and who were also trained to teach English as a second language. Critics complained that children were not being taught English; that academic content was being ignored; that students speaking a variety of languages were lumped together in a class that was taught in only one of those languages, typically, Spanish; and that anglophone children still benefited from the best teachers and the strongest curricula, while students in the bilingual classes had untrained teachers who didn't challenge them academically.

In the 1990s, education "reformers" tried replacing bilingual programs with English immersion – an updated name for the sink-or-swim approach whose many failures bilingual education sought to remedy. In 1998, unhappy over declining test scores and poor graduation rates, California voters overwhelmingly approved Proposition 227, which mandated one year of English instruction for nonanglophone students, after which they would be placed in regular

English-only classrooms. But as it had before, English-only instruction failed the state's English learners, and, in 2016, California again reversed course, allowing schools and parents to choose a variety of ways, including bilingual education, to ensure English mastery for students whose English proficiency is limited.[49]

## VATICAN 2.1

Most American schools still rely on some form of bilingual education for immigrant children, but a private, Catholic school in Wichita, Kansas, is not bound by Department of Education language policy or by *Lau v. Nichols*. St. Anne School declared itself an English-only campus, banning all foreign languages from classrooms and hallways, as well as the cafeteria and the playground. The goal was to reduce bullying among students and calm staff fears that students were making fun of them. This reflects a common form of language paranoia – "If I can't understand them, they must be talking about me" – that underlies many workplace English-only requirements as well.

St. Anne School, with many children from immigrant families, is affiliated with St. Anne Church, located next door, which offers a Spanish-language mass and sponsors a Spanish choir. The linguistic inclusiveness of the church reflects the spirit of Vatican II, which emphasized the importance of making religion available in the vernacular of the faithful. In contrast, in a letter to parents, St. Anne School framed its English-only policy as educational: "We require English to be spoken during school at all times! We are requesting that no native language other than English be spoken. Since all subjects are taught in English they need strengthening in that area. The more students are immersed in the English language the better the chance for improvement/success."[50]

But the principal also sent a letter to students suggesting a more punitive approach: "English is the language to be spoken during the school day. If this doesn't take place, consequences will follow."[51] When several students refused to sign a pledge to speak only English at school, they were expelled, though the school claimed that the students left voluntarily. Parents of four of these students then sued the school for illegal discrimination on the basis of race and national origin.

The school insisted that English immersion would improve students' academic success and prevent students from using language to exclude or make fun of other children. This despite the fact that schoolchildren can always form cliques or ridicule staff as well as one another in English without teachers being any the wiser. The school added that its English-only rule did not prevent the teaching of foreign languages at St. Anne. But even though 42 percent of the school's 243 students came from homes where Spanish or Vietnamese was spoken, the school offered no foreign-language instruction.

In his decision, Judge J. Thomas Marten ruled that St. Anne School was within its rights to prohibit foreign languages for disciplinary and educational reasons, and that such a policy did not create a hostile educational environment.[52] Nevertheless, Marten chided the school for not consulting parents, and he told both sides that they were wrong to make the matter of school rules a federal case: "It has divided a school. It has divided a congregation. It has divided the Hispanic community in a congregation, and it has touched a nerve across the country."

"Talking while Spanish" may be grounds for expulsion in a private school, where families must abide by school rules, but public schools designating an English-only policy do not have the same authority to control student speech. That doesn't always stop them from trying. In 2009, some teachers at Vineland High School North in New Jersey were said to be enforcing a "Classroom Protocol Contract" that forbade cursing, chewing gum, wearing coats or hoodies, or speaking foreign languages. The contract stated, "This is an English speaking school and classroom – any other language other than English will not be tolerated."[53] School officials insisted that the school had no general policy banning languages, but comments left on a local news site charged that the ban had been imposed by several teachers; that administrators knew about the policy and tolerated it; and that Spanish-speaking students were silenced, while those speaking Ukrainian were not.

Spanish was the target as well in 2007, when Robert Aumaugher, superintendent of the Esmeralda, Nevada, schools, promulgated an English-only policy for riding the school bus. In a letter to parents, Aumaugher stressed that fluency in English was necessary for success both in school and after graduation, adding that his no-Spanish policy would allow anglophone bus drivers to maintain order and discipline on the 90-minute ride to the high school in neighboring Nye county, and again on the 90-minute ride back (Esmeralda had closed its only high school some years earlier): "It is our belief that when a different language is being spoken and not understood by the driver it opens the door for a few to take advantage of the situation and exhibit disrespect. That we will not tolerate." When the American Civil Liberties Union warned that students' language rights were being abridged, Aumaugher relented. Instead of requiring English, he encouraged students to speak it for the first half of their ride, and use whatever language they wanted after that.[54]

And as recently as 2008, schools in Arthur, Illinois, still required English-only on the bus, a rule found alongside bans on swearing, weapons, and candy. Its position in the list of school bus don'ts reinforces the idea that the language restriction is disciplinary, not educational:

13. Obscene or profane language will not be used on the bus ...
14. No one is permitted to eat candy or food on the bus at any time.
15. *All pupils must speak English at all times while riding on the bus.*
16. Do not use or display a knife in any manner whatsoever while on the bus.[55]

Arthur abandoned this attempt to punish students for using languages other than English. And yet it remains the case that English-only classrooms – and school buses – persist, even in the absence of an official school policy.

## ENGLISH-ONLY ZONE

Even though rates of assimilation are strong among the post-1965 immigrants, continuing immigration means an increased public presence for non-English languages, not just in the schools, but in the office, on the street, and in the media. Since 1965, the US Census Bureau has reported a rising percentage of speakers of languages other than English in the United States, from 11 percent in 1980 to 21.9 percent in 2018 (to be sure, most users of another language report that they also speak English).[56]

Although such increases grab headlines, they are not surprising: when the nation's foreign-born population grows, so will the number of non-English speakers. But this poses no danger to English. Although learning a new language takes time, the new immigrants are learning English quickly: the 2018 American Community Survey reported that only 1.3 percent of Americans over five years old who speak a language other than English at home also report speaking no English at all.[57] This percentage has not changed since 2012. Currently, 3.6 million immigrants report they do not speak any English. But among their US-born children, the number who speak no English at all is less than 300,000, suggesting there is a very rapid acquisition of English in the second generation. Although nonanglophones represent an extremely small percentage of the total population, that is still almost 4 million people who depend on translators, whether professionals or family and friends, to deal with many daily activities until they acquire enough English to do so on their own.

As we have seen, schools have responded to the needs of nonanglophone students with bilingual education or English-only rules. Legislatures have also responded to the pressures of the new American multilingualism, though their official response is often restrictive. To date, thirty-one states have official language laws on their books. Two of these laws support some form of multilingualism. Hawaii privileges Hawaiian, the local language, alongside English, an immigrant tongue on the islands. New Mexico, which has had a large number of Spanish speakers since it was part of Mexico, along with a significant number of speakers of indigenous languages, promotes fluency both in English and in another language, any other language. Other states make only English official, though their impact varies. The Illinois official English law does not prevent state residents from receiving a variety of government services in languages other than English. But Arizona's law bars government employees from communicating in any language other than English in the course of their official duties (to satisfy federal requirements, the law makes exceptions for health and safety, along with international trade and the teaching of foreign languages). In addition, more than nineteen cities and towns have debated, or passed, local official English laws, including Farmers Branch, Texas; Clifton, New Jersey; Taneytown,

Maryland; Hazelton, Pennsylvania; and Lino Lakes, Minnesota. Voters in Nashville, Tennessee, rejected an official English measure in 2009. Many locales opting for official English have small, or even minuscule, non-English-speaking populations, as do states like Iowa and West Virginia, which also passed official English laws despite having relatively few nonanglophone residents. The principal goal in such cases is assimilation, but nonanglophones and those with limited English hear the law as another way of saying, "Go back where you came from," even if they were born in the United States.

Perhaps the most prominent of the new wave of nativist language measures was California's 1986 official English ballot initiative. California, a territory acquired by the United States from Mexico in 1848, has always been multilingual. In addition to Native Americans, its earliest European settlers were Spanish, and the area later became a magnet for Chinese immigration. The early history of the state shows a struggle between constitutional support for languages other than English and a sharp rejection of multilingualism. In the post-1965 era, the increased presence of non-English speakers led California voters to pass Proposition 63, a referendum that amended the state constitution to make English the official language.

California's language law contains a number of provisions that have been picked up by other states, and by the frequently proposed federal official English bill. It stresses the need "to preserve, protect and strengthen the English language," which suggests that English is both weak and in danger, though all evidence points to the unchallenged dominance of English both in the United States and globally. In addition, lawmakers may pass "no law which diminishes or ignores the role of English," suggesting that English must be protected from a democratically elected government. And, finally, the law contains a provision, called a private right of action, allowing anyone to sue the state for not enforcing the official language law:

> Any person who is a resident of or doing business in the State of California shall have standing to sue the State of California to enforce this section, and the Courts of record of the State of California shall have jurisdiction to hear cases brought to enforce this section. The Legislature may provide

reasonable and appropriate limitations on the time and manner of suits brought under this section.[58]

Arizona's official English requirements are more restrictive than those of California. The Arizona constitution requires all public employees to use English and only English on the job. Other languages are permitted in limited educational, commercial, or public health and safety contexts. A 1988 version of this provision was found to violate First Amendment speech protections. As Judge Stephen Reinhardt wrote, "speech in any language is still speech."[59] But the Supreme Court mooted the case on a technicality: the original plaintiff, a state employee who sued to protect her right to speak Spanish to clients who spoke little or no English, had left her job and none of the remaining parties had standing to sue.[60] Arizona's official language provision was revised in 2006 and remains in force, though its First Amendment implications remain untested.

In 1910, in anticipation of statehood, Arizona promoted official English while it was still a territory, requiring English in the public schools and stipulating that "the ability to read, write, speak, and understand the English language sufficiently well to conduct the duties of the office without the aid of an interpreter, shall be a necessary requirement for all State officers and members of the State Legislature."[61] The neighboring New Mexico Territory initially imposed identical English competency requirements for office holders. But in 1911, the House Committee on the Territories rejected the English requirements of both prospective states as unnecessary, since the southwest's Spanish Americans "largely now speak the English language."[62] The Committee also hinted that the language requirement might violate the Treaty of Guadalupe–Hidalgo, which guaranteed residents of the territories ceded by Mexico in 1848 "all the rights of citizens of the United States."[63]

In 1912, New Mexico dropped its language restriction for office holders, but Arizona did not. In 1988, when Arizona added its official English provision, it also expanded its long-time English-language rule to cover not just top state officials, but all government employees from the governor down to the local dog-catcher: "A person who is unable to speak, write and read the English language is not eligible to hold a state, county, city, town or precinct office in the state, whether elective or appointive, and no certificate of election or commission shall issue to a person so disqualified."[64] As a result, in 2012, a candidate for city council in the small, Spanish-speaking border town of San Luis, challenged the eligibility of his opponent, Alejandrina Cabrera, because she did not meet the expanded language requirement for elected and appointed officials. After a court-appointed expert interviewed Cabrera and determined that she possessed only survival-level English skills, a county judge removed her from the ballot.[65]

An additional provision of Arizona's official English law addresses discrimination not to protect speakers of minority languages, but rather to stand up for the rights of the majority: "A person shall not be discriminated against or penalized in any way because the person uses or attempts to use English in public or private communication."[66] The idea that English needs protection is common now, but it is not new. A 1921 Nebraska statute stated that public officials could not prohibit the use of English or discriminate against anyone who used English. Violators were subject to a fine of up to $100 (about $1,500 or £1,134 today) and up to thirty days in jail.[67] It is not clear, however, that there has ever been a case where a government official, elected or appointed, refused to speak English. Not at the founding, not during the First World War, and not at any time since then. Nor is it clear that anyone's right to speak English has ever been abridged by a government employee, either in Nebraska, or Iowa, or Arizona, or anywhere else in the United States. But enshrining in a state constitution the fear that the government could actually suppress English speakers suggests that such discrimination is not only possible, it is also common enough to require legal intervention. In keeping with this fear, the Arizona statute, like California's, gives individuals the right to sue if they feel their rights to use English are not being properly protected.

## THE ENGLISH LANGUAGE UNITY ACT

Since its founding, the United States, with no official language law, has maintained a higher percentage of speakers of its dominant language than many countries that impose a language on their populations. That does not stop lawmakers from trying to make English official not just in some states and cities, but also nationwide. To that end, from 1981 to

2001, proponents of official English sought to pass the English Language Amendment (ELA) to the US Constitution. That amendment would have required English for all state and federal acts, resolutions, votes, elections, records, and judicial proceedings – despite the fact that all of these are already in English.[68]

Here is the original version of the ELA, as introduced by California Senator Samuel I. Hayakawa:

Sec. 1. The English language shall be the official language of the United States.

Sec. 2. Neither the United States nor any State shall make or enforce any law which requires the use of any language other than English.

Sec. 3. This article shall apply to laws, ordinances, regulations, orders, programs, and policies.

Sec. 4. No order or decree shall be issued by any court of the United States or of any State requiring that any proceedings, or matters to which this article applies be in any language other than English.

Sec. 5. This article shall not prohibit educational instruction in a language other than English as required as a transitional method of making students who use a language other than English proficient in English.

Sec. 6. The Congress and the States shall have power to enforce this article by appropriate legislation.[69]

Senator Hayakawa, an immigrant from Canada of Japanese ancestry who had been an academic linguist and college president before he entered politics, argued in remarks accompanying his amendment that English was the glue holding Americans from different backgrounds together: "A common language can unify; separate languages can fracture and fragment a society. The American 'melting pot' has succeeded in creating a vibrant new culture among peoples of many different cultural backgrounds largely because of the widespread use of a common language, English." His amendment permitted transitional bilingual education, and it would not affect the use of foreign languages in religious services. And although the amendment doesn't say so, Hayakawa insisted that it would permit foreign languages where necessary for public health and safety, for example, a Chinese danger sign at a construction site in a local Chinatown, or a Japanese street sign in cities with significant numbers of Japanese-speaking residents and tourists, like Washington, DC, Los Angeles, or San Francisco. According to Hayakawa, such foreign-language signs are permissible, even desirable, "because they are also accompanied by street signs in English. They are also acceptable because they give a cosmopolitan flavor to those cities that have them and we are proud of the fact that we are a cosmopolitan culture."

The ELA never managed to garner enough support to win congressional approval, perhaps because English was already the de facto language of government, but also because legislators feared a backlash from ethnic voters. As a result, after twenty years with no action on the ELA, legislators proposed an official language statute that would require a simple majority in the House and Senate, plus presidential approval. But after another twenty years of trying, Congress has still not passed an official language bill.

In 2001, Representative Bob Stump, of Arizona, introduced the first such bill, the Declaration of Official English Act. Stump's bill picked up what had become the familiar formulas of official English legislation, requiring the federal government to "preserve and enhance the role of English," and denying people the right to expect the government or its representatives to communicate with them "in any language other than English." The bill included a section requiring enforcement of existing English proficiency requirements for naturalization – though there was no indication that existing requirements for English proficiency were being ignored – and it created exceptions for religious worship, international communication, law enforcement, terms of art (typically Latin legal phrases like *de facto* and *habeas corpus*), and scientific terminology. In addition, the bill would have repealed the Bilingual Education Act and the bilingual requirements of the Voting Rights Act of 1965. The federal bill also included a private right of action whose wording implies that not using English is actually harmful: "Whoever is injured by a violation of this chapter may, in a civil action, obtain appropriate relief."[70]

The sections on bilingual education and voting in the Declaration of Official English Act seemed inconsistent with the Fourteenth Amendment's equal protection clause and the 1964 Civil Rights Act's ban on discrimination based on national origin. To avoid constitutional challenges and gain more support, the proposed bill morphed into the slightly tamer English Language Unity Act, H.R. 997, which has been introduced in Congress without success from the early 2000s to the present. This bill gives federal workers "an affirmative obligation to preserve and enhance the role of English as the official language of the Federal Government." It requires English for any action that binds the government and any action required by law. It even mandates English for anything that is "subject to scrutiny by the press or the public." In the age of the smart phone video, that is a category that includes pretty much everything government workers and officials say or write both on and off the job, in their tweets, even in their sleep.

The English Language Unity Act contains the usual exceptions for health and safety, commerce, and diplomacy, even an exception for the Bureau of the Census as it conducts its constitutionally mandated population count every ten years. English is already required for citizenship, but H.R. 997 would establish a more rigorous standard to be met by future candidates for naturalization: "All citizens should be able to read and understand generally the English language text of the Declaration of Independence, the Constitution, and the laws of the United States."[71]

The current US naturalization law requires the ability to "read and write simple words and phrases" of English.[72] A stiffer test requiring the ability to decode the nation's founding documents and its laws would prove challenging even for speakers with English as their first language. The Declaration and the Constitution are written in an eighteenth-century English whose vocabulary and style may prove an impediment to the modern reader. As for understanding the laws, that too may be problematic, since legislation tends to be full of legalese. According to one common measurement of reading difficulty, prospective citizens would need almost a fifteenth-grade reading level to understand the Declaration of Independence and the Constitution. But national literacy assessments place the reading level of the average native English speaker at around the seventh or eighth grade, which means that H.R. 997 would require candidates for citizenship to know more English than their American-born peers, including some of the legislators supporting the measure.

## IS OFFICIAL ENGLISH NECESSARY?

The *raison d'être* of official English laws is the belief that the exclusive use of English is necessary to maintain national unity. This claim is difficult to prove. There are functional and dysfunctional monolingual nation-states, as well as functional and dysfunctional multilingual ones, suggesting that language is just one of many factors that impact national cohesion. Although the English Language Unity Act begins with a nod to the "rich diversity" of the American melting pot, it then privileges English as the great unifier: "Throughout the history of the United States, the common thread binding individuals of differing backgrounds has been the English language." This linguistic "thread that binds" is a common refrain of the English-only movement, which also likes to call English the "social glue" that holds together the disparate and centrifugal elements that make up American culture. Supporters of official English are quick to cite Canada and Belgium as states that failed because they did not unite behind one official language. But that is misleading.

Canada has two official languages – English and French. Belgium has Flemish (related to Dutch) and Walloon (a variety of French). And although both countries have internal squabbles, as all nations do, both seem to work well enough within their multilingual structure. Many other high-functioning states manage to maintain within their borders even more languages. India has one official language, Hindi, and English is granted special status, even though it is spoken by less than 5 percent of the population. But India also has twenty-two officially recognized languages, along with some 1,600 other local tongues. English is the official language of Nigeria, which has seven major regional languages and several hundred local languages as well. In countries like India and Nigeria, each very different from the United States, linguistic differences can and often do create problems at the local or national level. Though internal conflicts may be framed as demands for language rights – the right to speak the local lingo on the radio or to attend mother-tongue schools – they stand in for cultural and historical disagreements between the ethnic groups who speak these languages, and they may be deployed in the struggle for political clout or even independence. Their frictions may be rooted in colonialism and past military conflicts. In the end, a nation's dominant language embodies not the nature or spirit of the people, but the power of one group to enforce compliance or grant concessions. Even with many internal stresses, neither India nor Nigeria counts among the world's failed states. Another major multilingual nation is China, which has thrived for centuries. It is a unified political and cultural entity whose inhabitants speak what are conventionally referred to as dialects of Chinese, as well as a number of non-Sinitic regional and ethnic languages – some of which the present Chinese government has been accused of trying to suppress or eliminate in favor of Mandarin. But linguistically, the Chinese dialects form seven distinct, mutually unintelligible, regional languages and more than forty local ones, most of them sharing a common writing system.

There are also many nations separated by a common language: Northern Ireland and the Republic of Ireland; North and South Korea; the Scandinavian countries, where languages like Danish, Swedish, and Norwegian are varieties of a larger, umbrella language that would be called Scandinavian were it not for the political and historical differences that divide the region into separate countries. Then there are India and Pakistan, where Hindi and Urdu, two of the principal languages of these multilingual states, are also closely related to one another, though written with distinctly different scripts. The two countries are also separated by two frequently clashing religions. The language-as-social-glue claim fails closer to home, as well. Sharing a common language did not prevent the United States from breaking away from England in the eighteenth century; nor did the glue of English prevent the American Civil War. After that disruptive conflict, it took not English, but an army enforcing the Constitution and federal law to reconstruct the union.

Tellingly, today the official language issue pits competing ideological views of America against each other: either the United States is a nation of natives and immigrants, both forced and voluntary, who are finally free to pursue their individual differences and dreams while celebrating their union under a common political system. Or it is a melting pot, a crucible where cultures fuse under pressure to form a common and uniform mass. Competing language policies reflect this division: government either supports a person's right to choose whether to keep their native language, discard it for English, or become bilingual; or it forces nonanglophones to abandon their native tongues in favor of English only, encouraging a select few to acquire a limited knowledge of a culturally prized, economically advantageous or politically strategic foreign language later on, in school. In either case, the practical effect on the language of immigrants has been the same: Iowa's hostility toward German during the First World War led to a marked reduction of German on the streets. After the war, public use of immigrant languages, including German, picked up again, though not among the younger Americans of European ancestry, and foreign-language study never regained its prewar popularity. It was the cutting off of immigration, not a language ban, that ultimately led to the decline of monolingual German speakers and German–English bilingualism, and the loss of other immigrant languages as well.

Without laws forcing English on them, immigrants have always adopted English, and research – for example, studies by the Pew Hispanic Center – shows that the post-1965 immigrants continue to do so, often at an accelerated pace, even in border areas or other parts of the country where new immigrants continue to settle. This suggests that it is not necessary to cut off immigration to ensure the continued dominance of English, although lawmakers who support official English tend also to favor tightening controls on immigration.

Finally, official English laws won't speed the switch to English – it takes time, sometimes years, to learn a new language. Language acquisition may be affected by age, access to resources, and individual motivation and aptitude. Plus, official language laws can backfire, generating fear among some nonanglophones that their English is never going to be good enough, which in turn could cause some non-English speakers to give up trying.

The First World War fanned Americans' fear that anyone speaking a foreign language was a spy, while speaking English was a sign of loyalty. In contrast, in the lead-up to the Second World War, it was the Japanese who were suspicious of any outsider wanting to learn Japanese: "The police could not imagine that there was any purpose in learning it except to spy more effectively."[73] In either case, the language someone speaks may not reflect their political loyalties. Yet language remains an important shibboleth, a way to tell friend from foe. In 2017, the Pew

Research Center reported that the residents of many countries find language to be the most important marker of national identity. In the Netherlands, where Dutch is the official language, 84 percent of the people see speaking Dutch as a sign that you're truly Dutch. Of those surveyed in Britain, a nation without an official language, 81 percent regard English as the strongest marker of citizenship. This is in contrast to France and Italy, two countries with official languages, where 77 percent and 59 percent of the population, respectively, feel that proficiency in the official language is a sign of belonging. To compare, 70 percent of Americans find it is not where you were born, but whether you speak English that says, "you're one of us."[74]

Although people readily agree that English is the language of the United States, or that a knowledge of English is important for educational and economic success, throughout its many iterations the English Language Unity Act never garnered enough Congressional support to pass. Perhaps too many lawmakers saw official English as unnecessary, since the accelerated pace at which immigrants adopt English makes it clear that English, the most sought-after foreign language around the world, is certainly in no danger at home. Critics see the official English bill as too restrictive, sending immigrants the message that they're not welcome, a message often mistakenly directed by today's nativists at "immigrants" born in the United States. Some legislators agree with business leaders that enshrining monolingualism in the law imperils America's ability to compete in the global market. And some may simply fear that voting "yes" on official English could lose them the support of immigrants and the descendants of immigrants who form a significant part of their constituency.

Yet, despite a long history of failure to pass national language legislation, bills like the English Language Unity Act keep coming back. This suggests that a primary motive behind official language legislation is symbolic, not linguistic. English is not the common thread binding unlike elements. Instead, its use becomes a patriotic gesture, like flying the Stars and Stripes on national holidays.[75] That is what the Americanization movement had in mind with its slogan, "Speak the language of your flag." The problem is that flags make good symbols but languages do not. Snippets of English like the Pledge of Allegiance or the National

Anthem function well as public expressions of civic faith, though most often they are formulas to be gotten out of the way so the next part of the program can begin. But English as a whole is too variable and multifaceted to serve in the same capacity.

As we've seen, there is often an anti-immigrant side to official language legislation, one that operated in Iowa in 1918 and one that has been invoked often over the course of American history. But it is important to remember that English itself is an immigrant language in North America: it came ashore in the seventeenth century in Massachusetts and Virginia with undocumented refugees seeking a better life. Aaron Burr suggested as much in 1794 when he charged that the nativists of the federal period were trying to reconstitute a homogeneous Anglo-Saxon nation in the New World that had never existed in the British Isles, where English was initially an immigrant tongue as well.[76] But ignoring this history, today's new nativists use official English as a dog whistle for a darker, isolationist vision of America for Americans – and they've co-opted the term *Anglo-Saxon* as a synonym for "white supremacist." It is still publicly unacceptable to criticize people for their heritage, although one side in the 2016 American presidential campaign challenged that taboo, and public racism and xenophobia are on the rise, with anti-Asian sentiment exacerbated by the Covid-19 pandemic. But it remains acceptable to criticize or even ridicule people for their language – their errors, their accents, their limited fluency in English. Hence, the ability of mainstream television shows to "gently" satirize the immigrant, for example, Babu, on "Seinfeld," or Apu, on "The Simpsons" – even when critics object to these demeaning stereotypes. As a result, the not-so-subtle subtext of measures ranging from the English Language Unity Act, to state and local official language laws, to the English-only policies of individual schools and businesses, is always going to mean, "speak English or go back where you came from," even if where you came from is Trenton, or Kansas City, or Palo Alto.

An official language bill designed to unify can also divide, and that, perhaps, is what has doomed legislation like H.R. 997 from the start. But even if official English does become law one day, that won't simplify the linguistic situation in America. For one thing, it takes years, occasionally generations, for people to alter their language use. And for another, the world's economy will remain global despite any upswing in protectionist rhetoric around the world, and that means Americans will continue to interact with speakers in other countries whose English is different, or even non-existent, not just occasionally, but consistently. As a result, the language situation in the United States will remain complex, and we will need to continually rework our language laws and regulations not to control the shifting linguistic landscape, an enterprise doomed to failure, but simply to keep up with it.

And one last observation on the current official language landscape. German Americans were warned during the First World War to speak English for their own safety: law or no law, in states from Nebraska to Texas, people speaking foreign languages were beaten, tarred and feathered, made to kiss the flag, hauled before an inquisition, or hanged in effigy. One pastor was even strung up by an angry mob for speaking German, but police managed to intervene and cut him down before he died.[77] In 2017, Srinivas Kuchibhotla, an engineer from India, was shot dead in a bar in Olathe, Kansas, by an American nativist shouting "Go back to your own country." His murderer later explained that he thought Kuchibhotla was from Iran, as if shooting a Farsi speaker was more acceptable. In response, the Telangana American Telugu Association warned its members in a Facebook post to speak English, not Telugu, when they're out in public in the United States.[78] It seems that not much has changed in the course of a century. And Kansas provided one more in a growing number of examples where the Second Amendment silenced the First.

## CHAPTER 7

# Repeat After Me …

Speake the Speech, I pray you.

William Shakespeare, *Hamlet*, Act 3, sc. ii

The First Amendment prevents the government from interfering with your right to speak, with some significant exceptions. It also stops the government from compelling you to speak, though here, too, terms and conditions apply. Private employers may control job-related speech, even mandating specific words, phrases, even entire scripts. And most apps require you to agree to their terms of service before you can start using them. Accepting those requirements is technically voluntary. But if you want the job or the app, your assent is compelled; you must say the words, sign the agreement, click "OK" to continue.

On the other hand, in the United States the government cannot force you to salute the flag, sing the national anthem, or pray in public school. Nor can the government force you to say anything that violates a deeply held belief. Even so, there are some exceptions where the state, too, may compel speech. For example, in 2019, the Trump administration insti-tuted a gag rule prohibiting health-care providers from discussing abor-tion and compelling them instead to discuss nonabortion pregnancy alternatives with patients. The Biden administration reversed that rule, but future presidents could certainly reinstate it. Teachers may be barred from saying certain things or compelled to say others. For example, as part of a recent movement to restrict schools from teaching about race, sex, white supremacy, or other hot-button topics, which we will return to in the final chapter, a new Texas law requires teachers addressing controversial issues "to explore such issues from diverse and contending perspectives without giving deference to any one perspective."[1] One local school board official told teachers that the new law meant that they couldn't keep books on the Holocaust in classrooms or in the school library unless they also offered "reading materials that have opposing views." After the statement was widely reported in the national media, the School Superintendent relented, acknowledging that "there are not two sides of the Holocaust."[2]

In an earlier case with broad implications for speech protection, a commercial baker sued the Colorado Civil Rights Commission for ruling in 2012 that he must bake a wedding cake for a same-sex couple. The baker objected that doing so would compel him to "speak" in favor of the couple's union, violating his religious conviction that same-sex marriage is forbidden. *Masterpiece Cakeshop* v. *Colorado Civil Rights Commission* (2018) raised some thorny issues about whether the icing on a cake constitutes speech, and who is speaking, the baker or the customer, when a cake bears a message like "Congratulations!" In its decision in the case, the Supreme Court sidestepped the constitutional protection against compelled speech, finding instead that Colorado had failed to treat the baker's religious beliefs neutrally.[3] For now, this particular clash between free speech and antidiscrimination law remains unresolved.

Product warnings and nutritional labels are two forms of government-compelled speech that we encounter almost daily. The United States also requires English as the language of air traffic control, and if you sit in an airplane's exit row, it requires you to acknowledge, with words, that you are both willing and able to open the door in case of emergency. Finally, if you want a government job, you may be forced to take a loyalty oath. Such oaths became common for municipal, state, and federal government posts, including teaching at schools and universities, both public and private, during the red scare after the Second World War. Although some state loyalty oaths have been successfully challenged on First Amendment grounds for being overbroad or too intrusive, oaths that address a clear and present danger have been upheld. These typically require a prospective employee to swear that they do not advocate the overthrow of the government by force or violence, or that they have never knowingly joined a group advocating such illegal efforts.[4] In this chapter we will look at three examples of government-compelled speech in the United States: the presidential oath of office; the Miranda warning; and laws that define the meaning of certain words.

## THE PRESIDENTIAL OATH OF OFFICE: SO NICE, THEY
## DID IT TWICE

When it came time for Chief Justice John Roberts to administer the oath of office to president-elect Barack Obama on January 20, 2009, to use the language of political euphemism, mistakes were made. Roberts and Obama stumbled over mistimed phrasing. Then, trying to recover, the Chief Justice misspoke the words specified in the Constitution. As he tried to follow Roberts' lead, Obama also made mistakes in wording. Their confused recitation of the constitutionally mandated formula led to a second oath the next day. It is not clear whether the second oath was necessary, but they called a do-over just in case.

Article II of the Constitution, which outlines the duties of the president, specifies the words a president must say before becoming president: "Before he enter on the Execution of his Office, he shall take the following Oath or Affirmation: 'I do solemnly swear (or affirm) that I will faithfully execute the Office of President of the United States, and will to the best of my Ability, preserve, protect and defend the Constitution of the United States.'" The oath is a single, thirty-five word sentence, though it is customary for presidents to add the phrase "so help me God" at the end. Here is a transcript of the 2009 ceremony, indicating in italic type the slip-ups that occurred:

CHIEF JUSTICE ROBERTS: Please raise you right hand and repeat after me: I, Barack Hussein Obama ...

PRESIDENT-ELECT OBAMA: I, Barack ...

ROBERTS: ... do solemnly swear ...

OBAMA: I, Barack Hussein Obama, do solemnly swear ...

ROBERTS: ... that I will execute the office of president *to the United States faithfully* ...

OBAMA: ... that I will execute ...

ROBERTS: ... *faithfully the office* of president of the United States ...

OBAMA: ... the office of president of the United States *faithfully* ...

ROBERTS: ... and will to the best of my ability ...

OBAMA: ... and will to the best of my ability ...

ROBERTS: ... preserve, protect and defend the Constitution of the United States.

OBAMA: ... preserve, protect and defend the Constitution of the United States.

ROBERTS: So help you God?

OBAMA: So help me God.

ROBERTS: Congratulations, Mr. President.

Because of glitches in preparing for the ceremony, Obama was not told in advance when Roberts would pause to let him repeat the words.[5] Compounding the problem, instead of reading the oath from a card, Roberts spoke from memory. That led to mis-cues and mistimed phrasing, and it took several back-and-forths before they managed to synchronize instead of talking over one another. Then Roberts stumbled over some of the words: he said, *execute the office of President* to *the United States faithfully,* instead of the correct *faithfully execute the Office of President* of *the United States.* Backtracking, Roberts then said *faithfully the office of president,* leaving out the word *execute* that should have followed *faithfully.* Obama then pushed *faithfully* to the end of the phrase: *the office of president of the United States faithfully.* Ultimately, they both recovered and the rest of the oath went smoothly.

After the oath, President Obama delivered his inaugural address. Then he signed some executive orders as his first presidential acts, and the inauguration celebrations continued into the night. Was the botched oath a problem? Conservatives had already expressed their intention to thwart Obama's legislative program, and birthers were still questioning his very eligibility to serve as president. To make sure critics could not say that a misspoken oath left the country without a president, the White House asked Roberts to re-administer the oath the next day in a short, private ceremony.

The presidential oath had been flubbed before. In 1909, Chief Justice Melville Fuller misread the oath as he swore in William Howard Taft. The error was not publicized. As Taft later wrote, "In those days when there was no radio, it was observed only in the Senate chamber where

I took the oath."[6] Twenty years later, when Taft was Chief Justice of the United States, it was his turn to misspeak as he administered the oath to Herbert Hoover. This time the words were broadcast, and a schoolgirl wrote to Taft, who acknowledged his error but said he didn't think it mattered. Taft was Chief Justice, after all, and he had already been president, experiences that gave some weight both to his administration of the oath and to his interpretation of the Constitution. Then, when Justice Harlan Fiske Stone swore in Harry Truman, he misstated the president's name, though Truman then said his name correctly, so that was not a problem. And in 1964, Lyndon Johnson forgot to raise his right hand until the oath was half-way done, also not a problem since the Constitution requires no specific gesture to accompany the oath.

In addition, two previous presidents retook their oath of office, but not because of errors in performance. Calvin Coolidge was initially sworn in by his father, a notary public. Although the Constitution does not indicate who, if anyone, should administer the oath, Coolidge retook the oath before a federal judge the next day, just in case. And before that, Vice President Chester Arthur took the presidential oath privately, in his New York office, a day after President James Garfield died. Arthur then repeated the oath publicly, two days later, when he got to Washington (Amtrak was slow in those days, too).

The Constitution itself offers potentially conflicting guidance on the connection between the oath of office and the moment when the president actually starts work. Although Article II clearly specifies that the oath is to be taken "*before* he enter on the execution of his Office" (emphasis added), the equally valid Twentieth Amendment states that the president's term begins at noon on January 20 but does not mention the oath at all. This ensures a smooth transition of government and guarantees that there is not a second during which the country does not have a president. Similarly, the Twenty-Fifth Amendment provides that the vice president becomes president when the president dies, resigns, or is removed from office, again ensuring continuity. It, too, is silent about the need to take the oath of office first.

In short, Article II requires an oath, but the two amendments covering the presidential succession assume that becoming president is automatic, oath or no oath. In 2009, Barack Obama took the oath a few minutes after noon. Although a couple of people claimed – perhaps not altogether seriously – that in the brief span of time between noon and the completion of the oath, the country had no president, the Twentieth Amendment ensures an automatic transfer of authority to cover any gap. A 1985 memorandum from the White House Office of Legal Counsel supports this view that the oath itself is not the source of the president's power, though to play it safe, the memo also recommends that the oath should be taken as soon as possible.[7] That memo is merely advisory. No court has interpreted the ambiguous constitutional language of succession, or resolved any perceived conflict between Article II and the amendments. Still, President Obama's staff organized the retaking of the oath in order to avoid any controversy. Chief Justice Roberts, who told them, "I always believe in belt and suspenders," had no objection to the re-do.

We like to think that the law demands precision, with every *t* crossed and every *i* dotted, and that mandated formulas like the presidential oath must be repeated to the letter in order for them to take effect. But humans are fallible creatures. Custom dictates that the principals stand outdoors in frigid Washington weather, without hats, coats, and scarves, and before a massive audience: more than 1 million people were on the Mall in 2009, and millions around the world watched the swearing-in on television. That created some pressure for Roberts and Obama, and it is no surprise that even a well-rehearsed performance, by speakers as accomplished as they were known to be, can go awry.

We know that some formulas have no force unless they are pronounced correctly. In the magic world of Hogwarts, Hermione demonstrates to Ron that you cannot levitate a feather unless you give *Wingardium Leviosá* the proper stress. But in the muggle world of Washington, DC, where human laws apply, we are a lot more forgiving of performance errors. The drama of President Obama's first oath shows that even when the Constitution requires that a formula be repeated, judging whether that formula is effective if it is uttered incorrectly becomes a matter of interpretation. Strict constructionists like Hermione Granger might say, "It doesn't work if you say it wrong." But in the very few documented cases of misspoken presidential oaths, the mistakes either went unnoticed or they were considered too trivial to destabilize the presidency. Or, in the case of Obama's first oath, the words were repeated till they came out right.

## THE RIGHT TO REMAIN SILENT

The presidential oath of office mandates speech: say these thirty-five words, and you will become president (if you have been elected to the office, or you are in the line of succession). The Miranda warning – "You have the right to remain silent ..." – consists of words that police must say to anyone they arrest before they can begin questioning them. Ironically, its message, which must be spoken correctly to survive a court challenge, concerns not speech, but silence: you do not have to say anything if you've been arrested. Like the presidential oath, the source of the Miranda warning lies in the Constitution: the Fifth Amendment says, in part, "No person ... shall be compelled in any criminal case to be a witness against himself"; and the Sixth Amendment guarantees the right to counsel.

The popular distillation of those protections is a formula drummed into our heads by American television police dramas. As Chief Justice William Rehnquist observed in 2000, the phrase "you have the right to remain silent" has become "part of our national culture."[8] In the United States, its recognition factor is at least as high as the opening words of the national anthem, "Oh, say can you see?" and those of the Gettysburg Address, "Four score and seven years ago." The comedian Jerry Seinfeld said of the Miranda warning, "I mean is there anybody who doesn't know that by now?" And Justice Antonin Scalia found it implausible, "in the modern age of frequently dramatized 'Miranda' warnings," that any suspect would be unaware of the right to remain silent.[9] Even so, failure to Mirandize a suspect, or failure to say the words correctly, can sink a prosecution. But just like the presidential oath, the right to silence is not quite as straightforward as it seems.

The warning takes its name from the 1966 Supreme Court decision in *Miranda* v. *Arizona*. Ernesto Miranda had a long criminal record, serving time in juvenile facilities, in jails, and in a federal prison, for a variety of offenses, including attempted rape. For most of his life Miranda had difficulty holding down a job, and he had been dishonorably discharged from the Army after serving several months at hard labor for going AWOL and for Peeping Tom offenses. In 1963, he was arrested in Phoenix on suspicion of rape. After he was identified by the complaining

| Form 2000-66-D<br>Rev. Nov. 59 | CITY OF PHOENIX, ARIZONA<br>POLICE DEPARTMENT | Witness/Suspect<br>Statement |

SUBJECT: _Rape_    _DR. 63-08380_

STATEMENT OF: _ERNEST ARTHER MIRANDA_

TAKEN BY: _C Cooley #413 - W. Young #182_

DATE: _3-13-63_    TIME: _130 Pm_    PLACE TAKEN: _Interr Rm #2_

I, _Ernest A Miranda_, do hereby swear that I make this statement voluntarily and of my own free will, with no threats, coercion, or promises of immunity, and with full knowledge of my legal rights, understanding any statement I make may be used against me.

I, _Ernest A Miranda_, am _23_ years of age and have completed the _8th_ grade in school.

_Seen a girl walking up street stopped a little ahead of her got out of car walked towards her grabbed her by the arm and asked to get in the car. Got in car without force tied hands + ankles. Drove away_

7.1 This pre-printed waiver, with space left blank for a signature, appeared at the top of the handwritten statement that Miranda made after a two-hour police interrogation. It was common at the time for police to add such a waiver to confessions even when suspects had not been informed of their rights. Used by permission of the Arizona State Library.

witness, he was interrogated for two hours, at the end of which he wrote and signed a confession on a pre-printed form that is headed by a signed waiver of his rights, rights that are not specifically enumerated: "I Ernest A. Miranda do hereby swear that I make this statement voluntarily and of my own free will, with no threats, coercion, or promises of immunity, and with full knowledge of my legal rights, understanding any statement I make may be used against me."[10] What Miranda attested to in his waiver was not true: before questioning he had not been advised that he had any rights. It was only after he confessed that he was forced to sign his rights away without knowing what the rights that he had "voluntarily" given up actually were.

At Miranda's trial, his court-appointed lawyer asked for the confession to be thrown out, but the judge refused to do so. The jury convicted Miranda of kidnapping and rape, and he was sentenced to a term of twenty to thirty years in prison. The Arizona Supreme Court affirmed Miranda's conviction on appeal, but the US Supreme Court reversed that conviction. Splitting 5:4, the Court ruled that Miranda's confession was inadmissible because it was coerced: he had not been advised of his rights to silence and to an attorney.

At the same time, the Court found that the defendants in three other criminal cases, each convicted on the basis of confessions obtained during police interrogations, had been effectively denied their constitutional protections. The Court reversed those convictions, and it instructed law enforcement agencies at all levels to follow a set of guidelines to inform suspects of their right to silence and to an attorney during all future interrogations. The *Miranda* ruling was not retroactive – that would have jeopardized countless convictions – but it did apply to any cases that had not yet gone to trial. The Court did not specify the exact words that the police must use, though it did mandate what rights any warning must cover.

The *Miranda* opinion, written by Chief Justice Earl Warren, acknowledged that custodial interrogations – police questioning after a person has been placed under arrest – are inherently coercive. Because of this, the police must make anyone they question fully aware of their right against self-incrimination; their right to counsel, even if they can't afford an attorney; and their right to invoke their rights at any time, even if they have already started answering questions. In addition, the police must create an interview situation that is minimally intimidating. Additionally, if an arrest does lead to a trial, the government must demonstrate that defendants were made aware of their constitutional rights *before* questioning, and that any waiver of those rights, along with any confession or other statement made during interrogations, was given freely, without threats or promises. Finally, the Court stipulated that rights may only be waived knowingly and intelligently. In other words, speakers under arrest must be aware that they have waived their rights, and they must understand the consequences of giving up those rights.[11]

Warren illustrated the coercive nature of police questioning by describing at length the physically abusive interrogation techniques common in the past – the third degree, he called it, using the vernacular of Hollywood crime films, though the term goes back to the late-nineteenth century. He also criticized the psychologically manipulative techniques that replaced harsh lights and rubber hoses with carefully scripted scenarios like playing good cop/bad cop, interrogation techniques designed to elicit "inculpatory statements," that is, confessions.

Warren reasoned that police would pressure suspects to admit wrongdoing unless the accused were made aware of their rights prior to questioning. He cited as examples of particularly vulnerable and suggestible defendants two whose convictions the Court was reversing: Ernesto Miranda, described in the opinion as an "indigent Mexican defendant ... a seriously disturbed individual with pronounced sexual fantasies," and Roy Allen Stewart, "an indigent Los Angeles Negro who had dropped out of school in the sixth grade."[12] Stewart had been interrogated by police on nine separate occasions over the course of five days while jailed incommunicado in a cell at the station house, and he had never been advised of his rights during his time in custody. The Court emphasized that all defendants, not just those it termed "subnormal or woefully ignorant," must be informed of the constitutional protections against self-incrimination, and all must freely choose to waive or exercise their rights.[13]

The Fifth Amendment guarantee against self-incrimination derives from a seventeenth-century English law correcting the earlier practice of forcing confessions. That "Star Chamber" tactic was first used against criminals and later expanded to target heretics and political prisoners. Although the Fifth Amendment specifies that the right to silence applies "in any criminal case," the *Miranda* court made it clear that this protection extends not just to courtrooms, but to pre-trial police questioning as well, "enhanc[ing] the integrity of the factfinding processes in court" and protecting citizens from coercion by interrogators.[14] Warren concluded his opinion by citing Justice Brandeis' admonition in 1928 that the government should never break the law in order to secure a conviction: "Crime is contagious. If the Government becomes a lawbreaker, it breeds contempt for law; it invites every man to become a law unto himself; it invites anarchy."[15]

Dissenting from the *Miranda* majority, Justice John Marshall Harlan warned that the compelled warning would put an end to all confessions and the number of criminal convictions would plummet. But as Warren noted, the FBI already required its interrogators to inform subjects of their rights without hampering that agency's investigative ability. Warren also pointed out that in the four cases under review, there was sufficient evidence to obtain convictions even without the improperly obtained confessions.

Those reassurances did not stop the public outcry against the *Miranda* decision. The growing criticism reinforced an "impeach Earl Warren" campaign among conservatives who objected to the Warren court's decisions in cases like *Brown* v. *Board of Education* (1954),[16] which ended school segregation, and *Engel* v. *Vitale* (1962),[17] banning school-sponsored prayer in public schools. The outcry over *Miranda* led Senator Birch Bayh to conduct hearings around the country to determine whether the Constitution should be amended in order to sidestep the Court's decision. The author Truman Capote testified before Bayh's subcommittee that in "wailing about" criminals' rights, *Miranda* "totally ignore[s] the rights of the victims and of potential victims." Capote insisted that, had the *Miranda* decision come a few months earlier, it would have prevented the execution of Perry Smith and Dick Hickock, the brutal killers that he wrote about in his best-selling book, *In Cold Blood*.[18] Prosecutors, too, objected that *Miranda* would hamstring interrogations and gut their conviction rates, but that didn't happen. A study by the Los Angeles Police Department showed that after *Miranda*, confessions continued to occur in half of their cases, and that, as the Supreme Court had surmised, confessions played a role in only 10 percent of their convictions.[19]

Publicity surrounding the case turned Miranda's name into a household word. The phrase *Miranda warning* entered the English language within months of the decision and within five years, *Mirandize* had become a verb.[20] Miranda himself basked in his new-found fame, but he did so from his prison cell. After the Court's ruling, which vacated Miranda's conviction but did not exonerate him, he was quickly retried, this time without the tainted confession, and once again he was found guilty and sentenced to prison. Miranda was paroled in 1972, though he served time again later, on other charges, including parole violation. When he was out of prison, he sold autographed Miranda Warning cards for spare change.[21] Miranda had two of these cards with him when he was stabbed to death in a bar fight in 1976. A suspect was arrested and immediately Mirandized both in English and in Spanish, but police let him go when they learned that someone else had stabbed Miranda. Assuming that the real killer had returned to his native Mexico, they did not pursue the case further.[22]

"MIRANDA WARNINGS"

YOU HAVE THE RIGHT TO REMAIN SILENT.

ANYTHING YOU SAY CAN BE USED AGAINST YOU IN A COURT OF LAW.

YOU HAVE THE RIGHT TO THE PRESENCE OF AN ATTORNEY TO ASSIST YOU PRIOR TO QUESTIONING, AND TO BE WITH YOU DURING QUESTIONING, IF YOU SO DESIRE.

IF YOU CANNOT AFFORD AN ATTORNEY YOU HAVE THE RIGHT TO HAVE AN ATTORNEY APPOINTED FOR YOU PRIOR TO QUESTIONING.

DO YOU UNDERSTAND THESE RIGHTS?

WILL YOU VOLUNTARILY ANSWER MY QUESTIONS?

**7.2** Miranda Card signed by Ernesto Miranda and given to a police detective working undercover at the Duce, a bar in the red-light district in downtown Phoenix. Miranda, whose signature on this card was later verified against his signed confession, was unaware he had given the card to a detective. The warning on the card has seventy-eight words. Used by permission of the Phoenix Police Museum.

**DO YOU UNDERSTAND THESE RIGHTS?** During his 1968 presidential campaign, Richard Nixon blamed *Miranda* and the earlier decision in *Escobedo* v. *Illinois* (1964) affirming the right to counsel, for the nation's escalating crime rate: "The cumulative effect [of] these decisions has been to very nearly rule out the 'confession' as an effective and major tool in prosecution and law enforcement."[23] But fears that *Miranda* would handcuff the police – voiced by many law enforcement officials and legal scholars, and echoed by Nixon – proved unwarranted. In the months after the Supreme Court ruling, confession rates remained at their pre-*Miranda* levels, and today, almost half of all police interrogations still lead to voluntary confessions.[24] Although the motivation for such confessions may be an honest desire to come clean, or a hope that confessing will result in leniency, there is still a concern that many people who are read their rights do not understand them well enough to waive them intelligently, as *Miranda* requires:

> The ability of native speakers of English to understand their rights is affected by their level of education, their cognitive abilities, the context and manner of communication of the rights and the wording used to express individual rights. The problems are even greater among vulnerable populations, including juveniles and people with mental disorders ... [and] non-native speakers of English.[25]

Data shows that criminal defendants are much more likely to invoke their rights if they've had a previous conviction where they waived those rights, suggesting that they learn from their mistakes, not from the words of the Miranda warning.[26] Or at least, they learn from one mistake they made, not invoking their right to silence.

The *Miranda* decision did not mandate a specific formula or set of words for interrogators to use before questioning suspects. Instead, it required that any warning cover all of the following:

- the right to silence
- a reminder that any statements made may be used in court
- the right to counsel
- access to counsel for indigent suspects
- the assertion of these rights at any time – if a person asserts these rights during interrogation, the interrogation must stop.

Perhaps the most familiar Miranda warning is the version popularized by television police dramas like *Law and Order*:

> You have the right to remain silent. Anything you say can and will be used against you in a court of law.
> You have the right to speak to an attorney and to have an attorney present during any questioning.
> If you cannot afford a lawyer, one will be provided for you at government expense.
> Do you understand?

Surely this is the warning that Jerry Seinfeld and Antonin Scalia were referring to when they observed that everybody knows Miranda. But the *Law and Order* version is not the only one. There are at least 560 other variations on the right to silence and to counsel used at the federal, state, and local levels in the United States. Some of these may be harder to understand than others, and a warning that is too difficult is no warning at all.

The *Miranda* court found that understanding one's rights is as important as the enumeration of those rights. In addition to providing the essential categories that a warning must cover, the Court stressed that defendants may waive their right to silence or to an attorney only if they do so freely; without pressure, promises, or threats; *and with an intelligent understanding of what it is that they are doing.* The Court ordered interrogators to document the administration of the warning and its understanding, but just as it declined to make all warnings identical by dictating a formula, the Supreme Court did not specify how to administer the warning or how to determine a suspect's understanding of their rights.

Law enforcement agencies complied with *Miranda* by familiarizing their officers with the wording of their department's preferred text, sometimes making the warning available in more than one language. They began documenting the warning either by having the arrestee sign a form indicating their comprehension, or by recording the formal administration of the warning, along with the defendant's oral acknowledgment that they understood their rights. Or both. But sometimes defendants do not understand their rights, even if they say that they do. There are a number of factors that interfere with comprehension. The length and complexity of a warning can impact understanding. Miranda warnings range in length from a low of forty-nine words to as many as 547 (the *Law and Order* warning has fifty-eight words; the Miranda autograph card has seventy-eight), and they require reading levels that vary from third grade to college or beyond. Most criminal defendants have significantly lower literacy levels than the general adult population.[27]

Keeping a warning short doesn't guarantee comprehension: it is difficult to convey complex ideas like constitutional rights in a few words, and some of the terser Miranda warnings skimp on details that may prove important later on. For example, a warning that only says, "You have the right to a lawyer during questioning" omits the fact that defendants also have the right to consult a lawyer before questioning as well as when they are not being questioned. On the other hand, spelling these ideas out at length poses problems, too, since long texts may strain the ability of a person who has just been arrested to pay attention.

Most Miranda warnings are delivered orally, and that presents its own set of complications.[28] Under ideal circumstances, people have trouble following what a stranger tells them and remembering the details later, as anyone who asked for driving directions before the age of the smartphone can readily attest. But Miranda warnings are seldom given during ideal circumstances: at best they are inherently stressful, making it hard for defendants to pay attention to what is being said to them. The ability to understand a warning may also be impaired by injury, alcohol, drugs, mental illness, lack of competence, or limited English proficiency. And juvenile defendants may be at greater risk in terms of understanding Miranda and making a free and intelligent decision to waive their rights.

There are other impediments to understanding as well. Spoken or written, Miranda warnings are delivered out of context, in that they do not connect with any conversation up to that point. The person arrested must stop, focus on the warning for a few seconds, and keep the meaning of those words in mind while dealing with whatever happens next. And, finally, even though the Court did not require a uniform warning, Miranda warnings are necessarily formulaic. We tend to tune out formulas, especially when they are recited quickly and in a monotone, and we may skip over them when we read them. Such inattention impacts speech and reading even when we are relaxed; it is likely to be magnified for a person facing arrest.

Despite the mounting evidence that it may be difficult to understand a Miranda warning, and the requirement that defendants only waive their rights if they do so "intelligently," the courts typically require only objective proof that the defendant was Mirandized, and an objective indication by the defendant that they understand their rights. That's because it is virtually impossible to measure a defendant's comprehension, either when they are being warned or afterwards, in retrospect. Answering the question, "Do you understand these rights?" with a "Yes" does not mean that you understand your rights well enough to pass a test about them, let alone stay out of jail. But a one-word answer is all that is necessary to satisfy *Miranda.*

## REMAINING SILENT IS NOT ENOUGH

The enunciation and acknowledgment of Miranda rights is only part of the arrest process. An arrestee must also indicate *with words* whether they wish to invoke or waive those rights. The Supreme Court found in *Miranda* that "a knowing and intelligent waiver of these rights [cannot] be assumed on a silent record,"[29] just as it determined more explicitly, in

*Salinas* v. *Texas* (2013), that a defendant must speak in order to refuse to speak, a situation that would seem to be paradoxical.[30]

In *Salinas,* the Supreme Court took a step back from the sweeping protections that it granted in *Miranda.* But in *New York* v. *Quarles* (1984), the Supreme Court established a public safety exception permitting self-incrimination without a warning, if police questioning could prevent further harm.[31] In that case, the arresting officer followed rape suspect Benjamin Quarles into a supermarket. The officer believed that, when Quarles spotted police looking for him, he hid a gun somewhere in the store. After handcuffing Quarles, which effectively put him under arrest, the officer asked about the gun, and Quarles told him where to find it. Only then, once the gun was secured, did the officer read Quarles his rights. The trial judge threw out Quarles' statements about the gun, since he had been questioned about it after his arrest but before he had been Mirandized. But the Supreme Court reinstated that testimony. In his opinion in the case, Justice William Rehnquist acknowledged that the general Miranda rule encompasses the gathering of "testimonial evidence" from a suspect, but an exception must apply in cases where questioning the suspect could prevent a future danger to the public: "So long as the gun was concealed somewhere in the supermarket, with its actual whereabouts unknown, it obviously posed more than one danger to the public safety: an accomplice might make use of it, a customer or employee might later come upon it."[32] Although Rehnquist admitted that the public safety exception narrowed *Miranda,* he found no problem balancing a suspect's right to silence against the greater danger: "The need for answers to questions in a situation posing a threat to the public safety outweighs the need for the prophylactic rule protecting the Fifth Amendment's privilege against self-incrimination."

The public safety exception was first articulated in the context of criminal cases where an ongoing threat must be quickly defused. After 9/11, the exception was applied to terror suspects as well. A memorandum from Attorney General Eric Holder explains the reasoning behind this practice:

The magnitude and complexity of the threat often posed by terrorist organizations, particularly international terrorist organizations, and the nature of their attacks ... may warrant significantly more extensive public safety interrogation than would be permissible in an ordinary criminal case. ... The government's interest in obtaining this intelligence – lawfully but without *Miranda* warnings – outweighs the disadvantages of proceeding in this fashion.[33]

Almost everyone has heard of *Miranda*, but few people were aware of the public safety exception to *Miranda* until Dzhokhar Tsarnaev was arrested in the Boston Marathon terrorist bombing in 2013. Tsarnaev's brother, Tamerlan, thought to be the driving force behind the bombing, was killed during the arrest, and Dzhokhar was wounded. When Dzhokhar Tsarnaev woke up from surgery, federal agents, invoking the public safety exception, questioned the bomber about his motives, and whether he and his brother had worked alone, or were part of a group.

Tsarnaev was not read his rights until the next day, when he was arraigned at his hospital bedside by federal magistrate Marianne B. Bowler. Here is an excerpt from the transcript of the hearing in which Judge Bowler informed Tsarnaev about his right to silence, using a detailed version of the Miranda warning. Tsarnaev could not speak to indicate that he understood his rights because he had been shot in the throat during his arrest. Instead, he nodded – an objective indication of his understanding:

THE COURT: I am going to tell you about your constitutional rights.

You have the right under the Constitution of the United States to remain silent. Any statement made by you may be used against you in court, and you have the right not to have your own words used against you.

You may consult with an attorney prior to any questioning, and you may have the attorney present during questioning.

Counsel will be appointed without charge if you cannot afford counsel.

If you choose to make a statement or to answer questions without the assistance of counsel, you may stop answering at any time.

This right means you do not have to answer any questions put to you by law enforcement agents or by the Assistant United States Attorney, Mr. Weinreb.

I want to make it clear. You are not prohibited from making statements, but that if you do, they can be used against you. You are not required to make a statement at this initial appearance, and any statement you do make may be used against you.

Finally, if I ask you any questions here in this hearing or at any future hearing which you think might incriminate you, you have the right not to answer.

Do you understand everything I have said about your right to remain silent?

THE DEFENDANT: (Defendant nods affirmatively.)

THE COURT: Again I note that the defendant has nodded affirmatively.[34]

Tsarnaev was subsequently convicted of the bombing and sentenced to death, a sentence recently confirmed by the Supreme Court. Tsarnaev is currently in solitary confinement, not allowed to communicate with anyone he didn't know before he was jailed, or to communicate in any language other than English, a rule which treats speaking a language other than English as *prima facie* evidence of guilt.[35]

There is no doubt that *Miranda* made a major difference for speech in the context of the criminal justice system, changing police practice – not to mention popular culture – with the stroke of a pen. Criminal defendants must now be read their rights. FBI crime statistics show that in 2019, about nineteen people were Mirandized every minute. Each arrestee had to indicate their understanding of those rights, and whether or not they waived them.[36] But it is not clear that *Miranda* changed what arrestees do when it comes to speech and silence: advised about their right to silence, many speak anyway. A right to silence is not a mandate for silence, even when silence might be in a defendant's best interest.

To be sure, many defendants do understand their rights, or at least they have a general idea of what those rights are, if not from their own brushes with the law, then as Justice Scalia suggested, from watching police procedurals on television. But for vulnerable defendants who for various reasons do not understand their rights but say that they do, their acknowledgment of understanding is not done knowingly or intelligently, as *Miranda* requires. Instead, for them it is no better than the statement of understanding that Ernesto Miranda signed in his confession, even though he had no idea at the time what his rights to speech or silence were. As the *Miranda* court noted, and prosecutors continue to demonstrate, there is often enough evidence to prove guilt without a confession. That is why Miranda was re-convicted after the Supreme Court threw out his confession. The *Miranda* decision specifically applies to all defendants, not just vulnerable ones, which suggests that finding less perfunctory ways to assess whether defendants understand their rights to silence and to an attorney would not lower conviction rates.

## WHEN THE LAW WRITES THE DICTIONARY

To ensure that a law will be interpreted as intended, not left to the whims of dictionaries, lawyers, or even judges, statutes sometimes define their own words. Such definitions require us to accept a particular meaning and reject alternatives, and, as such, they constitute compelled speech. In the United States in 2019, 10 million people were Mirandized and no one took the presidential oath of office that year (ideally, the presidential oath is taken once every four years). In the same year, just over 2 million married. Yet over time, the legal definition of *marriage*, stipulating who can and who cannot wed, stands to impact just as many Americans as the right to remain silent. The 1996 Defense of Marriage Act (DOMA) excluded same-sex couples when it defined *marriage* in all federal laws, rules, and regulations, as "a legal union between one man and one woman as husband and wife":

Definition of "marriage" and "spouse." In determining the meaning of any Act of Congress, or of any ruling, regulation, or interpretation of the various administrative bureaus and agencies of the United States, the word "marriage" means only a legal union between one man and one woman as husband and wife, and the word "spouse" refers only to a person of the opposite sex who is a husband or a wife. (1 USC 1 § 7)

The law's very name – the Defense of Marriage Act – suggested that marriage was under attack. But DOMA didn't protect marriage. Instead, since laws about who may or may not marry are enacted by the states, not the federal government, it denied partners in legal same-sex marriages the recognition and benefits that married couples enjoy under more than a thousand federal laws.[37] Responding to the growing number of states recognizing same-sex marriage, other states opposed to this shift in public attitude enacted their own "Defense of Marriage" laws banning same-sex marriage. For example, in 2014, Tennessee, added this definition of marriage to its constitution:

> The historical institution and legal contract solemnizing the relationship of one (1) man and one (1) woman shall be the only legally recognized marital contract in this state. Any policy or law or judicial interpretation, purporting to define marriage as anything other than the historical institution and legal contract between one (1) man and one (1) woman, is contrary to the public policy of this state and shall be void and unenforceable in Tennessee.[38]

In addition to preventing same-sex marriage for its own residents, Tennessee refused to recognize legal same-sex marriages from other states. Clearly, having marriages that are legal in one state but not in another denies equal treatment under the law, as mandated by the Fourteenth Amendment. Problems multiply when the federal government also refuses to recognize a legal marriage, since many federal benefits depend on marital status.

In *United States* v. *Windsor* (2013), the Supreme Court declared that DOMA's definition of marriage, which "writes inequality into the entire United States Code," was unconstitutional. Two years later, in *Obergefell* v. *Hodges*, the Court applied that ruling to the states, invalidating laws in Michigan, Kentucky, Ohio, and Tennessee that defined *marriage* as the union of one man and one woman.[39] Statutory definitions of *marriage* could no longer ban same-sex marriage, but in 2017, Tennessee lawmakers tried to sidestep *Obergefell* by deleting the state-mandated definition of marriage, then requiring that, in any state statute, "undefined words shall be given their natural and ordinary meaning, without forced or subtle construction that would limit or extend the meaning of the language."[40]

That statement may seem innocuous on its face: it is a commonplace of legal interpretation that undefined words are supposed to be given their natural and ordinary meaning. But by prohibiting any "forced or subtle construction" of natural meaning, the bill's supporters meant same-sex marriage. The new law didn't say this directly, but its words borrow heavily from an earlier bill that sought to define spouses and parents as heterosexual, a definition that the Supreme Court had just found unconstitutional. According to that failed Tennessee proposal, "The words 'husband,' 'wife,' 'mother,' and 'father' shall be given their natural and ordinary meaning, without forced or subtle construction that would limit or extend the meaning of the language and that are based on the biological distinctions between men and women."[41]

Hoping to avoid a confrontation with the federal marriage ruling, the Tennessee law deleted references to heterosexual parents and spouses but left in "natural and ordinary," thereby suggesting that parents and spouses are naturally and ordinarily heterosexual. Then, in 2019, some Tennessee legislators went further by reinstating the one-man, one-woman definition of marriage, arguing that the Supreme Court had no authority to strike down the natural law of marriage any more than it could strike down the law of gravity.[42]

Tennessee's natural and ordinary meaning law ignores what we have seen repeatedly in this study, that any word's plain meaning may be disputed. Interpreting the statute is further complicated by the fact that the "natural and ordinary" meaning of a word like *marriage* is in flux, as can see by the evolving dictionary definitions of the word. Samuel Johnson, the eighteenth-century lexicographer whose definitions are often cited by the courts, defined *marriage* as "the act of uniting a man and a woman for life."[43] Noah Webster went a step further, grounding even civil marriage in religion:

MARRIAGE, n. ... The act of uniting a man and woman for life; wedlock; the legal union of a man and woman for life. Marriage is a contract both civil and religious, by which the parties engage to live together in mutual affection and fidelity, till death shall separate them. Marriage was instituted by God himself for the purpose of preventing the promiscuous intercourse of the sexes, for promoting domestic felicity, and for securing the maintenance and education of children.[44]

But later in the nineteenth century, dictionaries began to acknowledge the complexity of marriage. The *Century Dictionary* (1891) expanded

Johnson's "man-and-woman" definition by including both common law marriage and "plural marriage," or *polygamy*, in its definition of *marriage*. In the early twenty-first century, dictionaries began reflecting the more recent cultural and linguistic shift by adding same-sex marriage to their definitions. In 2003, *Merriam-Webster's Collegiate Dictionary* defined *marriage* as "(1) the state of being united to a person of the opposite sex as husband or wife in a consensual and contractual relationship recognized by law (2): the state of being united to a person of the same sex in a relationship like that of a traditional marriage."[45]

The *Oxford English Dictionary*, another favorite with judges, also added same-sex marriage to its definition: "The condition of being a husband or wife; the relation between persons married to each other; matrimony. The term is now sometimes used with reference to long-term relationships between partners of the same sex." In addition, the *OED* defined *gay marriage* in a separate entry: "a formal marriage bond contracted between two people of the same sex, often conferring legal rights; (also) the action of entering into such a relationship; the condition of marriage between partners of the same sex." And, in 2011, the *American Heritage Dictionary* added same-sex marriage to its definition: "The legal union of a man and woman as husband and wife, and in some jurisdictions, between two persons of the same sex, usually entailing legal obligations of each person to the other."[46]

Dictionaries broadened their definitions of *marriage* because speakers of English had broadened their use of the term to cover same-sex unions – even opponents of same-sex marriage must use the word *marriage* to refer to it – and because states were recognizing such unions as legal marriages. As a result, the "natural and ordinary" meaning of *marriage* can no longer refer only to the heterosexual unions specified by Johnson and Webster. Plus dictionaries cannot compel meaning – they do not have the power to force us to use the older sense of a word or to stop us from using a new one.

No nineteenth-century court would have extended the Fourteenth Amendment's guarantee of equal protection under the law to same-sex couples. The issue of same-sex marriage would not have come up then, either. But today's social climate is different. The *Windsor* court acknowledged the shifting meaning of *marriage*, and it interpreted the Fourteenth Amendment to include marriage protection. The need to read law flexibly and practically brings us back to where we started, the problem of interpretation.

## IT WILL BE NECESSARY, FIRST, TO INTERPRET THE LAW

Flexible interpretation – finding the spirit of the law, as Sergeant Saunders put it centuries ago – has always been central to legal meaning-making. As we saw in Chapter 2, the *Heller* court insisted that its reading of the Second Amendment reflected the original meaning, the one the framers had in mind, when they drafted it. But the legal scholar Richard Posner faulted Antonin Scalia for reading the amendment rigidly, when the framers believed that law must be interpreted flexibly in order to fit the legal text to current circumstances: "Scalia's entire analysis denies the legitimacy of flexible interpretation designed to adapt the Constitution (so far as the text permits) to current conditions. The irony is that the 'originalist' method would have yielded the opposite result."[47]

According to the eighteenth-century legal scholar William Blackstone, it was common practice to read laws loosely when necessary. Scalia bolstered his *Heller* opinion with references to Blackstone's legal commentaries, because Blackstone, who wrote about English common law, helped to shape the framers' thinking as they began crafting American law. But to show where Scalia went wrong on originalism, Posner cited Blackstone's example of how to read a law sensibly rather than literally. Here's what Blackstone said:

> Where words bear either none, or a very absurd signification, if literally understood, we must a little deviate from the received sense of them. Therefore the Bolognian law ... which enacted "that whoever drew blood in the streets should be punished with the utmost severity," was held after long debate not to extend to the surgeon, who opened the vein of a person that fell down in the street with a fit.[48]

Bloodletting, also called venesection or phlebotomy, was an all-purpose though ineffective medical treatment still popular even in Blackstone's enlightened times. It is said to have been used on both King George III and George Washington, and it possibly killed Washington, who was bled four times during his brief final illness.[49] In the last and possibly fatal bleed, his physician drew a quart of blood from the president, who may have been suffering from nothing worse than a sore throat. Bringing Blackstone's example of flexible legal interpretation up to date, a surgeon who opened the vein of someone having a seizure on the street in present-day Bologna would probably be arrested, since venesection is no longer an accepted medical practice.

As Posner indicated, if Blackstone's view of practical interpretation was widely held, and there is no reason to think that it wasn't, then the framers deliberately designed the Constitution for "loose construction" so that, when things changed in America, as everyone knew they would, the Constitution would not become "a straitjacket or a suicide pact." Posner is no outlier in calling for a practical rather than a rigid or literal interpretation of the law. Judge Learned Hand, who stressed the importance of *interpreting* the law, observed in 1945 that it was common practice for the courts to go beyond the text in order to reach a fair decision:

> The decisions are legion in which they [the courts] have refused to be bound by the letter, when it frustrates the patent purpose of the whole statute. ... It is true that the words used, even in their literal sense, are the primary, and ordinarily the most reliable, source of interpreting the meaning of any writing: be it a statute, a contract, or anything else. But it is one of the surest indexes of a mature and developed jurisprudence not to make a fortress out of the dictionary; but to remember that statutes always have some purpose or object to accomplish, whose sympathetic and imaginative discovery is the surest guide to their meaning.[50]

A long line of jurists from Saunders to Blackstone to the present have accepted the obligation so neatly phrased by Learned Hand: "It will be necessary, first, to interpret the law." Hand said this in an interpretation which was later overruled. That represents the next step in the process of making legal meaning: interpretations may always be revisited. Even Antonin Scalia's insistence on original meaning – that a law must mean only what it meant to those who drafted it or those who read it at the time it was enacted, assuming that such meaning is ascertainable – is still an interpretation and therefore subject to review.

Throughout this book we have seen that, in matters of language, the law revisits itself repeatedly, extending, narrowing, and occasionally reversing earlier interpretations. In determining what counts as seditious speech, obscene speech, or threatening speech, the First Amendment cases that we looked at redrew the boundary between protected and unprotected speech, and future cases are likely to keep tinkering with those categories and the blurred line that divides them, trying to get it right in the current context. There has been no change in the text of the First Amendment, but there has been an evolution in thinking about protected speech in the contexts of political protest and changing communication technologies. There has also been an increased focus on *intent* in threatening speech, even though the requisite level of intent has yet to be determined. As for obscenity, the Supreme Court has made it clear that obscene speech is always unprotected. But what counts as obscene depends entirely on time, place, and context, and on shifting standards of literary practice, social attitudes, and audience, and sometimes, when it comes to children in the audience, even time of day. Although there is a technical line in the law between protected and obscene speech, that line is drawn in shifting sands: you can't define obscenity, but you'll know it when you see it.

We have no way of knowing whether "you'll know it when you see it" is what the framers had in mind when they drafted the First Amendment, and just as the Second Amendment says nothing about the right to own a pistol but not an AK-47, the text of the First Amendment says nothing about obscenity, or indeed about any exceptions to protected speech. Nonetheless, the *practical* interpretation of the amendment infers from available evidence and common sense that there is some speech that is not protected, and obscene speech, when it can be identified, has always been a principal type of unprotected speech.

The ever-moving target of unprotected speech means that speakers may not always be able to know when or even if they can say what they want, and it may be difficult for them to predict in advance whether their words will violate the law. Were courts to establish unwavering distinctions between what is protected and what is not, that line would invite a deluge of hypothetical what-ifs to test it, because speakers naturally resist any attempt to regulate their language – the common "you're not the boss of me" response to language laws. Even for formulaic no-brainers like the mandated speech of the presidential oath and the Miranda warning, effectiveness and impact must be determined by external factors, judgments about whether an oath was taken properly, or whether the right to silence was understood and properly invoked or waived.

Official English laws do draw bright legal lines: it is generally evident when someone is using English and when they're not. But some of these laws may be blandly general, while others are framed as punitive – like the requirement that Dzhokhar Tsarnaev speak only English in prison, or that children must use English on a school bus – making the idea of official English ambiguous and the consequences for non-English speech uncertain. The Illinois official English law doesn't announce its purpose. It doesn't require, protect, or even encourage the use of English by anyone – resident, visitor, or government employee. It is symbolic, just as the Illinois state bird, the cardinal, is symbolic. But the meaning of a symbol may be difficult to pin down: you can know a cardinal by its appearance and its song, but what, exactly, does it mean for the cardinal to be the state bird? The Illinois official English provision sets no punishment for using any other language; it gives no right to sue if someone speaks Spanish or Telugu. Arizona's official English law regulates and restricts the speech of government employees. Although there are exceptions for trade, public health and safety, tourism, and education, for example, it is not always clear what sorts of speech fall within these categories. In addition, laws like Arizona's, along with the proposed federal English Language Unity Act, anticipate the need for legal interpretation by inviting citizens to sue if they perceive a violation.

The Constitution itself may be majestic and authoritative, but it too is subject both to interpretation and to revision. As we have seen, constitutional interpretation is an ongoing process. There is also a definite process established within the Constitution for modifying its text. Article V specifies how to amend "this Constitution," a procedure that is deliberately slow and cumbersome, presumably to prevent mistakes. Any amendment must be proposed by two-thirds of the House *and* the Senate, or by a constitutional convention proposed by two-thirds of the states (this second option has never been invoked). Once proposed, the amendment must be approved by three-fourths of the states in order to be ratified.

And just in case that lengthy, thoughtful, and deliberate process still produced a bad result, an amendment may also be repealed, a process that requires passing yet another amendment to replace it. In 1919, the Eighteenth Amendment – Prohibition – banned the manufacture, sale, or importation from abroad of "intoxicating liquors." Interestingly for our own consideration of official English, the campaign for prohibition played on the English-only feelings that came into focus during the First World War by calling attention to the presumed drunkenness of the enemy and emphasizing the German names of leading American brewers like Busch and Pabst.[51] But a dry America did not work well, except perhaps for a relatively small number of teetotalers, bootleggers, and Hollywood moviemakers cranking out gangster films, and so Prohibition was repealed in 1933 by the Twenty-First Amendment, which states in its first section, "The eighteenth article of amendment to the Constitution of the United States is hereby repealed."

Even constitutional amendments do not settle things once and for all, because they, too, have some wiggle room. According to the amendment that repealed Prohibition, the states retain the right to regulate or ban the sale of alcohol, and that means courts still have to interpret the law when an alcohol-related statutory challenge comes up. There is other constitutional wiggle room as well, for example, when the constitutionally-mandated presidential oath of office seems to contradict two amendments which specify how and when a president begins their term. Or when the Second Amendment does not specify which arms the people have a right to keep and bear; or where they can or cannot keep and bear them – in public, in private, openly, concealed, and with or without a license; or what *keep and bear arms* even means. Or when the First Amendment protects speech, and when, sometimes, it does not.

In the next and final chapter, I will examine the three most serious challenges today to our ability to say what we want: the clash between the First and Second amendments; the use of the First Amendment to suppress speech; and the growing digital erosion of our privacy.

## CHAPTER 8

# Will Free Speech Survive?

I ONCE SPECULATED THAT IF YOU HANDED OUT $10 bills at noon on busy Fifty-Seventh Street in Manhattan, passers-by would eagerly take one, but if you offered them a free poem, you would probably get a visit from Homeland Security.[1] That is because we trust paper money without checking to see if it is real, yet when a stranger offers us some words on paper, our first response is to avoid eye contact. It turns out my speculation about free verse had already been tested. In 1968, the poet John Giorno, a close friend of Andy Warhol, started Dial-a-Poem, a service where users called a toll-free number to hear a poet read from their work. Dial-a-Poem proved so popular it almost caused the local telephone exchange to crash. This was not bland greeting card verse. Some of the poems were edgy, raw, and socially aware, but no one was forced to listen against their will. Even so, concerned citizens lodged "complaints of indecency, claims that the poems incited violence," prompting the FBI to investigate poetry they suspected was up to no good. The story of Dial-a-Poem shows us that even speech that is literally free prompts attempts to silence it. The complaints of indecency and incitement cost Dial-a-Poem its funding, and the poetry hotline soon went dead.[2] But poetry is not dead, and new dial-a-poems keep springing up. If you prefer your verse hi-tech, there's even @PoetryHotline on Twitter, though no one's posted from that account recently.

We've seen throughout this book a continuing cycle: free speech leads to speech suppression, prompting speakers who are silenced to seek new ways to evade the limits placed on them. Today three forces threaten to limit speech, and they go well beyond ham-handed attempts to censor verse. The first pits guns against words, creating a showdown between the Second Amendment and the First. The second sees powerful speakers invoking their right to speak in order to silence other people's speech. Third, and perhaps the most subtle, the monitoring of our digital speech by government and business chills our ability to say what we want.

## MORE GUNS, LESS GRAMMAR

We began this book with a discussion of the Unite the Right protests in Charlottesville in 2017, where the Second Amendment clashed violently with the First. That was not a one-time event, more like the start of an undesirable tradition where the possession of legal firearms threatens to silence someone's legally protected speech.[3] In May, 2020, during the Covid-19 pandemic, Second Amendment extremists stormed the Michigan State House, brandishing military-style weapons to reinforce their protest of a state-wide public health lockdown.[4] Although the tooled-up protesters didn't shoot, and in Michigan it is legal to carry weapons openly inside the capitol building, their presence stopped the work of lawmakers. As in Charlottesville, protestors with guns were cheered on by President Trump, who insisted "these are very good people."[5] Some weeks later, after police arrested members of a right-wing group plotting to kidnap Michigan Governor Gretchen Whitmer, anti-Whitmer protestors again brought their guns to the capitol. A few days later, amid shouts of "Lock her up" in reference to Whitmer at a Michigan Trump rally, Trump seemed to encourage them by responding, "Lock them all up."[6] The increasing number of guns at protests have led to what Josh Marshall termed "murder safaris" like the one where three demonstrators were killed by a teenage, right-wing counter-protestor who had joined other out-of-towners traveling to Kenosha, Wisconsin, in 2020, ostensibly to protect private property.[7] And they stoked the insurrection of January 6, where caravans of people from all over the United States, some of them carrying weapons, used physical force to silence Congress and prevent the constitutionally mandated counting of Electoral College ballots for several hours – further evidence, if you need it, that guns and speech do not mix well.[8]

Adding to guns at protests, there has been an upsurge in armed voter intimidation in the United States. In some states, openly carrying a gun on the streets and inside offices, stores, and restaurants, is treated as a fundamental Second Amendment right. But in all states, voting is the epitome of political speech protected by the First Amendment. Openly carrying guns at the polls sets up a clash between the two amendments that could impact both the right to vote and the right to live. In the interests of public safety, six states and the District of Columbia prohibit guns at voting places, and another four ban concealed firearms there. Additionally, brandishing weapons anywhere or using them to intimidate is against the law.[9] But even though any form of voter intimidation is illegal under federal law, exactly what constitutes intimidation often remains vague.[10] Finally, if the Supreme Court decides in *New York State Rifle and Pistol Association* v. *Bruen* to expand the right to carry guns in public, it will create ever-greater opportunities for speech and guns to clash, and in such clashes, the presence of guns is likely to control the outcome.

## CANCELLING SPEECH

A survey by the Knight Foundation on post-2020 attitudes toward free speech offered a chilling take on the stand-off between speech rights and gun rights. One question asked respondents to pick the most important constitutional protection. The responses were sorted by various categories, including stated political affiliation (Democrat, Republican, Independent). Of Republicans, 26 percent picked the right to bear arms as most important; 13 per cent picked freedom of speech. That's two-to-one favoring gun rights over speech rights for the Republicans in this "representative" sample of 4,000 US adults. Although only 9 percent of Democrats selected freedom of speech as the most important right, just 1 percent of Democrats chose the right to bear arms. Democrats in this survey viewed free speech as nine times more important than having guns.[11] However it is not only "Second Amendment people" who suppress speech. Recent events have underscored the fact that "First Amendment people" do so too when they leverage free speech to suppress the speech of others.

Here's an example. In *Bostock* v. *Clayton County* (2020), the US Supreme Court ruled that "an employer who fires an individual merely for being gay or transgender violates Title VII" of the 1964 Civil Rights

Act.[12] That was a victory for opponents of gender discrimination. But in a section of his dissent in the case ominously headed "Freedom of Speech," Justice Samuel Alito addressed the conflict between the First Amendment and those antidiscrimination laws designed to protect the speech of people whose words have traditionally been ignored or actively suppressed. Justice Alito warned that *Bostock* compels speech in violation of the First Amendment by affecting "the way employers address their employees and the way teachers and school officials address students." To illustrate, he cited regulations requiring the use of gender pronouns, not just the traditional binaries *he* and *she*, but also nonbinary pronouns like singular *they, ze,* and *hir.*[13]

Alito's unusually long diatribe against pronouns is just one in a growing set of constitutional challenges to speech-related antidiscrimination measures. Conservative critics claim that pronoun mandates are a form of compelled speech forcing people to endorse a view of sex and gender that violates their beliefs, whether those beliefs are religious, scientific, or grammatical.[14] Alito's *Bostock* dissent raises the possibility that a First Amendment defense – "You can't make me say your pronouns!" – could neutralize a regulation designed to protect the speech of employees and students whose voices may otherwise be silenced by what the framers viewed as the tyranny of the majority. Taking another step toward invalidating an antidiscrimination regulation on First Amendment grounds, in March, 2021, a three-judge panel of the Sixth Circuit Court of Appeals ruled in *Meriwether* v. *Shawnee State University* that a professor at a public college could sue his employer for compelling him to say a transgender student's pronouns.[15] Shawnee State settled the case, a move that could give university faculty, and possibly other public employees, permission not just to ignore narrowly framed pronoun mandates, but also to verbally insult, demean, and discriminate at will.

*Bostock, Meriwether,* and other cases alleging gender discrimination go well beyond pronouns, raising the possibility that a conservative Supreme Court could strike down the language-based components of antidiscrimination law because hate speech is constitutionally protected in the United States. The Court could weaken rules forbidding discrimination based on accent, for example, while supporting those which ban the use of a language other than English. Allowing the First Amendment to shield language discrimination would protect the speech of the powerful while further suppressing voices that have been historically silenced or ignored. Instead of defending the words of those most in need of support, such action weaponizes the First Amendment *against* their speech. For Alito and many conservatives, that seems just fine.

Autocratic regimes do not hesitate to control speech, and this puts global media corporations in the precarious position of having to balance the freedom of users to say what they think against the freedom of these communication giants to operate in countries that enforce censorship. According to Amnesty International, Facebook earned more than a billion dollars from its Vietnamese operations in 2018. In 2021, a whistleblower charged that, in order to protect its market, Facebook complied with Hanoi's demands to censor antigovernment posts. In its defense, Facebook insisted that blocking a few posts actually protected the speech of most Vietnamese users, ensuring that "our services remain available for millions of people who rely on them every day."[16] Google faced a similar choice in China a decade earlier, initially complying with government demands to censor internet searches on forbidden topics and later, after strong negative reactions in the United States to that decision, shutting down its China-based servers rather than comply with censorship demands. These media platforms now face a similar attempt by powerful speakers in liberal democracies to suppress the online speech of critics, creating a tension between the freedom to speak truth to power and attempts by the likes of Facebook and Twitter to balance free speech against the need to regulate hate speech and other damaging content, while also protecting profits.

Any effort to restore balance by countering right-wing opinion is now damned as "cancel culture." More and more high-profile speakers with massive numbers of followers are complaining, "I'm being canceled," as they attempt to silence, in effect to cancel, their critics. In his acceptance speech to the Republican National Convention in 2020, Donald Trump called out cancel culture as one of the many "crimes" of the left: "The goal of cancel culture is to make decent Americans live in fear of being fired, expelled, shamed, humiliated, and driven from society as we know it."[17] This sense of *cancel*, meaning "to dismiss or reject a person," seems to originate in 1990s critiques of sexist and racist speech both face-to-face and online. The related *cancel culture* has been adopted by conservatives as a critique of "wokeness," a term that has been replacing *political correctness* in public discourse and is often used by conservatives to condemn progressive ideas. But there is no law against hypocrisy, and it turns out that many critics of cancel culture are also leading the efforts to shut down other people's speech. A week after his RNC speech, Trump himself called for the firing – cancelling – of reporters from three networks who had confirmed Trump's Memorial Day insults to service members who were wounded or taken prisoner, or who died in action. Trump then called on his followers to harass, or cancel, the publisher of the *Atlantic,* the magazine whose editor had first exposed Trump's insults.[18] When the powerful deploy the First Amendment to gag their critics, we generally call this censorship.

In the waning days of his presidency, Trump also threatened to use the law to punish Twitter for warning readers that some of his tweets were lies. But the law that Trump invoked, section 230 of the Communications Decency Act (CDA), explicitly exempts online platforms from the regulations governing other forms of publication: "It is the policy of the United States ... to preserve the vibrant and competitive free market that presently exists for the Internet and other interactive computer services, *unfettered by Federal or State regulation.*"[19] The CDA declares that these platforms are not publishers – a declaration that defies reality, since making text available to an audience either in print or through the spoken word is the very definition of publishing. But like the publishers of books, magazines, and newspapers, who decide what content to accept and what to reject, online platforms do set rules for what users may and may not post. Section 230 shields these platforms from liability for anything their users say, a practice not followed in the European Union or in many other countries, but it also encourages these "nonpublishers" to moderate online content by explicitly permitting them to flag or delete objectionable posts. That sort of monitoring is exactly what conventional publishers must also do. The only difference is that conventional publishers are liable for the speech they publish, while section 230 exempts online platforms from such liability.

Private companies are not generally obliged to honor the speech protections of the First Amendment, but the CDA specifically frees internet platforms from any obligation to publish their users' constitutionally-protected speech. They may legally remove any posts that are "obscene, lewd, lascivious, filthy, excessively violent, harassing, or otherwise objectionable, *whether or not such material is constitutionally protected.*" The law allows online platforms to shut down bots, fake accounts, terrorist speech, pornography, and anything else that violates either the law or a site's own terms of service, and it allowed Twitter to ban extreme right-wingers like Milo Yiannopoulos, Alex Jones, and Katie Hopkins for speech violating the platform's terms of service. After January 6, Twitter banned Trump as well.

In response to policing by mainstream media platforms who insist that they are viewpoint neutral but are blamed by both the left and right for favoring the other side, specifically conservative social media sites like Gab and Parler popped up to offer a "safe space" to right-wing speakers. Gab quickly became a haven for anti-Semites and neo-Nazis.[20] Parler's home page carried the slogan, "Read news, speak free. Control your experience," but it steered users to hard-right posts from Breitbart and the Daily Caller. Like all media platforms, Parler had what appeared to be ideologically neutral rules for the speech it bans, including defamation, incitement to violence, and pornography, and, like Facebook, it adopted the Holmes–Brandeis philosophy that the way to combat bad speech is not by deplatforming, but by encouraging more speech. But Parler too was criticized for making its space safe only for far-right speech. Its popularity soared in late 2020 after mainstream platforms began clamping down on right-wing election misinformation. But Parler soon blocked users with progressive points of view, furnishing yet another demonstration that truly neutral free speech absolutism whether online or off is hard to find.[21] Given its extremist proclivities, Parler itself was forced to shut down when, after January 6, its internet hosts booted it off the web.

The willingness of online platforms to let you say what you want is at best iffy. Facebook, for one, has consistently positioned itself as a defender of free speech online. But a company-sponsored independent audit of Facebook's impact on speech and civil rights found inconsistent handling of posts containing hate speech, incitement, and harassment. The audit concluded that Facebook, the largest online platform, operated a two-tier system in which it routinely deleted posts by ordinary users for violating speech standards, while it took no action against the offensive posts of political leaders because they were deemed newsworthy. The auditors concluded, "Elevating free expression is a good thing, but it should apply to everyone. When it means that powerful politicians do not have to abide by the same rules that everyone else does, a hierarchy of speech is created that privileges certain voices over less powerful voices."[22]

When Twitter began flagging Donald Trump's "stop the steal" posts after the 2020 election, Trump retaliated with an Executive Order threatening to revoke the site's immunity from liability for "stifling free and open debate by censoring certain viewpoints."[23] Trump claimed to be a victim of cancel culture despite the fact that he retained his audience of more than 87 million Twitter followers, and he himself routinely blocked users who disagreed with him, effectively silencing their ability to speak out on matters of public concern.[24] Eventually, even though the eyeballs he drew to the site were good for business, Trump's posts proved too destructive, and Twitter finally banned him for life. Facebook and Instagram, a platform owned by Facebook, banned Trump as well. However, Trump and other conservatives were not "canceled." They continued to draw massive audiences on Fox News and One America News, as well as plenty of ink in the mainstream media. But the Communications Decency Act specifically protects sites that engage in voluntary good-faith monitoring of user posts, which means the law encourages Twitter to do exactly what Trump complained that it did.[25] As for viewpoint balancing, Twitter reported that an analysis of its algorithms showed that Twitter was actually biased *in favor of* right-wing posts.[26]

Political extremes trying to silence one another in the name of free speech is nothing new, and it is ongoing. In 2021, the Conservative Political Action Committee Conference (CPAC) in Orlando, an annual gathering of far-right Republicans, adopted as its slogan, "America Uncanceled," implying that censorship was a tactic of progressives. But almost immediately CPAC announced that it was canceling a scheduled speaker whose views turned out to be too extreme even for that extreme group. Nor did CPAC cry "cancel culture" when that canceled speaker's Twitter account was also suspended.

Conservatives have recently expanded their efforts to "protect" free speech by banning speech in classrooms as well. In a blatant example of free-speech cynicism, in early 2021 the Iowa House of Representatives passed a bill to require free-speech training for all students, faculty, and staff in all public schools and colleges: "Each institution of higher education governed by the state board of regents shall provide training on free speech under the first amendment to the Constitution of the United States to all students, faculty, and staff on an annual basis."[27] The measure states that the function of education is to encourage freedom of thought, which in turn may expose individuals to "ideas and opinions the individual finds unwelcome, disagreeable, or even offensive." But in that same session, the Iowa House banned all state agencies – including public schools – from discussing "divisive concepts" like systemic racism or race and sex "scapegoating," or from "inhibiting the first amendment rights of students or faculty."[28] The first bill guarantees *all* free speech, regardless of viewpoint, but the second bans speech on social justice issues that conservatives are eager to suppress.

The Supreme Court has long insisted that the First Amendment is viewpoint-neutral, but other states whose leadership trends conservative have proposed or enacted "free-speech" measures similar to Iowa's, supporting right-wing speech, perceived to be endangered both in the public square and in the classroom. At the same time, they justify a ban on progressive speech by claiming, with no evidence, that schools are incubators of left-leaning ideologies. Similarly, in early 2021, the UK's Minister for Education proposed a "Free Speech Champion" for students. That champion would embrace "academic freedom, liberty, and the values of the Enlightenment" in order to protect university students and staff "who may feel unable to express their cultural, religious or political views without fear of repercussion."[29] But like the legislation in Iowa, Texas, and other US states, the move by the United Kingdom bolsters pious, nationalist conservatism at the expense of liberal, nonreligious, globalist thinking. The British free-speech bill supports academic freedom in a context where "students are not disadvantaged ... if they choose not to align with a certain viewpoint." And it would allow anyone who feels they can't express their views "to seek legal redress for the loss they have suffered." A related bill would limit speech at public protests, authorizing police to intervene if demonstrations and marches are noisy enough to cause "intimidation or harassment" or "serious unease, alarm or distress" to "persons in the vicinity." The wording of the policing bill is also viewpoint-neutral, but history suggests that law enforcement agencies are more likely to favor right-wing speech, and so making the police on-site adjudicators of acceptable speech may not be the best way to protect the people's right to speak their minds.[30]

Most schools and universities imagine themselves as sites where received ideas are challenged, modified, or confirmed, and where new ideas that emerge may be similarly tested. But the current wave of free-speech legislation positions schools and universities, not as intellectual marketplaces where good ideas drive out bad, but as the potential enemies of speech, to be watched, regulated, and sued whenever a speaker feels threatened. Hopefully, no matter what controls are in place, schools will remain incubators of competing and conflicting ideas rather than bastions of orthodoxy. But even though legislation to defend speech rights is facially neutral in its claim to protect all speakers, when the law is applied it has the potential to undermine the rights of less-powerful speakers, who will be reluctant to object, and certainly less willing or able to sue, because they fear the courts will support the government's agenda. A major goal of the First Amendment to the US Constitution is to protect such critical minority speech, online or off, from government interference, and any attempt to turn the amendment against such speech could reverse the continual broadening of protections for speech on matters of public interest since the decisions in *Schenck* and *Abrams* over a century ago.

To be sure, both extremes of the political spectrum try to impose their particular straitjacket on language, making all speakers more likely to self-censor. For example, blogs and social media posts – whether innocuous or provocative – attract trolls whose actions range from crass insults to the exposure of a speaker's personal details – a process called doxing – that can be annoying, disruptive, or in extreme cases, life threatening. Social media platforms address this with limited success. As for the classroom, many instructors – conservative, progressive, and middle-of-the-road – avoid sensitive issues and refrain from using specific words, even in an instructional setting, or risk offending students, administrators, parents, legislators and other pressure groups. The erosion of faculty speech protections is highlighted in recent laws echoing Oliver Wendell

Holmes' claim that teachers may be forbidden to teach many things.[31] For example, in 2021, Tennessee, a state which banned the teaching of evolution almost a century earlier, forbade the teaching of critical race theory (CRT) or anything touching on white privilege or structural racism, in any public school, despite the fact that CRT is a complex topic typically reserved for law schools and university courses on social policy and is never taught in elementary or high school. Four years earlier, Tennessee had passed a school free-speech law claiming to protect all speech, whether liberal or conservative, radical or traditional. Now, in a move that chills free speech, any school guilty of teaching about racism could face the loss of state funding.[32]

As we see from attempts in the United States and the United Kingdom to regulate the teaching of issues related to racism, sexism, and colonialism, to the extent that language instruction itself becomes sanitized, the classroom remains a primary arena for speech regulation by conservatives. Michael Hobbes has noted that the right has become preoccupied with amplifying a small number of incidents of supposed leftist speech suppression, distorting the facts and exaggerating their impact.[33] And the Knight Foundation survey confirms that, despite the many communication platforms available to them, respondents identifying as Republican are more likely than Democrats to claim that their freedom of speech is under attack, suggesting that the right's current cancel-culture paranoia has become so loud that it is coloring their view of their own ability to say what they want.[34]

In addition, despite Supreme Court protections for political speech regardless of viewpoint, including the speech of students and teachers, the attacks on classroom speech in the United States from the ideological right seem more organized, operating on a national level, and sponsored by wealthy activists who recruit observers to videotape and publicize online and in the right-wing press the words of instructors and other speakers they tar as too far left. In the United Kingdom, similar restrictions are coming from a powerful conservative government. It is true that the left also exposes teachers and students for speech transgressions ranging from pronoun resistance, to using racial slurs, to articulating conservative ideas. This also makes headlines and causes some speakers to watch their language out of fear of exposure and retribution.

But certainly today, speech pressure from progressives seems local, spo-radic, disorganized, and without the same degree of financial backing as the efforts from the right.

The present legal landscape suggests the possibility, perhaps the like-lihood in the United States, and possibly in the United Kingdom and Europe too, that free speech has become a major rallying cry *on the extreme right* for speech suppression in a paradoxical way, as conservatives assert their own speech rights, rights that have never been in doubt, in order to suppress what they regard as competing minority speech, both in the legal and the cultural arenas. But despite any pretense that their free speech initiatives support a level playing field, objective rational discourse is never the conservative aim. They are not trying to deregu-late the marketplace of ideas, though Oliver Wendell Holmes' ideal of a free-market, rational, Socratic dialogue never existed, not even in the agora during the golden age of Greece. Historically, speech has always been an arena where the socially, politically, and economically power-ful try to rig the marketplace of ideas to limit competition and control what's on offer. Even Socrates put his thumb on the scale, structuring his dialogues to prove that he was right and his interlocutors were wrong. And to punish Socrates for promoting his brand of rational speech, his more-powerful opponents canceled him with hemlock.

## PANOPTICON 2.0 IS WATCHING YOU

Another serious threat to saying what you want today is the erosion of privacy that accompanies our growing dependence on mobile and inter-net speech, not just for political discussion, but for all our work, study, and leisure-time communication.

The digital revolution has scaled up the invasion of privacy that accompanied the increasingly sophisticated communication technol-ogies of the nineteenth and twentieth centuries. The invention of the telephone in 1875 and the portable camera in the 1880s offered new ways for people to engage one another and share experiences and ideas. At the same time, these technologies allowed snoops to access private communications, a practice with the potential to chill otherwise pro-tected speech. Telephoto lenses first appeared in 1891, and in 1912, the

London lens maker Ross began to market them in England. The next year, Scotland Yard fitted a brand-new 11-in Ross Telecentric to a camera to spy on the activities of British suffragists and put their faces on wanted posters.[35] Today's surveillance technology is subtler and more sophisticated. Governments scan CCTV and social media to monitor people just going about their business as well as engaging in political activity and actual crime. The United Kingdom has roughly one surveillance camera for every fourteen people, and the average London resident is captured by CCTV some 300 times a day. However, only a minuscule fraction of that footage actually captures illegal behavior.[36] Mass surveillance combined with facial recognition software and simple crowd-sourcing helped to identify many of the January 6 domestic terrorists assaulting the US Capitol. In the United Kingdom, CCTV was instrumental in identifying the 7/7 bombers in London in 2005, as well as the police officer who kidnapped and murdered Sarah Everard in 2021. But digital surveillance remains fallible, often misidentifying targets and potentially sweeping up the innocent along with the guilty in its dragnet. This happened when vigilantes, poring over online videos from the 2013 Boston Marathon bombing, misidentified a number of suspects, some of whom were forced into hiding though they were just faces in the crowd and had nothing to do with that day's violence.[37]

Voice technology is deployed to suppress speech as well. Immediately popular, the telephone proved a boon both for commercial speech and for social interaction. Like the portable camera, it also became a tool for surveillance. Switchboard operators regularly monitored phone conversations, disconnecting callers for swearing and canceling the service of subscribers who violated the company's terms of service. In the United States, the police began tapping telephones in order to catch criminals, an investigative process that did not yet require a warrant. Some legislators considered phone taps an invasion of privacy, but in 1916, New York City police commissioner Arthur Woods assured a Senate hearing that the innocent had nothing to fear from his department's phone surveillance: "We will not listen in on any wire except we are convinced that a crime has been committed or that there is a good chance to prevent crime."[38] That same assurance – if you've done nothing wrong, you've got nothing to fear – continues to justify government monitoring of private telephone and internet communications in both the United States and the United Kingdom.[39]

But even if you have done nothing wrong, mass surveillance of digital, video, and voice communication makes people more likely to watch their words as well as their deeds when they think they're being observed – as we saw in 1918 when the Iowa woman found guilty of speaking German on a party line swore never to use the telephone again. Promoting this self-censorship was the primary goal of Jeremy Bentham's *panopticon.*

Bentham, the eighteenth-century utilitarian philosopher who promoted the social benefits of mass surveillance, designed a circular building where those to be observed, whether prisoners, workers, patients, or students, were placed in cells or rooms arrayed along an outside wall. An "inspector" sat in a booth at the center of the circle, unseen by those being watched, but able to see them. According to Bentham, even though this inspector could not observe every resident at every moment, simply knowing that they *could be seen* would be enough to make prisoners behave and keep workers and students on task.[40] The panopticon's physical design proved impractical, but the idea that behavior could be regulated by stripping away privacy lived on. Closed-circuit television both on our streets and inside public and private spaces is the modern, subtle, and more practical version 2.0 of that first architectural panopticon.

In the post-Bentham era, surveillance technology continued to impact speech. In an influential 1890 *Harvard Law Review* essay on "The Right to Privacy," Samuel D. Warren and Louis D. Brandeis warned that two new technologies of their day, the pocket "brownie" camera and the high-speed printing press, were encouraging newspapers to photograph and report on ordinary citizens, not just public figures like politicians and celebrities. These technologies exposed what had previously been the private words and deeds of people going about their daily tasks. As Warren and Brandeis put it, "Numerous mechanical devices threaten to make good the prediction that 'what is whispered in the closet shall be proclaimed from the house-tops.'"[41]

Brandeis was appointed to the US Supreme Court in time to join Oliver Wendell Holmes' dissent in *Abrams* in 1919. Nine years later, in *Olmstead* v. *United States*, the Court found that warrantless phone taps did not violate the Fourth Amendment's protection against illegal searches. Justice Brandeis, who by then had added telephones to his list of dangerous new spy technologies, dissented once again. Reprising his argument that technology erodes privacy, Brandeis warned that unchecked government surveillance of the private lives of ordinary people would increase as even newer technologies came along: "Ways may some day be developed by which the Government, without removing papers from secret drawers, can reproduce them in court, and by which it will be enabled to expose to a jury the most intimate occurrences of the home."[42]

Brandeis' dissent in *Olmstead* prompted Congress to outlaw warrantless wiretapping. Although the government has yet to perfect its ability to see inside locked drawers or read our minds, 130 years after Warren and Brandeis sketched out a right to be let alone, an onslaught of inventions threatens to make public our words and deeds. The mobile phone, which speeds our communications and allows us to access endless amounts of information, also tracks our location and exposes our behavior in ways that we are just beginning to understand. When we visit a web site, ads for that site pop up on other sites we visit as our data is instantly sold and resold on the off-chance that we might actually buy something. Plus the "track and trace" apps designed to keep us safe during the Covid pandemic monitor where we are and who we are with, but also who might be near by, behavioral data that would make Jeremy Bentham jump for joy, if such a thing could be imagined. It is also data that the app owners readily share with law enforcement as well as marketers.[43]

It is not just phones and computers tracking our locations, recording our keystrokes, exposing our words to government surveillance, or selling our clicks to the highest bidder, it is pretty much every gadget connected to the internet of things, the IoT. A smart home promises lower utility bills and the convenience of remote control for doors, lights, heat, even the oven, fridge, and washer, but it also offers anyone who can scrape that data legally or with a hack important clues about our habits and whereabouts. A smart doorbell tells us who's there, but in exchange for that added security it captures data about us and our visitors, data that the doorbell companies turn over to police and marketers without a second thought. Our voice commands tell a smart TV to find a movie or change the channel, but the convenience of not having to dig for the remote among the couch pillows comes with a caution not to whisper anything within range of the sensors that shouldn't be "proclaimed to the house-tops." And despite legal privacy protections, the digital speakers that find just the right song or read aloud from Wikipedia seem ready to rat us out, as this recent headline suggests: "Police Think Alexa May Have Witnessed a New Hampshire Double Homicide. Now They Want Amazon to Turn Her Over."[44]

Our digital books spy on us as well. Every time we open an iBook or Kindle, an invisible reader over our shoulder tracks our behavior. Ebooks offer convenience as a trade-off for this invasion of privacy: when we download one from Apple or Amazon, the company tracks our activity, noting where we stop and opening the book to that page when we resume, even if we've switched devices. That's because our reading data is stored in the company's proprietary cloud. But while it is in that cloud, Apple and Amazon – who call themselves "content providers" rather than publishers – analyze our preferences, our annotations, what words we looked up, our reading speed in words-per-minute, and when or whether we've finished the book, all to improve our reading experience but also to suggest other titles we might want to buy. And they "share" our data with publishers keen to shape what authors write to match reader preferences.

We have come to think of reading as a consummately private activity. Librarians in the United States regularly risk jail to avoid disclosing what their patrons read, but as Amazon says in its privacy statement, which covers Kindle books as well as other Amazon services, "We release account and other personal information when we believe release is appropriate to comply with the law."[45] In George Orwell's dystopian novel *1984*, Big Brother's telescreen worked two ways. Winston Smith watches it and it watches him: "It was one of those pictures which are so contrived that the eyes follow you about when you move. BIG BROTHER IS WATCHING YOU, the caption beneath it ran."[46] In the same way, our ebooks read us as we are reading them.

In January, 2010, Facebook creator Mark Zuckerberg declared that privacy was dead, by which he meant that people were eager to broadcast on social media what they once whispered in their closets.[47] To skeptics it seemed an exaggerated and self-serving claim: Facebook's insistence that people choose to live in Panopticon 2.0 justified new ways to maximize profits by compromising user privacy. Facing a backlash, Zuckerberg eventually declared his support for personal privacy, but it may be too late. At the very least, online tracking still generates a targeted ad, and at the worst, it could expose us to trolls, spam, and spyware, not to mention an ominous midnight knock at our digitally monitored front door.

As part of their duty to keep the public safe, governments track the online footprint of suspected criminals and terrorists, increasing their surveillance in response to such atrocities as the *Charlie Hebdo* murders and the January 6 insurrection. But today's omnibus surveillance promotes a sense of guilt even among the innocent. True, we increasingly trade our privacy and anonymity for the convenience that digital communication affords, but whether it is the government or the marketing department that is watching us, the possibility of being observed makes us think twice about what we are willing to write or read online. Yes, we typically click-to-agree as we trade away our right to privacy, but we do not really have a choice. For more and more people around the world, the alternative of living off the grid is neither practical nor reasonable. Whether we are talking about the portable film cameras and landlines of the 1890s or today's smartphones and gigabit Wi-Fi, participating in a technologically enhanced world forces a loss of privacy. More and more of our words are being monitored by a growing number of public and private observers, with or without a warrant or our informed consent. 1984 has come and gone, and we are still free to think as we like, but the continual erosion of our privacy means we may be less likely to post what we think.

The law can only go so far to protect or to limit language. Some time before he killed several people and severely wounded Representative Gabrielle Giffords in Tucson, in 2011, the conspiracy-obsessed assassin posted a YouTube video claiming that the government controls our grammar. It does not.[48] Laws and regulations may try to shape language, steering it in particular directions and "correcting" speakers when they cross the line. But the impact of law on language is generally indirect – most people do not have to worry about the legal definition of obscenity or a threat, or whether they are guilty of seditious speech, or if they may use a language other than English. Most of the do's and don'ts of language, the taboos and preferences, the quirks and innovations, the common practices, and the individual idiosyncrasies, come not from law, but from the social pressures that families, friends, and communities deploy to steer linguistic behavior toward acceptable norms.

And yet, though language laws operate mostly in the background, they impact everyone. When free speech and cancel culture grab headlines, or there is a proposal to make English official, or to ban a word, or a book, or a speaker, such actions spark animated discussion, as happened recently in the context of Black Lives Matter protests, white supremacist riots, immigration reform, same-sex marriage controversies, pronoun rights, mask and vaccine mandates, the toppling of memorial statues, the "cleansing" of books in school libraries, and the use of social media both by prominent speakers and by ordinary ones as well. Not to mention the impact on our speech of privacy-busting digital technologies. The boundary between protected and unprotected speech has shifted in the past and it continues to shift today. That shift may not always promote the common good, the ideal that Sergeant Saunders emphasized centuries ago. But it is vital for everyone, for those who have been deprived of a voice as well as for the powerful, to make sure that speech protections move us toward that common good. We must ensure that our hard-fought speech rights are not reversed by extremists intent on perverting constitutions and statutes that have been designed to protect speech equitably, not absolutely. Only then will the law continue to have a positive impact on what we can and cannot say and write.

# Notes

## FOREWORD

1. For a detailed study of Webster's nationalism, see Dennis Baron, *Grammar and Good Taste: Reforming the American Language.* Yale University Press, 1982.
2. Jody Gogody and Jonathan Stempel, "Sarah Palin Loses Defamation Lawsuit against New York Times," available at: Reuters.com., February 15, 2022.

## CHAPTER 1: FREE SPEECH, BUT …

1. Bruce L. Castor, David Schoen, and Michael T. van der Veen, "Trial Memorandum of Donald J. Trump, 45th President of the United States of America." *In re: Impeachment of Former President Donald J. Trump,* February 8, 2021, pp. 37–65. The other prong to the defense was that a president can't be impeached after they are out of office, although the Senate had already rejected that argument.
2. Keith L. Alexander, "Prosecutors break down charges, convictions for 725 arrested so far in Jan. 6 attack on US Capitol," *Washington Post,* December 31, 2021.
3. Jack Brewster, "Sen. Ron Johnson on Capitol Riot: 'This Didn't Seem Like An Armed Insurrection to Me,'" *Forbes,* February 15, 2021.
4. Brittany Shammas, "A GOP Congressman Compared Capitol Rioters to Tourists. Photos Show Him Barricading a Door," *Washington Post,* May 18, 2021.
5. Republican National Committee, "Resolution to formally censure Liz Cheney and Adam Kinzinger and to no longer support them as members of the Republican Party," February 4, 2022, available at: washingtonpost.com. The Committee later claimed that the resolution's original wording referred only to protestors "that had nothing to do with violence at the Capitol," but the motion as adopted, which had been carefully vetted before the vote, did not contain that wording. Geoffrey Orr, "In Censure of Cheney and Kinzinger, RNC Calls Events of January 6 'Legitimate Political Discourse,'" available at: CNN.com, February 4, 2022.
6. Grace Seegers and Cassidy McDonald, "McConnell Says Trump Was 'Practically and Morally Responsible' for Riot after Voting Not Guilty," CBS News, February 14, 2021.

7. Although the term *heckler's veto* was coined in the 1960s, the case of *Terminiello* v. *Chicago*, 337 US 1 (1949), offers an early example. Shortly after the end of the Second World War, Terminiello delivered an angry fascist rant at a Chicago speaking engagement, causing a crowd outside to riot. The Supreme Court reversed Terminiello's conviction for disturbing the peace. Justice Douglas said in his opinion that speech fulfills "its high purpose when it induces a condition of unrest, creates dissatisfaction with conditions as they are, or even stirs people to anger."

8. Maggie Haberman, "Trump Told Crowd 'You Will Never Take Back Our Country With Weakness,'" *New York Times*, January 6, 2021 (updated January 15).

9. Sara Pauff, "Muscogee Schools: Mother Arrested for Cursing Edgewood Elementary Principal on the First Day of School," *Ledger-Enquirer* (Columbus, GA), August 10, 2010.

10. *Salinas* v. *Texas*, 133 US 2174 (2013).

11. 40 USC § 6137.

12. *District of Columbia* v. *Heller*, 554 US 570 (2008).

13. ACLU-VA 2017. Complaint for Declaratory and Injunctive Relief and Damages, available at: acluva.org.

14. City of Charlottesville, Brief in Opposition to Plaintiff's Motion for a Preliminary Injunction or Temporary Restraining Order, Civil Case No. 3:17-cv-00056-GEC, August 11, 2017, p. 13; this post, entered into the trial record, has since been removed from Facebook.

15. *Village of Skokie* v. *National Socialist Party of America*, 69 Ill. 2d 605, 619 (1978).

16. David Frum, "The Chilling Effect of Openly Displayed Firearms," *The Atlantic*, August 16, 2017, available at: atlantic.com.

17. Code of Virginia, § 18.2-282. Pointing, holding, or brandishing firearm, air- or gas-operated weapon or object similar in appearance; see at: penalty.law.lis.virginia .gov.

18. ACLU, "Shall We Defend Free Speech for Nazis in America?" New York, NY: American Civil Liberties Union, October, 1934.

19. Claire G. Gastanaga, "ACLU of Virginia Response to Governor's Allegations that ACLU Is Responsible for Violence in Charlottesville," 2017a, available at: acluva.org.

20. Joe Palazzolo, "ACLU Will No Longer Defend Hate Groups Protesting with Firearms," *Wall Street Journal*, August 17, 2017.

21. Carolyn Shapiro and Cody Jacobs, "Outlaw Firearms at Public Rallies, Demonstrations," *USA Today*, August 31, 2017.

22. Akhil Reed Amar, *America's Unwritten Constitution*. New York: Basic Books, 1994.

23. Its decision in *New York State Rifle and Pistol Association* v. *Bruen*, 20-843, is due in 2022.

24. *Nix* v. *Hedden*, 149 US 304, 1893.

25. James Madison, *Federalist* 37, "Concerning the Difficulties of the Convention in Devising a Proper Form of Government," *Daily Advertiser*, January 11, 1788, available at: www .congress.gov.

26. The historian Jonathan Gienapp has documented these and other examples of the framers' uncertainty, immediately following ratification, over the precise meaning of

the Constitution's words. Jonathan Gienapp, *The Second Creation: Fixing the American Constitution in the Founding Era*. Harvard University Press, 2018.

27. Edmund Plowden, *The Commentaries, or Reports of Edmund Plowden ... Containing, Divers Cases upon Matters of Law*. London, 1571 (rpt. 1816).

28. William Baude and Stephen E. Sachs, "The Law of Interpretation," *Harvard Law Review* 130 (2017): 1079, 1081–1149.

## CHAPTER 2: GUNS AND GRAMMAR

1. *District of Columbia* v. *Heller*, 554 US 570 (2008).

2. Dennis Baron, "Corpus Evidence Illuminates the Meaning of Bear Arms," *Hastings Constitutional Quarterly* 46(3) (2019): 509–522.

3. *Aymette* v. *State of Tennessee*, 21 Tenn., 2 Humphreys 154 (1840).

4. *English* v. *State of Texas*, 35 Tex. 473, 14 Am. Rep. 374 (1872).

5. *Nunn* v. *State of Georgia*, 1 Kelly 243 (Ga. 1846). It is not clear that Lumpkin would have extended Second Amendment rights to Georgia's enslaved population, over 691,000 people, constituting about 60 percent of the state's population according to the 1840 Census, but his wording does not exclude them. See at: www2.census.gov.

6. *Andrews* v. *State of Tennessee*, 50 Tenn. 165 (1871).

7. *United States* v. *Miller*, 307 US 174 (1939).

8. Brian Frye, "The Peculiar Story of United States v. Miller," *NYU Journal of Law and Liberty* 3 (2008): 48–82.

9. *United States* v. *Emerson*, 270 F.3d 203 (2001).

10. Theodore Olson, "In the Case of Emerson v. United States," Brief for the United States in Opposition, 2001.

11. *Silveira* v. *Lockyer*, 312 F.3d 1052 (2002).

12. *Parker et al.* v. *District of Columbia*, 478 F. 3d 370, 401 (2007).

13. Neil H. Cogan (ed.), *The Complete Bill of Rights: The Drafts, Debates, Sources, and Origins*. New York: Oxford University Press, 1997.

14. Cogan, *Complete Bill of Rights*, p. 171.

15. Baron, "Corpus Evidence Illuminates the Meaning of Bear Arms"; see also, Brigham Young University Law, Corpus Linguistics: Corpus of Early Modern English (COEME); Corpus of Founding Era American English (COFEA), 2018, available at: https://lawncl.byu.edu

16. The five databases are newspapers.com; newspaperarchive.com; britishnewspaperarchive.co.uk; Readex America's Historical Newspapers; and chroniclingamerica.loc.gov.

17. Garry Wills, "To Keep and Bear Arms," *New York Review of Books*, September 21, 1995, available at: www.nybooks.com/articles/1720.

18. Oral Arguments, *District of Columbia* v. *Heller*, 2008, pp. 36–37, available at: www.supremecourtus.gov.

19. Jeffrey L. Jones, "Public Believes Americans Have Right to Own Guns," *News Gallup*, March 27, 2008, available at: https://news.gallup.com.

20. *District of Columbia* v. *Heller*, 554 US 570 (2008).

21. Richard Posner, "In Defense of Looseness," *The New Republic*, August 27, 2008, available at: www.newrepublic.com.
22. *District of Columbia* v. *Heller* 554 US 570 (2008), emphasis added.
23. The Duke Center for Firearms Law database, available at: firearmslaw.duke.edu, contains the texts of hundreds of these early statutes.
24. *State of Vermont* v. *Max Misch*, 2021 VT 10, No. 2019-266.
25. Horace Greeley, Editorial, *New York Daily Tribune*, December 30, 1857, p. 4.
26. Eddie Izzard, "The Gun Thing," 2007, available at: http://www.youtube.com.
27. *Brandenburg* v. *Ohio*, 395 US 444 (1969).
28. For various arguments on this question, see the Brennan Center for Justice seminar "Does the 2nd Amendment Threaten the 1st?" September 14, 2021, available at: www.youtube.com.

## CHAPTER 3: A CLEAR AND PRESENT DANGER

1. *Schenck* v. *United States*, 249 US 47 (1919).
2. *Tinker* v. *Des Moines*, 393 US 503 (1969).
3. 40 USC § 5104(f).
4. *Hodge* v. *Talkin*, 13-5250 (2015), US Court of Appeals, District of Columbia Circuit.
5. Supreme Court Regulation 7 (approved 2013), available at: www.supremecourt.gov.
6. United Kingdom Protection of Freedoms Act, 2012, available at: www.legislation.gov.uk.
7. "Freedom of Expression and Information," Article 11, European Charter of Fundamental Rights. *Official Journal of the European Union* C 303/17 – 14.12.2007, 2007, available at: fra.europa.eu/en/eu-charter.
8. "'Act of War': New Charlie Hebdo Edition Triggers Muslims' Anger, Threats," January 14, 2015, available at: www.rt.com.
9. Polly Toynbee, "On Charlie Hebdo Pope Francis is Using the Wife-Beater's Defence," *The Guardian*, January 16, 2015.
10. Eric Conan, "Que Reste-t-il de 'l'Esprit du 11 Janvier'?" *Marianne*. February 11, 2015.
11. Salman Rushdie, Speech at the University of Vermont. January 14, 2015. Associated Press video, available at: www.youtube.com.
12. Emmanuel Todd, *Qui est Charlie?* Paris: Seuil, 2015.
13. Garry Trudeau, "The Abuse of Satire," *The Atlantic*, April 11, 2015.
14. 2015 PEN/TONI and James C. Goodale, Freedom of Expression Courage Award, March 27, 2015, available at: https://pen.org.
15. Glenn Greenwald, "204 PEN Writers (Thus Far) Have Objected to the Charlie Hebdo Award – Not Just 6," available at: theintercept.com, April 30, 2015.
16. Rushdie commented on the PEN blog, "Courage in Continuing," April 27, 2015, available at: pen.com; Adam Gopnik, "PEN Has Every Right to Honor Charlie Hebdo," *The New Yorker*, April 27, 2015.
17. Dominique Sopo, "Message à Ceux Qui Ne Veulent Pas 'Être Charlie' Prétextant que Charlie Est Raciste et Islamophobe," 2015, available at: https://sos-racisme.org.

18. Jennifer Scheussler, "After Protests, Charlie Hebdo Members Receive Standing Ovation at PEN Gala," *New York Times*, May 6, 2015.

19. Alex Griswold, "Media that Censored *Charlie Hebdo*'s Muhammad have No Problem With Terrorist God Cover," available at: mediaite.com, January 7, 2016; Sydney Smith, "Charlie Hebdo's Anniversary Cartoon of God: Associated Press and Others not Using 'L'Assassin Court Toujours' Cover Image," available at: iMediaEthics.org, January 8, 2016.

20. Sedition Act, 1798, s. 2; *US Statutes at Large*, vol. I, pp. 596–597.

21. Debate on the Sedition Act in the House of Representatives, *Annals of Congress*, 5th Congress, 2nd Session, July 10, 1798: 2139–2172.

22. Gordon T. Belt, "The Sedition Act of 1798: a Brief History of Arrests, Indictments, Mistreatment and Abuse," First Amendment Center, 2011, available at: www.firstamendmentcenter.org.

23. Robert M. La Follette, "Free Speech in Wartime," 65th *Congressional Record* 1st Session: 787–786, October 6, 1917.

24. Espionage Act, 1917.

25. Sedition Act, 1918. Amendment to Section 3 of the Espionage Act of June 15, 1917. United States, *Statutes at Large*, Washington, DC, 1918, vol. XL, pp 553 ff.

26. Clyde E. Willis, *Students Guide to Landmark Congressional Laws on the First Amendment*. Westport, CT: Greenwood, 2002, p. 23.

27. Zechariah Chaffee, "Freedom of Speech in War Time," *Harvard Law Review* 32 (1919): 932–973.

28. Michael Selig, "United States v. Motion Picture Film The Spirit of '76," *Journal of Popular Film and Television* 10(4) (2013): 168–174.

29. *United States v. The Spirit of '76*, 252 F. 946 (S.D. Cal. 1917), at 948; it was common in the early days of film to refer to movies as "plays," and we still refer to movie scripts as "screenplays."

30. Indictment, National Archives id. 7595374; *United States v. Masses Publishing Company* 252 F. 232 (1918).

31. Floyd Dell, "Story of the *Masses* Trial," *The Liberator*, June, 1918, pp. 7–18.

32. Dell, "Story of the *Masses* Trial," p. 7.

33. *Masses v. Patten*, 244 F. 535 (1917). Learned Hand, the judge in the *Masses* injunction trial, was the cousin of Augustus Hand, the judge in the *Masses* conspiracy trial.

34. *Masses v. Patten*, p. 538

35. *Masses v. Patten*, p. 539.

36. *Masses v. Patten*, p. 540.

37. *United States v. Masses Publishing Company*, 252 F. 232 (1918).

38. Geoffrey R. Stone, "Judge Learned Hand and the Espionage Act of 1917: A Mystery Unraveled," *University of Chicago Law Review* 70 (2003): 335–358.

39. *Debs v. United States*, 249 US 211 (1919).

40. Art Young, *The Masses*, August, 1917, p. 33.

41. Charles Schenck, "Wake Up America," 1918. National Archives, available at: http://recordsofrights.org. Several examples are reprinted in *Schenck v. United States*, 249 US 47 (1919), Transcript of Record, File Date: 5/3/1918.

42. Schenck, "Wake Up America," verso.

43. Henry J. Gibbons and Henry John Nelson, "Brief for Plaintiffs in Error," *Schenck* v. *United States*, 1918, pp. 10–11.

44. Willis, *Students Guide to Landmark Congressional Laws on the First Amendment*, p. 21; Stephen M. Feldman, *Free Expression and Democracy in America: A History*. Chicago: University of Chicago Press, 2008, p. 250.

45. *United States* v. *Zimmerman*, cited by Henry J. Gibbons and Henry John Nelson, "Brief for Plaintiffs in Error," *Schenck* v. *United States*, 1918, pp. 10–11.

46. Supreme Court of the United States, Transcript of Record, *Charles T. Schenck* v. *The United States of America*, Washington, DC, May 22, 1918, pp. 42–43.

47. *United States* v. *Eastman et al.*, April 25, 1918, cited by Gibbons and Nelson 1918, p. 13.

48. *Schenck* v. *United States*, 249 US 47 (1919), p. 51.

49. *Schenck* v. *United States*, p. 52; emphasis added; internal citations omitted.

50. The Sedition Act, "An Act To Amend Section Three, Title One, of the Act Entitled 'An Act to Punish Acts of Interference with the Foreign Relations, the Neutrality, and the Foreign Commerce of the United States, to Punish Espionage, and Better to Enforce the Criminal Laws of the United States, and for Other Purposes, Approved June Fifteenth, Nineteen Hundred and Seventeen,' and for Other Purposes," 65th Congress, Session II, Ch. 75, 1918, 40 Statutes: 553–554. Approved, May 16, 1918.

51. Zechariah Chaffee, "A Contemporary State Trial: The United States Versus Jacob Abrams et al.," *Harvard Law Review* 33 (1920): 747–774.

52. Translation of the leaflet by Dr. Chana Kronfeld, in Richard Polenberg, *Fighting Faiths: The Abrams Case, the Supreme Court, and Free Speech*. Ithaca, NY: Cornell University Press, 1987, p. 54; this translation differs from the more militant and less-accurate translation made for the trial court.

53. "Free Speech Does Not Protect Disloyalty," *The New York Times*, September 13, 1918, p. 15.

54. Chaffee, "A Contemporary State Trial," p. 761.

55. "Long Prison Terms for the Bolsheviki," *New York Times*, October 26, 1918, p. 18.

56. Transcript of Record, *Jacob Abrams et al. v. United States*, Supreme Court of the United States, October Term, 1918, p. 243.

57. *Abrams* v. *United States*, 250 US 616 (1919).

58. *Abrams*, Dissent, p. 628.

59. *Abrams*, Dissent, pp. 628–629.

60. *Abrams*, Dissent, p. 629.

61. *Abrams*, Dissent, p. 630.

62. *Whitney* v. *California*, 274 US 357 (1927), at 374; Holmes joined Brandeis in the concurrence.

63. *Brandenburg* v. *Ohio*, 395 US 444, 447 (1969).

64. *Whitney* v. *California*, Opinion, p. 371.

65. *Whitney* v. *California*, J. Brandeis concurring, pp. 375–376.

66. *Whitney* v. *California*, p. 377; emphasis added.

67. The Smith Act. An Act To Prohibit Certain Subversive Activities; to Amend Certain Provisions of Law with Respect to the Admission and Deportation of Aliens; to Require the Fingerprinting and Registration of Aliens; and for Other Purposes. *US Statutes at Large*, vol. 54, ch. 439, June 28, 1940, pp. 670–676.

68. *United States* v. *Dennis*, 183 F.2d 201 (1950).

69. *Dennis* v. *United States*, 341 US 491 (1951).

70. *Brandenburg* v. *Ohio*, 395 US 444 (1969).

71. Ohio Rev. Code Ann. § 2923.13.

72. *Brandenburg*, 395 US 444 (1969), at 447.

73. *Kashiya Nwanguma et al.* v. *Donald J. Trump et al.*, Civil Action No. 3:16-cv-247-DJH. Louisville Division, US District Court, Western District of Kentucky (2016).

74. *Nwanguma et al.* v. *Donald J. Trump et al.*, File No. 18a0202p 06, US Court of Appeals for the Sixth Circuit, September 11, 2018.

75. *Lander* v. *Seaver*, 32 Vt. 114 (1859).

76. *Tinker* v. *Des Moines Independent Community School District*, 393 US 503 (1969).

77. *Meyer* v. *Nebraska*, 262 US 390 (1923).

78. *Bethel School District No. 403 et al.* v. *Fraser, a Minor, et al.*, 478 US 675 (1986).

79. *Cohen* v. *California*, 403 US 15 (1971).

80. *Hazelwood School District et al.* v. *Kuhlmeier et al.*, 484 US 260 (1988).

81. *Morse* v. *Frederick*, 127 US 2618 (2007).

82. *Heidi Zamecnik and Alexander Nuxoll* v. *Indian Prairie School District #294 et al.*, 636 F.3d 874 (2011).

83. *Mahanoy Area School District* v. *B. L., a Minor, by and through Her Father, Levy et al.*, No. 20-255, 2021.

## CHAPTER 4: STRONG LANGUAGE

1. Martin Fricker, "Foul-Mouthed Yob Banned from Swearing in Public Anywhere in Britain," *The Mirror*, July 14, 2016, available at: www.mirror.co.uk.

2. "Q675: Can a Person Be Arrested for Just Swearing in the Street?" available at: www.askthe.police.uk/content/Q675.htm.

3. Lauren Collins, "The Pub that Banned Swearing," *The New Yorker*, January 15, 2018.

4. *Wisconsin* v. *Breitzman*, Wisconsin Court of Appeals, District 1, 2015AP1610-CR, August 16, 2016. The conversation was overheard and reported by someone her son was talking with on the phone.

5. Evann Gastaldo, "Mom Arrested for Swearing in Front of Kids," *USA Today*, August 15, 2014.

6. *People* v. *Bruce*, Municipal Court for San Francisco and San Francisco County F54134, March 5, 1962.

7. *Cohen* v. *California*, 403 US 15 (1971).

8. *Jacobellis* v. *Ohio*, 378 US 184 (1964) (emphasis added).

9. Cary G. Osborn, "Banned Books in New Mexico," *Donaana County Historical Society Historical Review* 2013: 23–26.

10. Alison Flood, "'Oral Sex' Definition Prompts Dictionary Ban in US Schools," *The Guardian*, January 25, 2010.

11. Reed Smoot, Bronson Cutting, et al., Senate Debates on the Smoot–Hawley Tariff, 71–72 *Congressional Record*, 1929–1930, p. 5498. To be fair, the survey found that the dictionary was the second most-common introduction to sex.

12. Noah Webster, *The Holy Bible, Containing the Old and New Testaments, in the Common Version. with Amendments of the Language.* New Haven, CT: Durrie & Peck, 1833.

13. David Cressy, *Literacy and the Social Order: Reading and Writing in Tudor and Stuart England.* Cambridge: Cambridge University Press, 1980.

14. Samuel Smith, "Corrupt Literature," Debate in the House of Commons, Hansard, HC Deb 08, May 8, 1888, vol. 325, cc1707–1725.

15. Anthony Cummins, "Emile Zola's Cheap English Dress: The Vizetelly Translations, late-Victorian Print Culture, and the Crisis of Literary Value," *Review of English Studies* NS 60(243) (2008): 108–132.

16. *Regina* v. *Hicklin*, L.R. 3 Q.B. 360 (1868).

17. The Vizetelly press cuttings summarized here, along with a synopsis of the hearing, were published by the National Vigilance Association in a pamphlet, *Pernicious Literature: Debate in the House of Commons; Trial and Conviction for Sale of Zola's Novels,* 1889.

18. Samuel Smith, "Pernicious Literature," *The Standard,* July 28, 1888, rpt. in National Vigilance Association, pp. 28–29.

19. "An act relating to the postal laws," Statutes at Large, vol. 13, 38th Congress, 1st Session; ch. LXXIX, sec. 16, p. 507; March 3, 1865.

20. The Comstock Act, officially known as "An Act for the Suppression of Trade in, and Circulation of, Obscene Literature and Articles of Immoral Use," 42nd Congress, Session III, ch. 258, pp. 598–600. Approved March 3, 1873.

21. Stephen M. Feldman, *Free Expression and Democracy in America: A History.* Chicago: University of Chicago Press, 2008, p. 213.

22. Reed Smoot, Bronson Cutting, et al., 1929–1930, *Congressional Record,* October 10, 1929, p. 4433.

23. Paul S. Boyer, *Purity in Print: Book Censorship in America from the Gilded Age to the Computer Age.* Madison: University of Wisconsin Press, 2002.

24. Reed Smoot, Bronson Cutting, et al., Senate Debates on the Smoot–Hawley Tariff. 71–72 *Congressional Record,* 1929–1930, pp. 4433–4472; 5375–5520.

25. 71–72 *Congressional Record,* p. 4433.

26. 71–72 *Congressional Record,* p. 4435.

27. 71–72 *Congressional Record,* p. 4446.

28. 71–72 *Congressional Record,* p. 4470.

29. 71–72 *Congressional Record,* p. 5414.

30. 71–72 *Congressional Record,* p. 5414.

31. 71–72 *Congressional Record,* p. 5416.

32. 71–72 *Congressional Record.*

33. 71–72 *Congressional Record,* p. 5417.

34. 71–72 *Congressional Record,* pp. 5418–5419.

35. 71–72 *Congressional Record,* pp. 5431–5432.

36. 71–72 *Congressional Record.*

37. 71–72 *Congressional Record,* pp. 5432–5433.

38. 71–72 *Congressional Record,* p. 5490.

39. 71–72 *Congressional Record,* p. 5494.

40. Boyer, *Purity in Print*, p. 226.

41. 71–72 *Congressional Record*, p. 5493.

42. 71–72 *Congressional Record*, p. 5498.

43. 71–72 *Congressional Record*, p. 5509.

44. *United States* v. *One Book Called "Ulysses"*, 5 F.Supp. 182 (S.D.N.Y., 1933).

45. Obscene Publications Act of 1959, UK Public General Acts, 1959, c. 66 (7–8 Eliz 2).

46. Obscene Publications Act of 1959, sec. 1 [1] (emphasis added).

47. *Regina* v. *Penguin Books Ltd.*, Crim. L.R. 176 (1960); also known as *Queen* v. *Penguin Books Ltd.*

48. C. H. Rolph (ed.), *The Trial of Lady Chatterley*. Harmondsworth and Baltimore, MD: Penguin Books, 1961.

49. Rolph, *The Trial of Lady Chatterley*, p. 17.

50. Mollie Panter-Downs, "The Lady at the Old Bailey," *The New Yorker*, November 19, 1960.

51. Roy Jenkins, "Lady Chatterley," *The Spectator*, August 26, 1960, p. 307.

52. *Grove Press, Inc.* v. *Christenberry*, 175 F.Supp. 488 (S.D.N.Y. 1959).

53. *Roth* v. *United States*, 354 US 476 (1957).

54. *Miller* v. *California*, 413 US 15 (1973), at 24.

55. WorldCat lists a few libraries holding one or two very early issues, and a seller on eBay is asking $49.99 for a copy of the July, 1929, number. *Jim Jam Jems* apparently ceased publication some time between 1929 and 1930.

56. Michelle Pautz, "The Decline in Average Weekly Cinema Attendance: 1930–2000," *Issues in Political Economy* 11 (2002): n.p., available at: http://org.elon.edu/ipe/pautz2.pdf.

57. "Say Picture Shows Corrupt Children," *New York Times*, December 24, 1908, p. 4.

58. *Federal Motion Picture Commission Briefs*, Washington, DC: Government Printing Office, 1916, p. 41.

59. Samantha Barbas, "How the Movies Became Speech," *Rutgers Law Review* 64(3) (2012): 665–745.

60. *Mutual Film Corporation* v. *Industrial Commission of Ohio*, 236 US 230 (1915).

61. *Burstyn* v. *Wilson*, 343 US 495 (1952).

62. A Bill to Establish an Official National Censorship of Motion Pictures in Interstate and Foreign Commerce and in the District of Columbia and the Territories and All Other Places under National Jurisdiction, S. 4941, s. 4; 51 *Congressional Record*, March 18, 1914, p. 5022.

63. *Federal Motion Picture Commission Briefs*, Washington, DC: Government Printing Office, 1916, p. 11.

64. *Federal Motion Picture Commission Hearings*, Washington, DC: Government Printing Office, 1934, p. 33.

65. *Federal Motion Picture Commission Hearings*, Washington, DC: Government Printing Office, 1916, p. 9.

66. Brief of the Motion Picture Board of Trade; *Federal Motion Picture Commission Briefs*, Washington, DC: Government Printing Office, 1916, p. 20.

67. *Federal Motion Picture Commission Hearings*, 1916, p. 75.

68. *Federal Motion Picture Commission Hearings*, 1916, p. 78.

69. Report of the Chicago Motion Picture Censorship Commission, 1920, p. 183.

70. Report of the Chicago Motion Picture Censorship Commission, 1920, pp. 121, 131–140.

71. A Bill to Create a Commission to Be Known as the Federal Motion Picture Commission, and Defining Its Powers and Duties, H. R. 6821, 68th Congress, 1st Session, introduced February 9, 1924, pp. 9–11.

72. Ibid., pp. 11–12.

73. 68 *Congressional Record*, February 14, 1925, p. 3742.

74. 67 *Congressional Record*, July 2, 1926, p. 12842.

75. A Bill to Protect the Motion-Picture Industry ... and to Provide for the Manufacture of Wholesome Motion Pictures, H.R. 9986. 72 *Congressional Record*, March 25, 1930, p. 6105.

76. 72 *Congressional Record*, May 26, 1930, p. 9606.

77. Report, Chicago Motion Picture Censorship Commission, 1920, p. 124.

78. A Bill to Create a Commission to Be Known as the Federal Motion Picture Commission, p. 51. See also, A Bill to Protect the Motion-Picture industry ... to Provide for the Manufacture of Wholesome Motion Pictures, both Silent and Talking, at the Sources of Production; to Create a Federal Motion Picture Commission, to Define Its Powers; and for Other Purposes, H.R. 9986, 71st Congress, 2nd Session, introduced February 17, 1930, pp. 27–28.

79. 67 *Congressional Record*, December 19, 1925, p. 1192; see also, 72 *Congressional Record*, May 26, 1930, p. 9606.

80. *Federal Motion Picture Commission Hearings*, 1934, p. 3 (emphasis added).

81. Will Hays, "Code to Govern the Making of Talking, Synchronized and Silent Motion Pictures," 1930, Preamble, III.

82. Barbas, "How the Movies Became Speech," p. 707.

83. David. O. Selznick, *Memo from David O. Selznick*, ed. Rudy Behrman (New York: Viking, 1972). Reprinted in *Letters of Note*, available at: www.lettersofnote.com/2012/02/damn.html.

84. The exception was added on November 1, 1939, one week after Selznick appealed, though Hays fined Selznick $5,000 for violating the code, see at: https://production-code.dhwritings.com.

85. US Supreme Court Transcript of Record, No. 456, April 22, 1914.

86. 44 *United States Statutes at Large*, Stat. 1172; quoted in *Pacifica* v. *Federal Communications Commission*, 438 US 736 (1978), at 735.

87. *Pacifica* v. *FCC*, at 746.

88. *Federal Communications Commission* v. *Fox*, 567 US 239 (2012), Oral Arguments, January 10, 2012, p. 23.

89. *FCC* v. *Fox*, Oral Arguments, p. 27.

## CHAPTER 5: THREAT LEVEL: ORANGE

1. *Elonis* v. *United States*, 135 US 2001 (2015).

2. Matthew P. Doyle, Tweet, March 23, 2016. @MatthewDoyle31.

3. "Man Charged after Tweet 'Confronting Muslim Woman' on Brussels Attacks," *The Guardian*, March 25, 2016.

4. Crown Prosecution Service, "Social Media: Guidelines on Prosecuting Cases Involving Communications Sent via Social Media," revised August 21, 2018, available at: www.cps .gov.uk.

5. Naomi LaChance, "After Dallas Shootings, Police Arrest People for Criticizing Cops on Facebook and Twitter," *The Intercept*, July 12, 2016, available at: https://theintercept .com; Matt Mahoney, "Norwalk Man Posts Threats to Police on Social Media," Fox61 .com. July 10, 2016.

6. Justin Jouvenal, "A 12-Year-Old Girl is Facing Criminal Charges for Using Certain Emoji. She's not Alone," *Washington Post*, February 27, 2016, A1.

7. Diana Crandall, "Feminist Columnist Jessica Valenti Quits Social Media after Trolls Threaten to Rape her 5-Year-Old Daughter," *New York Daily News*, July 27, 2016.

8. Twitter, Rules and Policies, 2020, available at: https://help.twitter.com/en/ rules-and-policies/twitter-rules.

9. Twitter, Terms of Service, 2020, available at: https://twitter.com/tos?lang=en#restrictions.

10. Amanda Lenhart et al., *Online Harassment, Digital Abuse, and Cyberstalking in America*, Data and Society Research Institute and the Center for Innovative Public Health Research, 2016.

11. "Evergreen Park Woman Accused of Threatening to Shoot Cops in Facebook Post," *Chicago Tribune*, July 8, 2016.

12. George Hunter, "Detroit Police Arrest Four for Threats Against Cops," *Detroit News*, July 11, 2016.

13. Clarence Thomas, J., Dissent, *Elonis* v. *United States*, 135 US 2001 (2015).

14. *Watts* v. *United States*, 394 US 705 (1969).

15. Charles Slack, *Liberty's First Crisis: Adams, Jefferson, and the Misfits Who Saved Free Speech*. New York: Atlantic Monthly Press, 2015.

16. *Herald of Liberty* (Washington, PA), November 3, 1800, p. 3.

17. Presidential Threat Law, "An Act to Punish Persons Who Make Threats against the President of the United States," 64th Congress, Session II, p. 919, approved February 14, 1917 (emphasis added); now expanded and amended in 18 USC § 871 to cover threats against the vice president, the president-elect, and others in the presidential line of succession.

18. *United States* v. *Stickrath*, 242 F. 151 (1917).

19. Untitled News Article, *Dayton Daily News*, May 10, 1917, p. 15; "Uttered against President," *Fulton County Tribune*, July 6, 1917, p. 6.

20. *United States* v. *Metzdorf*, 252 F. 933 (1918).

21. *Ragansky* v. *United States*, 253 F. 643, 645 (1918); the trial transcript has disappeared, but the appeal recounts the details. Ragansky, whose other details are unknown, is identified in contemporary newspaper reports of the trial as "a Lithuanian."

22. *Ragansky* v. *United States*, 1918 (emphasis added).

23. *Watts* v. *United States*, 394 US 705 (1969).

24. Stuart Auerbach, "Grand Jury Will Sift Case of Threat to LBJ," *Washington Post,* August 30, 1966, p. A8.
25. *Watts* v. *United States,* 402 F.2d 676 (1968).
26. *Watts* v. *United States* (1968).
27. Edwin Webb, Remarks in Debate on the Presidential Threat Bill, 53 *Congressional Record,* p. 9377, 1916.
28. Webb, 53 *Congressional Record,* p. 9378.
29. *Clark* v. *United States,*250 F. 449 (1918).
30. *Watts* v. *United States,* 394 US 705 (1969).
31. *Elonis* v. *United States,* 135 US 2001 (2015).
32. 18 USC § 875 (c).
33. Editorial Board, "The Court and Online Threats," *New York Times,* June 1, 2015.
34. Oral Arguments, *Elonis* v. *United States,* December 1, 2014, p. 59.
35. Brief for the United States in Opposition to Petition for *Certiorari, Elonis* v. *United States,* 2014, p. 3.
36. Opposition to Petition for *Certiorari, Elonis* v. *United States,* p. 8.
37. Oral Arguments, *Elonis* v. *United States,* December 1, 2014, p. 59.
38. Brief for the Petitioner, *Elonis* v. *United States,* p. 55.
39. Oral Arguments, *Elonis* v. *United States,* p. 27.
40. Oral Arguments, *Elonis* v. *United States,* p. 46.
41. Oral Arguments, *Elonis* v. *United States,* p. 53.
42. Brief for the Petitioner, *Elonis* v. *United States,* pp. 21–22.
43. Oral Arguments, *Elonis* v. *United States,* p. 4.
44. *Abrams* v. *United States,* 250 US 616 (1919).
45. Third Circuit Court of Appeals Rehearing, *Elonis* v. *United States;* Oral Arguments, 2016, (tape) beginning at 15:40.
46. Third Circuit Court of Appeals Rehearing, *Elonis* v. *United States,* beginning at 35:30.
47. Third Circuit Court of Appeals; Opinion, *Elonis* v. *United States,* 2016, p. 16.
48. Third Circuit Court of Appeals; Opinion, *Elonis* v. *United States,* pp. 18–20.
49. Brent Kendall, "Man in Facebook Threat Case Scrutinized for Note to Prosecutor," *Wall Street Journal,* December 2, 2014.
50. *Virginia* v. *Black,* 538 US 343 (2003).
51. Interstate Threats Clarification Act of 2016, S.2552.
52. Manny Fernandez and Ashley Southall, "Dallas Gunman Killed after Attack on Police Headquarters," *New York Times,* June 13, 2015.
53. Jackie Alemany, Emma Brown, Alice Crites, Tom Jackman, Tom Hamburger, Peter Hermann, Spencer S. Hsu, Isaac Stanley-Becker, Julie Tate, Elise Viebeck, and Cleve Wootson, "Red Flags," *Washington Post,* October 31, 2021.
54. Sean Sullivan and Isaac Stanley-Becker, "Trump Appears to Encourage Gun Owners to Take Action if Clinton Appoints Anti-Gun Judges," *Washington Post,* August 9, 2016.
55. Michael Crowley, "Trump's Long Dalliance with Violent Rhetoric," *Politico,* August 10, 2016, available at: www.politico.com; Kate Somers-Dawes, "All the Times Trump Has Called for Violence at His Rallies," Mashable.com, March 12, 2016.

56. Crowley, "Trump's Long Dalliance with Violent Rhetoric."

57. Tweet, @realDonaldTrump, August 9, 2016.

58. Customs and Border Protection, available at: www.cbp.gov/about.

59. Department of Homeland Security, "Analyst's Desktop Binder," 2011, available at: https://epic.org/foia/epic-v-dhs-media-monitoring/Analyst-Desktop-Binder-RE-DACTED.pdf.

60. "Caution on Twitter Urged as Tourists Barred from US," British Broadcasting Corporation, March 8, 2012, available at: www.bbc.com/news/technology-16810312.

61. Emily Banting, "A Tweet Got Me Deported," *The Sun*, January 17, 2012, p. 15.

62. Richard Hartley-Parkinson, "'I'm Going to Destroy America and Dig up Marilyn Monroe,'" *Daily Mail*, January 31, 2012.

63. Andrew Parker, "US Tweeted Us like Terrorists; Held for Twitter Jokes," *The Sun*, January 30, 2012, p. 17.

64. Leigh Bryan, "Tweetorists," July 26, 2016, available at: www.youtube.com.

## CHAPTER 6: AMERICA'S WAR ON LANGUAGE

1. Frederick C. Luebke, "Legal Restrictions on Foreign Languages in the Great Plains States 1917–1923," in *Languages in Conflict*, ed. Paul Schach. Lincoln, NE: University of Nebraska Press, 1980, pp. 1–19.

2. Trading with the Enemy Act. An Act To Define, Regulate, and Punish Trading with the Enemy, and for Other Purposes, 65th Congress, ch. 106, sec. 19, pp. 425–426, enacted October 6, 1917. *United States Statutes at Large.*

3. "To Strike Germany from Map of US," *New York Times*, June 2, 1918, p. 56.

4. *Daily Gate City and Constitution-Democrat*, Keokuk, Iowa, June 12, 1918, p. 5, citing the *Des Moines Register*.

5. "Michaelis of U.S. Throws off Name," *Tampa Times*, August 15, 1917, p. 2.

6. Advertisement, *The Plain Speaker*, Hazleton, PA, September 7, 1918, p. 5.

7. "Liberty Measles at West Point," *New York Times*, February 8, 1918. Contrast this to the current demonization of disease, from the "Asian flu" epidemic of the 1950s to the more recent outbreaks of "Ebola" and the "Wuhan" or "China" virus.

8. Cheryl Gay Stolberg, "An Order of Fries Please, but Do Hold the 'French,'" *New York Times*, March, 12, 2003, p. A1.

9. Richard (Lord) Acton, *To Go Free: A Treasury of Iowa's Legal Heritage*. Ames: Iowa State University Press, 1995.

10. Steven Wrede, "The Americanization of Scott County 1914–1918," *Annals of Iowa* 44 (1979): 627–638.

11. Acton, *To Go Free*, p. 225.

12. William L. Harding, 1918. Proclamation. Iowa City: Iowa State Archives, May 23, 1918.

13. "Harding's Edict Closes Churches," Ottumwa *Semi-weekly Courier*, June 4, 1918, p. 1.

14. "One Language Idea Popular," *Quad-City Times*, Davenport, Iowa, June 2, 1918, p. 19. According to Luebke, "Legal Restrictions on Foreign Languages in the Great Plains States 1917–1923,"similar sentiments were voiced by rabid patriots in Oklahoma as well.

15. "Harding Explains Edict," *Evening Times-Republican*, Marshalltown, Iowa, June 3, 1918, p. 3.

16. Nancy Derr, "Babel Proclamation," *Palimpsest* 60(4) (July/August, 1979): 98–115.

17. "Fine 4 Women for Speaking German Tongue," *Quad-City Times*, Davenport, Iowa, June 14, 1918, p. 6.

18. "Topics of the Times," *Times-Republican*, Marshalltown, Iowa, July 5, 1918, p. 6.

19. "Colonel for 'Knockout,'" *New York Times*, May 28, 1918, p. 8.

20. Judd Legum and Aaron Rupar, "Rep. King Designs Electrified Fence for Southern Border: 'We Do This with Livestock All the Time,'" *Think Progress*, July 13, 2006, available at: https://archive.thinkprogress.org. King was eventually voted out of office for his extremist views.

21. "Marshal Foch and the Law," *New York Times*, July 30, 1921, p. 6.

22. See, for example, the letter from Mrs. M. Leon, "Why German-Jargon (Yiddish) Should Stop," *The Modern View*, St. Louis, MO, July 12, 1918, p. 6.

23. "Only One Language Here," *The American Israelite*, rpt. in the *Kansas City* (MO) *Times*, August 31, 1918, p. 12.

24. A Bill To Define the National and Official Language of the Government and People of the United States of America, H.R. 14136, 67th Congress, 4th Session. Introduced by Washington Jay McCormick (R., Montana) on February 1, 1923, and referred to the Committee on the Judiciary, where it languished. For McCormick's "mental emancipation of '23," see "Language by Legislation," *The Nation*, April 11, 1923, p. 408.

25. An Act Establishing the American Language as the Official Language of the State of Illinois, S.B. 15, approved June 19, 1923. *Revised Statutes of the State of Illinois Embracing All General Laws of the State of Illinois in Force July 1, 1923*, ch. 17b, p. 234.

26. "It's legal – We Speak English," *Chicago Tribune*, September 24, 1969, p. 3.

27. Ulysses S. Grant, Eighth Annual Message to Congress, December 5, 1876, available at: www.presidency.ucsb.edu.

28. An Act To Establish a Bureau of Immigration and Naturalization, and to Provide for a Uniform Rule for the Naturalization of Aliens Throughout the United States, United States Statutes at Large, 59th Congress, Session I 1906; ch. 3592, sec. 8, p. 599; approved June 29, 1906.

29. Ibid., "Petition for Naturalization," p. 604.

30. Charles McNary, Memorial, 64 *Congressional Record*, February 19, 1923, pp. 3931–3932.

31. Kenneth McKellar, 65 *Congressional Record*, April 9, 1924, pp. 5958–5959.

32. John Shields, 65 *Congressional Record*, April 16, 1924, pp. 6461–6462.

33. A Bill to Regulate Immigration and Insure the Use of the English Language by Those Coming to the United States; H.R. 4089, introduced by Walter Lineberger, December 20, 1923.

34. An Act To Revise and Codify the Nationality Laws of the United States into a Comprehensive Nationality Code, H.R. 9980, October 14, 1940; sec. 304, *United States Statutes at Large*, 76th Congress, ch. 876, p. 1140.

35. An Act To Amend the Immigration and Nationality Act, and for Other Purposes. PL 89-236, October 3, 1965, 79 *United States Statutes at Large*, pp. 911–922.

36. Kenji Hakuta, *Mirror of Language*.New York: Basic Books, 1986.

37. *Meyer* v. *Nebraska*, 262 US 390 (1923).

38. Israel Zangwill, *The Melting-Pot.* New York: Macmillan, 1909.

39. Woodrow Wilson, "Americanism and the Foreign Born," Address at Convention Hall, Philadelphia, May 10, 1915.

40. Woodrow Wilson, "Address of President Wilson to the Citizenship Convention," Washington, DC, July 13, 1916.

41. Franklin K. Lane, "What America Means," *Americanization Bulletin* 1(6) (February 1, 1919), pp. 2, 4, 8.

42. "Americanization Division on the 'Melting Pot' Phrase," *Americanization Bulletin* 1(6) (February 1, 1919), p. 7.

43. This and other statements about the Club's language efforts come from the unpublished archives of the Chicago Woman's Club held by the Chicago History Museum.

44. "Guide to American Speech Week," National Council of Teachers of English, Chicago (1919) 1921, p. 32.

45. Governor Henry Allen (Kansas), in "Guide to American Speech Week," National Council of Teachers of English, Chicago (1919) 1921, pp. 16–17.

46. Dennis Baron, *The English-Only Question: An Official Language for Americans?* New Haven, CT: Yale University Press, 1990, p. 171.

47. *Lau* v. *Nichols*, 414 US 563 (1974).

48. Office of Civil Rights, "Identification of Discrimination and Denial of Services on the Basis of National Origin," *Federal Register* 35(139) (June 18, 1970): 11595–11596.

49. SB 1174 (Chapter 753, Statutes of 2014), English Language Education, California Proposition 58, Non-English Languages Allowed in Public Education (2016), available at: https://ballotpedia.org.

50. Letter from Principal Sr. Margaret Nugent, Exhibit A, *Adam Silva et al.* v. *St. Anne Catholic School, Wichita, Kansas et al.*, Complaint, 08-1143-JTM (2008).

51. Letter from Principal Sr. Margaret Nugent, Exhibit B, *Adam Silva et al.* v. *St. Anne Catholic School, Wichita, Kansas et al.*, Complaint, 08-1143-JTM (2008).

52. *Adam Silva et al.* v. *St. Anne Catholic School, Wichita, Kansas et al.*, 595 F.Supp. 2d 1171 (2009).

53. Ted Greenberg, "'English-Only' Contract Stirs Controversy at N.J. School." NBC 10 (Philadelphia), February 6, 2009. The online comments are no longer available.

54. Lee Rowland and Maggie McLetchie, Letter to Robert Aumaugher, American Civil Liberties Union, January 31, 2008.

55. "School Bus Rules, Regulations," Arthur 2008 Back-to-School Supplement, *Arthur* (IL) *Graphic*, p. 8.

56. "Language Spoken at Home," Table S1601, American Community Survey, 2018, available at: https://data.census.gov.

57. "Nativity by Language Spoken at Home by Ability to Speak English for the Population 5 Years and Over," Table B16005, American Community Survey, 2018, available at: https://data.census.gov.

58. State of California Constitution, Article III, sec. 6, 2018.

59. *Yniguez* v. *Arizonans for Official English*, 69 F.3rd 920 (1995).

60. *Arizonans for Official English et al.* v. *Arizona et al.*, 520 US 43, 1997.

61. Constitution of the State of Arizona, proposed, December 9, 1910, Arizona Memory Project, available at: https://azmemory.azlibrary.gov. The state officers covered by the law were the governor, treasurer, auditor, secretary of state, and superintendent of schools.
62. "Constitutions of New Mexico and Arizona," House of Representatives Report No. 33, 62nd Congress, 1st Session. May 12, 1911, p. 5.
63. Treaty of Guadalupe–Hidalgo, 1848, Art. IX.
64. Arizona Revised Statutes 38–201 (1988).
65. Marc Lacey, "Arizona Candidate Challenged over English Skills," *New York Times,* January 25, 2012.
66. Arizona Constitution, 2006, Art. XXVIII, sec. 3b.
67. Compiled Statutes of the State of Nebraska, 1922, ch. 63, Art. 15, sec. 6460–6461.
68. "Proposing an Amendment to the Constitution of the United States Establishing English as the Official Language of the United States," H.J. Res. 16, 107th Congress, 1st Session, February 13, 2001, informally known as the English Language Amendment (ELA).
69. English Language Amendment, S.J.R. 72, CR 97, April 27, 1981, in 127 *Congressional Record,* 97th Congress, 1st Session, pp. 7444–7445.
70. A Bill To Amend Title 4, United States Code, to Declare English as the Official Language of the Government of the United States, H.R. 3333, 107th Congress, 1st Session, November 16, 2001. That provision is repeated in the current version of the bill, H.R.997, introduced in 2021.
71. A Bill To Declare English as the Official Language of the United States, H.R. 997, 117th Congress, 1st Session, February 11, 2021.
72. 8 USC § 1423.
73. "Japs Can't Say 'Yes,'" *Good Morning* (newspaper of the US Submarine Service), December 29, 1943, p. 1.
74. Bruce Stokes, "What It Takes to Truly Be 'One of Us,'" Pew Research Center, Washington, DC, 2017, available at: http://assets.pewresearch.org.
75. See, for example, Geoffrey Nunberg, "Lingo Jingo: English-Only and the New Nativism," *The American Prospect* 8(33) (July/August, 1997).
76. Roger G. Kennedy, *Burr, Hamilton, and Jefferson: A Study in Character.* New York: Oxford University Press, 2000, p. 159.
77. Luebke, "Legal Restrictions on Foreign Languages in the Great Plains States 1917–1923," pp. 1–19.
78. Press Trust of India, "Telugu Community in US Asked to Converse in English in Public," CNN News18, February 28, 2017, available at: www.news18.com.

## CHAPTER 7: REPEAT AFTER ME ...

1. State of Texas. H.B. 3979, "A Bill To Be Entitled An Act Relating to Civics Instruction Public School Students and Instruction Policies in Public Schools," September 1, 2021.
2. Meryl Kornfield and Timothy Bella, "Texas School Official Tells Teachers That Holocaust Books Should Be Countered with 'Opposing' Views," *Washington Post,* October 15, 2021.

3. *Masterpiece Cakeshop* v. *Colorado Civil Rights Commission*, 584 US___ (2018).

4. Employment Restrictions and Loyalty Oaths, Legal Information Institute, available at: www.law.cornell.edu.

5. Jeffery Toobin, *The Oath: The Obama White House and the Supreme Court.* New York: Doubleday, 2012.

6. Toobin, *The Oath*, p. 3.

7. Toobin, *The Oath*, p. 3.

8. *Dickerson* v. *United States*, 530 US 428, 443 (2000).

9. *Brogan* v. *United States*, 522 US 398 (1998).

10. *Miranda* v. *Arizona*, 384 US 436, 492 (1966).

11. *Miranda* v. *Arizona*, at 444–445.

12. *Miranda* v. *Arizona*, at 457.

13. *Miranda* v. *Arizona*, at 468.

14. *Miranda* v. *Arizona*, at 466.

15. *Olmstead* v. *United States*, 277 US 438 (1928).

16. *Brown* v. *Board of Education*, 347 US 483 (1954).

17. *Engel* v. *Vitale*, 370 US 421 (1962).

18. John MacKenzie, "Capote Assails Crime Decision," *Boston Globe*, July 22, 1966, p. 2.

19. Fred P. Graham, "The Law: How to Make Sure a Confession Stands Up," *New York Times*, February 26, 1967, p. E12.

20. Graham, "The Law" (emphasis added). *California Reporter* 96 (1971), 128/1 (emphasis in the original); cited in the *Oxford English Dictionary*.

21. Brent Whiting, "Run-of-the-Mill Phoenix Rape Case Made Legal History," *Arizona Republic*, May 27, 2013.

22. "'Miranda Card' Read to Suspect in Slaying of '66 Court Figure," *New York Times*, February 2, 1976, p. 14.

23. *Escobedo* v. *Illinois*, 378 US 478 (1964); H. Mitchell Caldwell and Michael S. Lief, "You Have the Right to Remain Silent," *American Heritage* 57(4) (August/September, 2006).

24. Richard Rogers, Kimberly S. Harrison, Lisa L. Hazelwood, and Kenneth W. Sewell, "Knowing and Intelligent: A Study of Miranda Warnings in Mentally Disordered Defendants," *Law and Human Behavior* 31(4) (2007): 401–418.

25. Communication of Rights Group, "Guidelines for Communicating Rights to Non-Native Speakers of English in Australia, England and Wales, and the USA," 2016, available at: www.aaal.org.

26. Richard A. Leo, "The Impact of Miranda Revisited," *Journal of Criminal Law and Criminology* 86 (1996): 621–692.

27. Irwin S. Kirsch, Ann Jungeblut, Lynn Jenkins, and Andrew Kolstad, *Adult Literacy in America*. Washington, DC: National Center for Education Statistics, 1992.

28. Rogers et al., "Knowing and Intelligent."

29. *Miranda* v. *Arizona*, at 499.

30. *Salinas* v. *Texas*, 133 US 2174 (2013).

31. *New York* v. *Quarles*, 467 US 649 (1984).

32. *New York* v. *Quarles*, at 657.

33. Eric Holder, "Guidance for Conducting Interviews without Providing *Miranda* Warnings in Arrests of Terrorism Suspects," Memorandum, Office of the Attorney General, Washington, DC, October 19, 2010, available at: www.justice.gov.

34. "Transcript of the Boston Bombing Suspect's Bedside Hearing," *New York Times*, April 22, 2013.

35. *United States* v. *Tsarnaev*, No. 20-442, decided March 4, 2022.

36. Federal Bureau of Investigation, "Crime in the United States, 2019: Arrest Tables," 2019, available at: https://ucr.fbi.gov/crime-in-the-u.s/2019. Statistics are not yet posted for more recent years.

37. *United States* v. *Windsor*, 570 US 744 (2013).

38. The Constitution of the State of Tennessee, Art. XI, § 18, November 4, 2014.

39. *Obergefell* v. *Hodges*, 135 US 2071 (2015).

40. Tennessee Code Annotated, § 1-3-105(b).

41. An Act to Amend Tennessee Code Annotated, Title 1, Chapter 3, Relative to Construction of Statutes, Senate Bill 30, introduced February 8, 2017, available at: https://legiscan.com/TN/text/HB0033/id/1454392.

42. An Act to Amend Tennessee Code Annotated, Title 36, Relative to the "Tennessee Natural Marriage Defense Act," Tennessee House Bill 1369, introduced February 6, 2019, available at: http://wapp.capitol.tn.gov. Despite the reference to the law of gravity, Tennessee had a strong track record in rejecting science: it had banned the teaching of evolution in 1925. That law was finally repealed in 1967, but in 2012 the state passed a new law allowing the teaching of creationism alongside evolution, and many local districts now require "both sides" to be taught.

43. Samuel Johnson, *Dictionary of the English Language*. London, 1755.

44. Noah Webster, *An American Dictionary of the English Language*, 1828.

45. *Merriam-Webster's Collegiate Dictionary*, 11th ed., Springfield, MA: Merriam-Webster, 2003.

46. *American Heritage Dictionary of the English Language*, 5th ed., Boston, MA: Houghton Mifflin Harcourt, 2011.

47. Richard Posner, "In Defense of Looseness," *The New Republic*, August 27, 2008.

48. William Blackstone, *Commentaries on the Laws of England*, 1765; rpt. the Avalon Project, New Haven, CT: Yale University, I:60.

49. "The Death of George Washington," *The Digital Encyclopedia of George Washington*, Fred W. Smith National Library for the Study of George Washington at Mount Vernon, available at: www.mountvernon.org.

50. *Cabell* v. *Markham*, 148 F.2d 737 (1945).

51. Stephen M. Feldman, *Free Expression and Democracy in America: A History*. Chicago: University of Chicago Press, 2008, p. 195.

## CHAPTER 8: WILL FREE SPEECH SURVIVE?

1. Dennis Baron, *A Better Pencil: Readers, Writers, and the Digital Revolution*. New York: Oxford University Press, 2009, p. 119.

2. Ralf Webb, "He's a Poet and the FBI Know It: How John Giorno's Dial-a-Poem Alarmed the Feds," *The Guardian*, October 18, 2021.

3. Mary Anne Franks has also looked at Charlottesville in her account of First and Second Amendment clashes, *The Cult of the Constitution: Our Deadly Devotion to Guns and Free Speech*, Stanford: Stanford University Press, 2019.

4. Bryan Armen Grayan, "'Swastikas and Nooses': Governor Slams 'Racism' of Michigan Lockdown Protest," *The Guardian*, May 4, 2020.

5. Grayan, "'Swastikas and Nooses.'"

6. Todd Spangler, "Trump Downplays Plot against Whitmer at Michigan Rally, Crowd Chants 'Lock Her Up,'" *Detroit Free Press*, October 17, 2020.

7. Josh Marshall, "Thinking about Rittenhouse and Right Wing Murder Safaris," *Talking Points Memo*, November 12, 2021, available at: tpm.com. Kyle Rittenhouse, the protestor, successfully pled self-defense and quickly became a darling of the far right.

8. For a discussion of First and Second Amendment clashes, see, for example, Franks, *The Cult of the Constitution*.

9. Giffords Law Center, "Preventing Armed Voter Intimidation: A State-by-State Analysis," September, 2020, available at: https://giffords.org.

10. Shaila Dewan, "Armed Observers, Chants of '4 More Years' at Polls: Is that Legal?" *New York Times*, October 30, 2020.

11. "Free Expression in America Post-2020," Knight Foundation-Ipsos, 2022, p. 13.

12. *Bostock* v. *Clayton County, Georgia*, US Supreme Court, No. 17-1618, June 15, 2020. Title VII of the 1964 Civil Rights Act prohibits discrimination in employment, including discrimination "based on race, color, religion, sex, or national origin."

13. For a detailed history of gender pronouns in English, including their legal functions, see Dennis Baron, *What's Your Pronoun? Beyond He and She*. New York: Norton/Liveright, 2020.

14. Baron, *What's Your Pronoun?* pp. 140–145.

15. *Nicholas K. Meriwether* v. *Trustees of Shawnee State University and Jane Doe*, No. 20-3289, US Court of Appeals for the Sixth Circuit, March 26, 2021. In its decision the court made clear that the First Amendment's broad protections apply only to higher education faculty, not to teachers in elementary or high schools.

16. Elizabeth Dwoskin, Tory Newmyer, and Shibani Mahtani, "The Case Against Mark Zuckerberg: Insiders Say Facebook's CEO Chose Growth over Safety," *Washington Post*, October 26, 2021.

17. "Transcript: Donald Trump's RNC speech," CNN Politics, August 28, 2020, available at: www.cnn.com.

18. Matthew Gertz, tweet, September 6 , 2020, rpt. at cnn.com; the *Atlantic* story referenced is Jeffrey Goldberg, "Trump: Americans Who Died in War Are 'Losers' and 'Suckers,'" *The Atlantic*, September 3, 2020.

19. 47 USC § 230 (emphasis added).

20. Chloe Hadavas, "What's the Deal with Parler?" *Slate*, July 3, 2020.

21. James Wellemeyer, "Conservatives are Flocking to a New 'Free Speech' Social Media App that has Started Banning Liberal Users," NBC News, July 2, 2020, available at: www .nbcnews.com.

22. Laura W. Murphy, Introduction, Facebook's Civil Rights Audit, July 8, 2020, p. 9, available at: https://about.fb.com/wp-content/uploads/2020/07/Civil-Rights-Audit-Final-Report.pdf. This puts Facebook in a bind, because controversial and extremist right-wing posts generate the most clicks, making them very profitable for a company whose aim is to increase its user base along with its profit margin.

23. Donald J. Trump, Executive Order on Preventing Online Censorship, May 28, 2020, available at: www.whitehouse.gov/presidential-actions/executive-order-preventing-online-censorship.

24. See, for example, *Knight First Amendment Institute et al.* v. *Donald J. Trump et al.*, No. 18-1691, US District Court of Appeals for the Second Circuit, 2019, affirming a lower court decision that Trump did not have a constitutional right to block followers on Twitter.

25. Mike Masnick, editor of the Techdirt blog, details the many ways in which section 230 has been misinterpreted in his post, "Hello! You've Been Referred Here Because You're Wrong About Section 230 of the Communications Decency Act," June 23, 2020, available at: www.techdirt.com.

26. Rumman Chowdhury and Lucas Bell, "Examining Algorithmic Amplification of Political Content on Twitter," October 22, 2021, available at: blog.twitter.com.

27. An Act Providing for Training, Prohibitions, and Requirements Relating to First Amendment Rights at School Districts and Universities Governed by the State Board of Regents, Iowa House File 744, March 16, 2021.

28. An Act Providing for Requirements Related to Racism or Sexism Trainings. Iowa House File 802, March 16, 2021. 9.

29. Department for Education, "Higher Education: Free Speech and Academic Freedom," February 21, 2021.

30. "Police, Crime, Sentencing and Courts Bill," Bill 268, available at: https://publications.parliament.uk/pa/bills/cbill/58-01/0268/200268.pdf, p. 46; Jennifer Brown and Sally Lipscombe, "Police, Crime, Sentencing and Courts Bill 2019–21: Part 3 and 4 – Public Order and Unauthorised Encampments," House of Commons Briefing Paper 9164, March 12, 2021, available at: https://commonslibrary.parliament.uk.

31. Oliver Wendell Holmes, dissent in *Meyer* v. *Nebraska*, 262 US 390 (1923).

32. Foundation for Individual Rights in Education, "Comprehensive Campus Free Speech Bill Becomes Law in Tennessee," May 10, 2017; Natalie Allison, "Tennessee Bans Public Schools from Teaching Critical Race Theory amid National Debate," *The Tennessean*, May 6, 2021.

33. Michael Hobbes, "The Methods of Moral Panic Journalism," available at: https://michaelhobbes.substack.com, October 21, 2021.

34. Knight Foundation, "Free Expression in America Post-2020," p. 24. The Knight-Ipsos survey also reveals a general free-speech malaise: most Americans, regardless of their political affiliation, feel that their own speech rights are not as robust as those of competing groups.

35. Dominic Casciani, "Spy Pictures of Suffragettes Revealed," *BBCNews Magazine Online*, October 3, 2003, available at: news.bbc.co.uk.

36. Mark Townsend, "How CCTV Played a Vital Role in Tracking Sarah Everard – and Her Killer," *The Observer*, October 2, 2021.

37. Dave Lee, "Boston Bombing: How Internet Detectives Got It Very Wrong," BBC News, April 19, 2013, available at: bbc.com.
38. "Police Head's Testimony: Wire Spying a Necessity to Detect Crime Here," *New York Times*, May 5, 1916, p. 1.
39. For example, when NSA spying on domestic communications was revealed in 2013, President Obama reassured Americans that no one was listening to their calls. Jared A. Favole and Peter Nicholas, "Obama: 'Nobody is Listening to Your Telephone Calls,'" *Wall St. Journal*, June 7, 2013. C. B. Farr, Director General of the UK's domestic surveillance agency, was even more insistent that "any member of the public who does not associate with potential terrorists or serious criminals or individuals who are potentially involved in actions which could raise national security issues for the UK can be assured that none of the interception agencies which I inspect has the slightest interest in examining their emails, their phone or postal communications or their use of the internet, and they do not do so to any extent which could reasonably be regarded as significant." Charles Blandford Farr, "Witness Statement," Investigatory Powers Tribunal between Privacy International and Various Parties, IPT/13/92/CH, May 16, 2014.
40. Jeremy Bentham, *Panopticon: or, The Inspection-House*. Dublin, 1791.
41. Samuel D. Warren and Louis D. Brandeis, "The Right to Privacy," *Harvard Law Review* 4(5) (December 15, 1890): 193–220.
42. *Olmstead v. United States*, 277 US 438 (1928). Although the Court's majority in *Olmstead* confirmed that warrantless wiretaps were constitutional, in 1933 Congress passed legislation banning the practice.
43. See, for example, Zeynep Tufekci's critique of cell-phone monitoring of student behavior in her essay, "The Pandemic is No Excuse to Surveil Students," *The Atlantic*, September 4, 2020.
44. Meagan Flynn, "Police Think Alexa May Have Witnessed a New Hampshire Double Homicide. Now They Want Amazon to Turn Her Over," *Washington Post*, November 14, 2018.
45. "Amazon Privacy Notice," updated January 1, 2020.
46. George Orwell, *1984*. Secker & Warburg, 1949, p. 1.
47. Bobbie Johnson, "Privacy No Longer a Social Norm, says Facebook Founder," *The Guardian*, January 11, 2010.
48. Dennis Baron, "The Government Does Not Control Your Grammar," *The Web of Language*, January 19, 2011, available at: https://blogs.illinois.edu/view/25/42015.

# References

ACLU. 1934. "Shall We Defend Free Speech for Nazis in America?" New York: American Civil Liberties Union, October.

ACLU-VA 2017. Complaint for Declaratory and Injunctive Relief and Damages, available at: https://acluva.org/wp-content/uploads/2017/08/Kessler-Complaint20170810.pdf.

"'Act of War': New Charlie Hebdo Edition Triggers Muslims' Anger, Threats." 2015. Available at: www.rt.com, January 14.

Acton, Richard, Lord. 1995. *To Go Free: A Treasury of Iowa's Legal Heritage.* Ames, IA: Iowa State University Press.

Address. 1787. The Address and Reasons of Dissent of the Minority of the Convention of the State of Pennsylvania, to Their Constituents. Early American Imprints, ser. 1, No. 20619.

Alemany, Jackie, Emma Brown, Alice Crites, Tom Jackman, Tom Hamburger, Peter Hermann, Spencer S. Hsu, Isaac Stanley-Becker, Julie Tate, Elise Viebeck, and Cleve Wootson. 2021. "Red Flags," *Washington Post,* October 31.

Alexander, Keith L. 2021. "Prosecutors Break Down Charges, Convictions for 725 Arrested So Far in Jan. 6 Attack on US Capitol," *Washington Post,* December 31.

Allison, Natalie. 2021. "Tennessee Bans Public Schools from Teaching Critical Race Theory amid National Debate," *The Tennessean,* May 6.

Amar, Akhil Reed. 1994. *America's Unwritten Constitution.* New York: Basic Books.

Amazon. 2020. "Amazon Privacy Notice," updated January 1, available at: www.amazon.com/gp/help.

American Community Survey. 2018. "Language Spoken at Home," Table S1601, available at: https://data.census.gov.

  2018. "Nativity by Language Spoken at Home by Ability to Speak English for the Population 5 Years and Over," Table B16005, available at: https://data.census.gov.

*American Heritage Dictionary of the English Language.* 2011. 5th ed., Boston, MA: Houghton Mifflin Harcourt.

"Americanization Division on the 'Melting Pot' Phrase." 1919. *Americanization Bulletin* 1(6) (February 1): 7.

# REFERENCES

An Act Establishing the American Language as the Official Language of the State of Illinois. 1923. S.B. 15, approved June 19. *Revised Statutes of the State of Illinois Embracing All General Laws of the State of Illinois in Force July 1, 1923*, ch. 17b, p. 234.

"An Act Relating to the Postal Laws." 1865. Statutes at Large, vol. 13, 38th Congress, 1st Session, ch. LXXIX, sec. 16, p. 507; March 3.

Act To Amend the Immigration and Nationality Act, and for Other Purposes. 1965. PL 89-236, October 3, 79 *United States Statutes at Large*, pp. 911–22.

"An Act To Establish a Bureau of Immigration and Naturalization, and to Provide for a Uniform Rule for the Naturalization of Aliens throughout the United States." 1906. *United States Statutes at Large*, 59th Congress, Session I, ch. 3592, sec. 8, p. 599; approved June 29.

"An Act To Punish Persons Who Make Threats against the President of the United States." 1917. 64th Congress, Session II, p. 919, approved February 14.

Act To Revise and Codify the Nationality Laws of the United States into a Comprehensive Nationality Code. 1940. H.R. 9980, sec. 304, *United States Statutes at Large*, 76th Congress, ch. 876, p. 1140, October 14.

Annals of Congress. 1798. Debate on the Sedition Act in the House of Representatives. 5th Congress, 2nd Session, July 10: 2139–72.

Arizona, State of. 1910. Constitution. Arizona Memory Project, available at: https://azmemory.azlibrary.gov/digital/collection/statepubs/id/19457/rec/2.

2006. Constitution.

Arthur (Illinois) *Graphic*. 2008. Arthur Back-to-School Supplement, "School Bus Rules, Regulations," August, p. 8.

"Ask the Police." n.d. "Q675: Can a person be arrested for just swearing in the street?" available at: www.askthe.police.uk/content/Q675.htm.

Auerbach, Stuart. 1966. "Grand Jury Will Sift Case of Threat to LBJ," *Washington Post*, August 30, p. A8.

Banting, Emily. 2012. "A Tweet Got Me Deported," *The Sun*, January 17, p. 15.

Barbas, Samantha. 2012. "How the Movies Became Speech," *Rutgers Law Review* 64(3): 665–745.

Baron, Dennis. 1982. *Grammar and Good Taste: Reforming the American Language*. New Haven, CT: Yale University Press.

1990. *The English-Only Question: An Official Language for Americans?* New Haven, CT: Yale University Press.

2007. "Can Commas Shoot Down Gun Control?" *Los Angeles Times*, March 22.

2009. *A Better Pencil: Readers, Writers, and the Digital Revolution*. New York: Oxford University Press.

2011. "The Government Does Not Control Your Grammar," *The Web of Language*, January 19, available at: https://blogs.illinois.edu/view/25/42015.

2019. "Corpus Evidence Illuminates the Meaning of Bear Arms," *Hastings Constitutional Quarterly* 46(3): 509–522.

2020. *What's Your Pronoun? Beyond He and She*. New York: Norton/Liveright.

Baron, Dennis, Richard W. Bailey, Jeffrey P. Kaplan, and Charles M. Dyke. 2008. *Brief for Professors of Linguistics and English … in Support of Petitioners. District of Columbia v. Heller* 554 US 270.

Baude, William and Stephen E. Sachs. 2017. "The Law of Interpretation," *Harvard Law Review* 130:1079, 1081–1149.

Belt, Gordon T. 2011. "The Sedition Act of 1798: a Brief History of Arrests, Indictments, Mistreatment and Abuse," First Amendment Center, available at: firstamendmentcenter.org.

Bentham, Jeremy. 1791. *Panopticon: or, the Inspection-House.* Dublin.

Bill To Amend Title 4, United States Code, to Declare English as the Official Language of the Government of the United States. 2001. H.R. 3333, 107th Congress, 1st Session, November 16.

Bill to Create a Commission to Be Known as the Federal Motion Picture Commission, and Defining Its Powers and Duties. 1924. H.R. 6821, 68th Congress, 1st Session, introduced February 9, pp. 9–11.

Bill to Define the National and Official Language of the Government and People of the United States of America. 1923. H.R. 14136, 67th Congress, 4th Session.

Bill to Establish an Official National Censorship of Motion Pictures in Interstate and Foreign Commerce and in the District of Columbia and the Territories and All Other Places under National Jurisdiction. 1914. S. 4941, s. 4; 51 *Congressional Record*, March 18, p. 5022.

Bill to Protect the Motion-Picture Industry … and to Provide for the Manufacture of Wholesome Motion Pictures. 1930. H.R. 9986. 72 *Congressional Record*, March 25, p. 6105.

Bill to Regulate Immigration and Insure the Use of the English Language by Those Coming to the United States. 1923. H.R. 4089, December 20.

Blackstone, William. 1765. *Commentaries on the Laws of England*, The Avalon Project. New Haven, CT: Yale University.

Boyer, Paul S. 2002. *Purity in Print: Book Censorship in America from the Gilded Age to the Computer Age.* Madison, WI: University of Wisconsin Press.

Brennan Center for Justice. 2021. "Does the 2nd Amendment Threaten the 1st?" September 14, available at: www.youtube.com.

Brewster, Jack. 2021. "Sen. Ron Johnson on Capitol Riot: 'This Didn't Seem Like An Armed Insurrection To Me,'" *Forbes*, February 15.

Brown, Jennifer and Sally Lipscombe. 2021. "Police, Crime, Sentencing and Courts Bill 2019–21: Parts 3 and 4 – Public Order and Unauthorised Encampments," House of Commons Briefing Paper 9164. March 12, available at: https://commonslibrary.parliament.uk/research-briefings/cbp-9164.

Bryan, Leigh. 2016. "Tweetorists," *YouTube*, July 26, available at: www.youtube.com/watch?v=vrE1wqJJNI4.

Burger, Warren. 1990. "The Right to Bear Arms," *Parade Magazine*, January 4, p. 4. Reprinted in Annette T. Rottenberg and Donna Haisty Winchell (eds.), *Elements of Argument: A Text and Reader.* New York: Macmillan, 2011, pp. 377–379.

1991. Interview by Charlayne Hunter-Gault of C. J. Warren Burger, *The Mac-Neill/Lehrer News Hour*, December 16. The program was devoted to the 200th anniversary of the Bill of Rights. Transcript from Lexis/Nexis.

Brigham Young University Law School. 2018. Corpus Linguistics: Corpus of Early Modern English (COEME); Corpus of Founding Era American English (COFEA), available at: https://lawncl.byu.edu.

Caldwell, H. Mitchell and Michael S. Lief. 2006. "You Have the Right to Remain Silent," *American Heritage* 57(4) (August/September), available at: www.americanheritage.com/content/"you-have-right-remain-silent"?page=show.

California, State of. 2018. Constitution. Article III, sec. 6, 2018.

Casciani, Dominic. 2003. "Spy Pictures of Suffragettes Revealed," *BBCNews Magazine Online*, October 3, available at: news.bbc.co.uk.

Castor, Bruce L., David Schoen, and Michael T. van der Veen. 2021. "Trial Memorandum of Donald J. Trump, 45th President of the United States of America," *In re: Impeachment of Former President Donald J. Trump*, February 8.

"Caution on Twitter Urged as Tourists Barred from US." 2012. *BBC*, March 8, available at: www.bbc.com/news/technology-16810312.

Chaffee, Zechariah. 1919. "Freedom of Speech in War Time," *Harvard Law Review* 32: 932–973.

1920. "A Contemporary State Trial: The United States versus Jacob Abrams et al.," *Harvard Law Review* 33: 747–774.

Chicago Motion Picture Censorship Commission. 1920. *Report*. Chicago.

Chowdhury, Rumman and Lucas Bell. 2021. "Examining Algorithmic Amplification of Political Content on Twitter," available at: https://blog.twitter.com/en_us/topics/company/2021/rml-politicalcontent.

Chrisafis, Angelique. 2015. "French Dissenters Jailed after Crackdown on Speech That Glorifies Terrorism," *The Guardian*, January 30.

City of Charlottesville. 2017. Brief in Opposition to Plaintiff's Motion for a Preliminary Injunction or Temporary Restraining Order. Civil Case No. 3:17-cv-00056-GEC. August 11.

Cogan, Neil H. (ed.). 1997. *The Complete Bill of Rights: The Drafts, Debates, Sources, and Origins*. New York: Oxford University Press.

Collins, Lauren. 2018. "The Pub That Banned Swearing," *The New Yorker*, January 15.

"Colonel for 'Knockout.'" 1918. *New York Times*, May 28, p. 8.

Communication of Rights Group. 2016. "Guidelines for Communicating Rights to Non-Native Speakers of English in Australia, England and Wales, and the USA," available at: www.aaal.org.

Comstock Act, The. 1873. "An Act for the Suppression of Trade in, and Circulation of, Obscene Literature and Articles of Immoral Use," 42nd Congress, Session III, ch. 258, pp. 598–600. Approved March 3.

Conan, Eric. 2015. "Que Reste-t-il de 'l'Esprit du 11 Janvier'?" *Marianne*, February 11.

"The Confessional Unmasked; Shewing the Depravity of the Romish Priesthood, the Iniquity of the Confessional, and the Questions Put to Females in Confession." 1867. London: Protestant Electoral Union.

Crandall, Diana. 2016. "Feminist Columnist Jessica Valenti Quits Social Media after Trolls Threaten to Rape her 5-Year-Old Daughter," *New York Daily News*, July 27.

Cressy, David. 1980. *Literacy and the Social Order: Reading and Writing in Tudor and Stuart England.* Cambridge: Cambridge University Press.

Crowley, Michael. 2016. "Trump's Long Dalliance with Violent Rhetoric," *Politico*, August 10.

Crown Prosecution Service. 2018. "Social Media: Guidelines on Prosecuting Cases Involving Communications Sent via Social Media," revised August 21, available at: www.cps.gov.uk/legal-guidance.

Cummins, Anthony. 2008. "Emile Zola's Cheap English Dress: The Vizetelly Translations, late-Victorian Print Culture, and the Crisis of Literary Value," *Review of English Studies* NS 60(243): 108–132.

Customs and Border Protection. 2018. "About," available at: www.cbp.gov/about.

*Dayton Daily News.* 1917. Untitled Article, May 10, p. 15.

"Death of George Washington, The." n.d. *The Digital Encyclopedia of George Washington*, Fred W. Smith National Library for the Study of George Washington at Mount Vernon, available at: www.mountvernon.org/library.

Dell, Floyd. 1918. "Story of the *Masses* Trial," *The Liberator*, June, 7–18.

Demorand, Nicholas. 2017. Tweet. @ndemorand, January 22.

Department for Education. 2021. "Higher Education: Free Speech and Academic Freedom," February 21, available at: www.gov.uk/official-documents.

Department of Homeland Security. 2011. "Analyst's Desktop Binder," available at: http://epic.org/foia/epic-v-dhs-media-monitoring/Analyst-Desktop-Binder-REDACTED.pdf.

Derr, Nancy. 1979. "Babel Proclamation," *Palimpsest* 60(4) (July/August): 98–115.

Dewan, Shaila. 2020. "Armed Observers, Chants of '4 More Years' at Polls: Is That Legal?" *New York Times*, October 30.

Doyle, Matthew P. 2016. Tweet, @MatthewDoyle31, March 23.

Duke Center for Firearms Law. 2021. Database of Firearms Laws, available at: firearmslaw.duke.edu.

Dwoskin, Elizabeth, Tory Newmyer, and Shibani Mahtani. 2021. "The Case Against Mark Zuckerberg: Insiders Say Facebook's CEO Chose Growth over Safety," *Washington Post*, October 26.

Eastman, Max. 1919. "The Trial of Eugene Debs," *The Liberator* 1: 5–12.

Editorial Board. 2015. "The Court and Online Threats," *New York Times*, June 1.

English Language Amendment. 1981. S. J. R. 72, CR 97. 127 *Congressional Record*, 97th Congress, 1st Session, April 27, pp. 7444–7445.

2001. "Proposing an Amendment to the Constitution of the United States Establishing English as the Official Language of the United States," H.J. Res. 16, 107th Congress, 1st Session, February 13.

English Language Unity Act. 2001. "A Bill To Amend Title 4, United States Code, to Declare English as the Official Language of the Government of the United States," H.R. 3333, 107th Congress, 1st Session, November 16.

2021. "A Bill to Declare English as the Official Language of the United States," H.R. 997, 117th Congress, 1st Session, February 11.

Espionage Act. 1917. "An Act to Punish Acts of Interference with the Foreign Relations, the Neutrality, and the Foreign Commerce of the United States, to punish espionage, and better to enforce the criminal laws of the United States, and for Other Purposes." H. R. 291, June 15. 65 *Congressional Record* 1st Session, ch. 30, pp. 217–219.

European Charter. 2000. "Freedom of Expression and Information," Article 11, available at: www.europarl.europa.eu/charter/pdf/text_en.pdf.

"Evergreen Park Woman Accused of Threatening to Shoot Cops in Facebook Post." 2016. *Chicago Tribune*, July 8.

Farr, Charles Blandford. 2014. "Witness Statement," Investigatory Powers Tribunal between Privacy International and Various Parties, IPT/13/92/CH, May 16, available at: www.privacyinternational.org/sites/privacyinternational.org/files/downloads/press-releases/witness_st_of_charles_blandford_farr.pdf.

Favole, Jared A. and Peter Nicholas. 2013. "Obama: 'Nobody is Listening to Your Telephone Calls,'" *Wall St. Journal*, June 7.

Federal Bureau of Investigation. 2019. "Crime in the United States, 2019: Arrest Tables," available at: https://ucr.fbi.gov/crime-in-the-US.

*Federal Motion Picture Commission Briefs*. 1916. Washington, DC: Government Printing Office.

*Federal Motion Picture Commission Hearings*. 1916. Washington, DC: Government Printing Office.

*Federal Motion Picture Commission Hearings*. 1926. Washington, DC: Government Printing Office.

*Federal Motion Picture Commission Hearings*. 1934. Washington, DC: Government Printing Office.

Feldman, Stephen M. 2008. *Free Expression and Democracy in America: A History*. Chicago, IL: University of Chicago Press.

Fernandez, Manny and Ashley Southall. 2015. "Dallas Gunman Killed after Attack on Police Headquarters," *New York Times*, June 13.

"Fine 4 Women for Speaking German Tongue." 1918. *Quad-City Times*, Davenport, Iowa, June 14, p. 6.

Flood, Alison. 2010. "'Oral Sex' Definition Prompts Dictionary Ban in US Schools," *The Guardian*, January 25.

Flynn, Meagan. 2018. "Police Think Alexa May Have Witnessed a New Hampshire Double Homicide. Now They Want Amazon to Turn Her Over," *Washington Post*, November 14.

Foundation for Individual Rights in Education. 2017. "Comprehensive Campus Free Speech Bill Becomes Law in Tennessee," May 10.

Franks, Mary Anne. 2019. *The Cult of the Constitution: Our Deadly Devotion to Guns and Free Speech.* Stanford, CA: Stanford University Press.

"Free Speech Does Not Protect Disloyalty." 1918. *The New York Times,* September 13, p. 15.

Fricker, Martin. 2016. "Foul-Mouthed Yob Banned from Swearing in Public Anywhere in Britain," *The Mirror,* July 14.

Frum, David. 2017. "The Chilling Effect of Openly Displayed Firearms," *The Atlantic,* August 16, available at: www.theatlantic.com.

Frye, Brian. 2008. "The Peculiar Story of United States v. Miller," *NYU Journal of Law and Liberty* 3: 48–82.

Gardiner, Beck, Mahana Mansfield, Ian Anderson, Josh Holder, Dan Louter, and Monica Ulmanu. 2016. "The Dark Side of Guardian Comments," *The Guardian,* April 12.

Gastaldo, Evann. 2014. "Mom Arrested for Swearing in Front of Kids," *USA Today,* August 15.

Gastanaga, Claire G. 2017a. "ACLU of Virginia Response to Governor's Allegations That ACLU Is Responsible for Violence in Charlottesville," available at: acluva.org/20108.

2017b. "Why We Represented the Alt-Right in Charlottesville," available at: https://acluva.org/20191.

Gertz, Matthew. 2020. Tweet, September 6, available at: www.cnn.com/2020/08/28/politics/donald-trump-speech-transcript/index.html.

Gibbons, Henry J. and Henry John Nelson. 1918. "Brief for Plaintiffs in Error," *Schenck* v. *United States,* available at: http://fair-use.org/supreme-court/1917/schenck-v-united-states/brief-of-plaintiffs-in-error.php.

Gienapp, Jonathan. 2018. *The Second Creation: Fixing the American Constitution in the Founding Era.* Cambridge, MA: Harvard University Press.

Giffords Law Center. 2020. "Preventing Armed Voter Intimidation: A State-by-State Analysis," September, available at: giffords.org.

Gogody, Jody and Jonathan Stempel. 2022. "Sarah Palin Loses Defamation Lawsuit against New York Times," Reuters.com., February 15.

Goldberg, Jeffrey. 2020. "Trump: Americans Who Died in War Are 'Losers' and 'Suckers,'" *The Atlantic,* September 3.

Gopnik, Adam. 2015. "PEN Has Every Right to Honor Charlie Hebdo," *The New Yorker,* April 27.

Graham, Fred P. 1967. "The Law: How to Make Sure A Confession Stands Up," *New York Times,* February 26, p. E12.

Grant, Ulysses S. 1876. Eighth Annual Message to Congress, December 5, available at: www.presidency.ucsb.edu/ws/?pid=29517.

Grayan, Bryan Armen. 2020. "'Swastikas and Nooses': Governor Slams 'Racism' of Michigan Lockdown Protest," *The Guardian,* May 4.

Greeley, Horace. 1857. Editorial, *New York Daily Tribune*, December 30, p. 4.

Greenberg, Ted. 2009. "'English-only' Contract Stirs Controversy at N.J. School," NBC 10 (Philadelphia), February 6, available at: www.nbcphiladelphia.com.

Greenwald, Glen. 2015. "204 PEN Writers (Thus Far) Have Objected to the Charlie Hebdo Award – Not Just 6," available at: theintercept.com, April 30.

Griswold, Alex. 2016. "Media that Censored *Charlie Hebdo*'s Muhammad have No Problem with Terrorist God Cover," available at: mediaite.com, January 7.

Haberman, Maggie. 2021. "Trump Told Crowd 'You Will Never Take Back Our Country With Weakness,'" *New York Times*, January 6, updated January 15.

Hadavas, Chloe. 2020. "What's the Deal with Parler?" *Slate*, July 3.

Hakuta, Kenji. 1986. *Mirror of Language*. New York: Basic Books.

Harding, William L. 1918. "The Babel Proclamation." Iowa City, IA: Iowa State Archives.

"Harding's Edict Closes Churches." 1918. Ottumwa *Semi-weekly Courier*, June 4, p. 1.

"Harding Explains Edict." 1918. *Evening Times-Republican*, Marshalltown, Iowa, June 3, 1918, p. 3.

Hartley-Parkinson, Richard. 2012. "'I'm Going to Destroy America and Dig up Marilyn Monroe,'" *Daily Mail*, January 31.

Hays, Will. 1930. "Code to Govern the Making of Talking, Synchronized and Silent Motion Pictures," available at: http://productioncode.dhwritings.com.

Heckman, Horace. 1925. "Pernicious Effects of Motion Pictures on Children," 68 *Congressional Record*, February 14, p. 3742.

*Herald of Liberty* (Washington, PA). 1800. Untitled Article, November 3, p. 3.

Hobbes, Michael. 2021. "The Methods of Moral-Panic Journalism," available at: michaelhobbes.substack.com, October 21.

Holder, Eric. 2010. "Guidance for Conducting Interviews Without Providing *Miranda* Warnings in Arrests of Terrorism Suspects," Memorandum, Office of the Attorney General, Washington, DC, October 19, available at: https://www.justice.gov/sites/default/files/oip/legacy/2014/07/23/ag-memo-miranda-rights.pdf.

Hudson, Grant M. 1930. "A Bill to Protect the Motion-Picture Industry ... and to Provide for the Manufacture of Wholesome Motion Pictures," H.R. 9986. 72 *Congressional Record*, March 25, p. 6105.

Hunter, George. 2016. "Detroit Police Arrest Four for Threats Against Cops," *Detroit News*, July 11.

Immigration Act. 1940. "An Act to Revise and Codify the Nationality Laws of the United States into a Comprehensive Nationality Code," H.R. 9980, October 14; sec. 304, *United States Statutes at Large*, 76th Congress, ch. 876, p. 1140.

1965. "An Act to Amend the Immigration and Nationality Act, and for Other Purposes," PL 89-236, October 3, 79 *United States Statutes at Large*, pp. 911–922.

Indictment. 1918. *United States* v. *Masses Publishing Company*, 252 F. 232 (1918), National Archives id. 7595374.

"Interstate Threats Clarification Act." 2016. S.2552.

Iowa, State of. 2021a. An Act Providing for Training, Prohibitions, and Requirements Relating to First Amendment Rights at School Districts and Universities Governed by the State Board of Regents, House File 744, March 16, available at: www.legis.iowa.gov/docs/publications/LGI/89/HF744.pdf.

2021b. An Act Providing for Requirements Related to Racism or Sexism Trainings, House File 802, March 16, available at: https://www.legis.iowa.gov/legislation/BillBook?ba=HF%20802&ga=89.

Isaac, Mike. 2016. "Twitter Bars Milo Yiannopoulos in Wake of Leslie Jones's Reports of Abuse," *New York Times*, July 20.

"It's Legal – We speak English." 1969. *Chicago Tribune*, September 24, p. 3.

Izzard, Eddie. 2007. "The Gun Thing," available at: www.youtube.com.

"Japs Can't Say 'Yes.'" 1943. *Good Morning* (newspaper of the Submarine Service), December 29, p. 1.

Jenkins, Roy. 1960. "Lady Chatterley," Letter to the *Spectator*, August 26, p. 307.

Johnson, Bobbie. 2010. "Privacy no Longer a Social Norm, says Facebook Founder," *The Guardian*, January 11.

Johnson, Samuel. 1755. *Dictionary of the English Language*. London.

Jones, Jeffrey L. 2008. "Public Believes Americans Have Right to Own Guns," *News Gallup*, March 27, available at: news.gallup.com/poll/105721.

Journal of the Senate of the United States of America. 1789–1793. Friday, September 4, 1789, available at: www.memory.loc.gov.

Jouvenal, Justin. 2016. "A 12-Year-Old Girl is Facing Criminal Charges for Using Certain Emoji. She's Not Alone," *Washington Post*, February 27, A1.

Kendall, Brent. 2014. "Man in Facebook Threat Case Scrutinized for Note to Prosecutor," *Wall Street Journal*, December 2.

Kennedy, Roger G. 2000. *Burr, Hamilton, and Jefferson: A Study in Character*. New York: Oxford University Press.

Kirsch, Irwin S., Ann Jungeblut, Lynn Jenkins, and Andrew Kolstad. 1992. *Adult Literacy in America*. Washington, DC: National Center for Education Statistics.

Knight Foundation-Ipsos. 2022. "Free Expression in America Post-2020: A Landmark Survey of Americans' Views on Speech Rights," Miami, FL, available at: knightfoundation.org.

Kornfield, Meryl and Timothy Bella. 2021. "Texas School Official Tells Teachers That Holocaust Books Should Be Countered with 'Opposing' Views," *Washington Post*, October 15.

Lacey, Marc. 2012. "Arizona Candidate Challenged Over English Skills," *New York Times*, January 25.

LaChance, Naomi. 2016. "After Dallas Shootings, Police Arrest People for Criticizing Cops on Facebook and Twitter," *The Intercept*, available at: theintercept.com/2016/07/12.

La Follette, Robert M. 1917. "Free Speech in Wartime," 65 *Congressional Record* 1st Session: 787–786, October 6.

Lane, Frankin K. 1919. "What America Means," *Americanization Bulletin* 1(6) (February 1): 2, 4, 8.

"Language by Legislation." 1923. *The Nation*, April 11, p. 408.

Lee, Dave. 2013. "Boston Bombing: How Internet Detectives Got It Very Wrong," BBC News, April 19, available at: bbc.com.

Legal Information Institute. 2021. "Employment Restrictions and Loyalty Oaths," available at: www.law.cornell.edu/constitution-conan.

Legum, Judd and Aaron Rupar. 2006. "Rep. King Designs Electrified Fence for Southern Border: 'We Do This with Livestock All the Time,'" *Think Progress*, July 13, available at: archive.thinkprogress.org.

Lenhart, Amanda, Michelle Ybarra, Kathryn Zickuhr, and Myeshia Price-Feeney. 2016. *Online Harassment, Digital Abuse, and Cyberstalking in America*. Data and Society Research Institute and the Center for Innovative Public Health Research.

Leo, Richard A. 1996. "The Impact of Miranda Revisited," *Journal of Criminal Law and Criminology* 86: 621–692.

Leon, M. 1918. "Why German-Jargon (Yiddish) Should Stop," *The Modern View*, St. Louis, MO, July 12, p. 6.

"Liberty Measles at West Point." 1918. *New York Times*, February 8.

Lineberger, Walter, 1923. "A Bill to Regulate Immigration and Insure the Use of the English Language by Those Coming to the United States," H.R. 4089, introduced, December 20.

Lithwick, Dahlia and Mark Joseph Stern. 2017. "The Guns Won," *Slate*, August 14, available at: www.slate.com.

"Long Prison Terms for the Bolsheviki." 1918. *New York Times*, October 26, p. 18.

Luebke, Frederick C. 1980. "Legal Restrictions on Foreign Languages in the Great Plains States 1917–1923," in *Languages in Conflict*, ed. Paul Schach. Lincoln, NE: University of Nebraska Press, 1–19.

MacKenzie, John. 1966. "Capote Assails Crime Decision," *Boston Globe*, July 22, p. 2.

Madison, James. 1788a. *Federalist* 37, "Concerning the Difficulties of the Convention in Devising a Proper Form of Government," *Daily Advertiser*, January 11, available at: www.congress.gov.

1788b. *Federalist* 46. "The Influence of the State and Federal Governments Compared," *New York Packet*, January 29, available at: www.congress.gov.

Mahoney, Matt. 2016. "Norwalk Man Posts Threats to Police on Social Media," available at: Fox61.com, July 10.

"Man Charged After Tweet 'Confronting Muslim Woman' on Brussels Attacks." 2016. *The Guardian*, March 25.

"Marshal Foch and the Law." 1921. Topics of the Times, *New York Times*, July 30, p. 6.

Marshall, Josh. 2021. "Thinking About Rittenhouse and Right Wing Murder Safaris," *Talking Points Memo*, November 12, available at: tpm.com.

Masnick, Mike. 2020. "Hello! You've Been Referred Here Because You're Wrong About Section 230 of the Communications Decency Act," June 23, available at: www.techdirt.com.

McCormick, Washington Jay. 1923. A Bill to Define the National and Official Language of the Government and People of the United States of America, H.R. 14136, 67th Congress, 4th Session.

McKellar, Kenneth. 1923. "Remarks," 65 *Congressional Record*, April 9, 1924, pp. 5958–5959

McNary, Charles. 1923. "Memorial," 64 *Congressional Record*, February 19, pp. 3931–3932.

Meisner, Jason. 2016. "Feds Agree to Drop Online Threat Case Against Former UIC Student," *Chicago Tribune*, July 27.

*Merriam-Webster's Collegiate Dictionary*. 2003. 11th ed., Springfield, MA: Merriam-Webster.

"Michaelis of U.S. Throws off Name." 1917. *Tampa Times*, August 15, p. 2.

"'Miranda Card' Read to Suspect in Slaying of '66 Court Figure," *New York Times*, February 2, p. 14.

Murphy, Laura W. 2020. "Facebook's Civil Rights Audit," July 8, available at: https://about.fb.com/wp-content/uploads/2020/07/Civil-Rights-Audit-Final-Report.pdf.

National Council of Teachers of English. 1921 (1919). "*Guide to American Speech Week.*" Chicago: NCTE.

National Vigilance Association. 1889. *Pernicious Literature: Debate in the House of Commons; Trial and Conviction for Sale of Zola's Novels.*

Nebraska, State of. 1922. Compiled Statutes, Ch. 63, Art. 15, sec. 6460–6461.

"Non-English Languages Allowed in Public Education." 2016. California Proposition 58, to Amend SB 1174 (Chapter 753, Statutes of 2014), available at: ballotpedia.org.

Nugent, Sr. Margaret. 2008. "Letter." Exhibit B, *Adam Silva et al. v. St. Anne Catholic School, Wichita, Kansas et al.*, Complaint, 08-1143-JTM.

Nunberg, Geoffrey. 1997. "Lingo Jingo: English-Only and the New Nativism," *American Prospect* 8(33) (July/August): 40.

Obscene Publications Act of 1959. United Kingdom Public General Acts, 1959, c. 66 (7–8 Eliz 2), available at: www.legislation.gov.uk.

Office of Civil Rights. 1970. "Identification of Discrimination and Denial of Services on the Basis of National Origin," *Federal Register* 35(139) (June 18): 11595–11596.

Ohio, State of. Revised Code Annotated, § 2923.13.

Olson, Theodore. 2001. "In the Case of Emerson v. United States," Brief for the United States in Opposition.

"One Language Idea Popular." 1918. *Quad-City Times*, Davenport, Iowa, June 2, p. 19.

"Only One Language Here." 1918. Editorial, *The American Israelite*, rpt. in the *Kansas City* (MO) *Times*, August 31, p. 12.

Oppenheim, Maya. 2016. "Labour MP Jess Phillips Builds 'Panic Room' at Her Constituency Office," *The Independent*, August 17.

Orwell, George. 1949. *1984*. London: Secker & Warburg.

Osborn, Cary G. 2013. "Banned Books in New Mexico," *Donaana County Historical Society Historical Review*, pp. 23–26.

Overby, Peter. 2012. "NRA: 'Only Thing That Stops a Bad Guy with a Gun is a Good Guy with a Gun,'" *All Things Considered*, National Public Radio. December 12, available at: www.npr.org.

Palazzolo, Joe. 2017. "ACLU Will No Longer Defend Hate Groups Protesting with Firearms," *Wall Street Journal*, August 17.

Panter-Downs, Mollie. 1960. "The Lady at the Old Bailey," *New Yorker*, November 19.

Parker, Andrew. 2012. "US Tweeted Us Like Terrorists; Held for Twitter Jokes," *The Sun*, January 30, p. 17.

Pauff, Sara. 2010. "Muscogee Schools: Mother Arrested for Cursing Edgewood Elementary Principal on the First Day of School," *Ledger-Enquirer* (Columbus, GA), August 10.

Pautz, Michelle. 2002. "The Decline in Average Weekly Cinema Attendance: 1930–2000," *Issues in Political Economy* 11: n.p., available at: http://org.elon.edu/ipe/pautz2.pdf.

PEN American Center. 2015. PEN/TONI and James C. Goodale Freedom of Expression Courage Award, March 27, available at: https://pen.org.

"Picture Shows All Put Out of Business." 1908. *New York Times*, December 25, p. 1.

Plowden, Edmund. 1571. *Les comentaries, ou les reportes de Edmunde Plowden … en les temps des raygnes le roye Edwarde le size, le roigne Mary, le roy & roigne Phillipp & Mary, & le roigne Elizabeth*. London.

1816. *The Commentaries, or Reports of Edmund Plowden … Containing Divers Cases upon Matters of Law*. London.

Polenberg, Richard. 1987. *Fighting Faiths: The Abrams Case, the Supreme Court, and Free Speech*. Ithaca, NY: Cornell University Press.

"Police, Crime, Sentencing and Courts Bill." 2021. Bill 268-EN, "A Bill to Make Provision about the Police and Other Emergency Workers," March 12, available at: publications.parliament.uk.

"Police Head's Testimony: Wire Spying a Necessity to Detect Crime Here." 1916. *New York Times*, May 5, p. 1.

Posner, Richard. 2008. "In Defense of Looseness," *The New Republic*, August 27.

2012. "The Incoherence of Antonin Scalia," *The New Republic*, August 24.

"Presidential Threat Law." 1917. "An Act to Punish Persons Who Make Threats Against the President of the United States," 64th Congress, Session II, p. 919, approved February 14.

Press Trust of India. 2017. "Telugu Community in US Asked to Converse in English in Public," February 28, available at: CNN News18.com.

Principe, Craig Matthew. 2012. "What Were They Thinking?: Competing Culpability Standards for Punishing Threats Made to the President," *American University Criminal Law Brief* 7(2): 39–54.

*Public Statutes at Large of the United States of America.* 1845. Boston: Little & Brown, available at: memory.loc.gov.

Republican National Committee. 2022. Committee on Resolutions, "Resolution to formally censure Liz Cheney and Adam Kinzinger and to no longer support them as members of the Republican Party," February 4, available at: washingtonpost.com.

Rogers, Richard, Kimberly S. Harrison, Lisa L. Hazelwood, and Kenneth W. Sewell. 2007. "Knowing and Intelligent: A Study of Miranda Warnings in Mentally Disordered Defendants," *Law and Human Behavior* 31(4): 401–418.

Rolph, C. H. (ed.). 1961. *The Trial of Lady Chatterley.* Harmondsworth: Penguin.

Rosenberg, Eli. 2018. "Texas Official Says That Fewer Doors Could Mean Fewer School Shootings," *Washington Post,* May 19.

Rowland, Lee and Maggie McLetchie. 2008. Letter to Robert Aumaugher, American Civil Liberties Union, January 31, available at: www.aclu.org.

Rushdie, Salman. 2015. Speech at the University of Vermont. January 14. Associated Press video, available at: youtube.com.

——— 2015. "Courage in Continuing," available at: pen.org, April 27.

"Say Picture Shows Corrupt Children." 1908. *New York Times,* December 24, p. 4.

Schenck, Charles. 1918. "Wake Up America," Pamphlet, National Archives, available at: http://recordsofrights.org/records/307/wake-up-america-your-liberties-are-in-danger/0.

Scheussler, Jennifer. 2015. "After Protests, Charlie Hebdo Members Receive Standing Ovation at PEN Gala," *New York Times,* May 6, available at: www.nytimes.com/2015/05/06/nyregion/after-protests-charlie-hebdo-members-receive-standing-ovation-at-pen-gala.html.

"Sedition Act." 1918. "An Act to Amend Section Three, Title One, of the Act Entitled 'An Act to Punish Acts of Interference with the Foreign Relations, the Neutrality, and the Foreign Commerce of the United States, to Punish Espionage, and Better to Enforce the Criminal laws of the United States, and for Other Purposes,' Approved June Fifteenth, Nineteen Hundred and Seventeen, and for Other Purposes," 65th Congress, Session II, Ch. 75, 40 Statutes: 553–554. Approved, May 16, available at: www.loc.gov/law.

Seegers, Grace and Cassidy McDonald. 2021. "McConnell Says Trump Was 'Practically and Morally Responsible' for Riot after Voting Not Guilty," February 14, available at: CBSNews.com.

Selig, Michael. 2013. "United States v. Motion Picture Film The Spirit of '76," *Journal of Popular Film and Television* 10(4): 168–174.

Selznick, David. O. 1972. *Memo from David O. Selznick*, ed. Rudy Behrman. New York: Viking. Reprinted in *Letters of Note*, available at: www.lettersofnote .com/2012/02/damn.html.

Shammas, Brittany. 2021. "A GOP Congressman Compared Capitol Rioters to Tourists. Photos Show Him Barricading a Door," *Washington Post*, May 18.

Shapiro, Carolyn and Cody Jacobs. 2017. "Outlaw Firearms at Public Rallies, Demonstrations," *USA Today*, August 31.

Sheehan, Dan. 2016. "Lehigh Valley Man Loses Latest Court Fight Over Violent Facebook Posts," *The Morning Call*, Allenton, PA, October 29, available at: www.mcall.com.

Shields, John. 1924. "Remarks," 65 *Congressional Record*, April 16, pp. 6461–6462.

Slack, Charles. 2015. *Liberty's First Crisis: Adams, Jefferson, and the Misfits Who Saved Free Speech*. New York: Atlantic Monthly Press.

Smith Act. 1940. An Act to Prohibit Certain Subversive Activities; to Amend Certain Provisions of Law with Respect to the Admission and Deportation of Aliens; to Require the Fingerprinting and Registration of Aliens; and for Other Purposes, *United States Statutes at Large*, vol. 54, ch. 439, June 28, 1940, pp. 670–676.

Smith, Hoke and Dudley Hughes. 1914. "A Bill to Establish an Official National Censorship of Motion Pictures in Interstate and Foreign Commerce and in the District of Columbia and the Territories and all Other Places Under National Jurisdiction," S. 4941, s. 4; 51 *Congressional Record*, March 18, p. 5022.

Smith, Samuel. 1888. "Corrupt Literature," Debate in the House of Commons, *Hansard*, HC Deb 8 May, vol. 325, cc1707–25.

1888. "Pernicious Literature," *The Standard*, July 28; rpt. in National Vigilance Association, 1889, pp. 28–29.

Smith, Sydney. 2016. "Charlie Hebdo's Anniversary Cartoon of God: Associated Press and Others not Using 'L'Assassin Court Toujours' Cover Image," January 8, available at: iMediaEthics.org.

Smoot, Reed, Bronson Cutting et al., 1929–1930. Senate Debates on the Smoot–Hawley Tariff, 71–72 *Congressional Record*, 4433–4472, 5375.

Somers-Dawes, Kate. 2016. "All the Times Trump Has Called for Violence at His Rallies," March 12, available at: *mashable.com*.

Sopo, Dominique. 2015. "Message à Ceux Qui Ne Veulent Pas 'Être Charlie' Prétextant que Charlie Est Raciste et Islamophobe," available at: sos-racisme .org.

Spangler, Todd. 2020. "Trump Downplays Plot Against Whitmer at Michigan Rally, Crowd Chants 'Lock Her Up,'" *Detroit Free Press*, October 17.

Stokes, Bruce. 2017. "What It Takes to Truly Be 'One of Us,'" Pew Research Center, Washington, DC, February 1.

Stolberg, Cheryl Gay. 2003. "An Order of Fries Please, But Do Hold the 'French,'" *New York Times*, March 21, p. A1.

Stone, Geoffrey R. 2003. "Judge Learned Hand and the Espionage Act of 1917: A Mystery Unraveled," *University of Chicago Law Review* 70: 335–358.

Sullivan, Sean and Isaac Stanley-Becker. 2016. "Trump Appears to Encourage Gun Owners to Take Action if Clinton Appoints Anti-Gun Judges," *Washington Post*, August 9.

Supreme Court. 2008. Oral Arguments. *District of Columbia* v. *Heller*, available at: www.supremecourtus.gov/oral_arguments.

Supreme Court Regulation 7. 2013. Available at: www.supremecourt.gov/publicinfo/ buildingregulations.aspx.

Tennessee, State of. 2014. The Constitution of the State of Tennessee, Article XI, § 18, November 4.

2017. An Act to Amend Tennessee Code Annotated, Title 1, Chapter 3, Relative to Construction of Statutes, Senate Bill 30, introduced February 8, available at: https://legiscan.com/TN/text/HB0033/id/1454392.

2019. An Act to Amend Tennessee Code Annotated, Title 36, Relative to the "Tennessee Natural Marriage Defense Act," Tennessee House Bill 1369, introduced February 6, available at: wapp.capitol.tn.gov.

Texas, State of. 2021. H.B. 3979, "A Bill To Be Entitled An Act Relating to Civics Instruction Public School Students and Instruction Policies in Public Schools," September 1.

Todd, Emmanuel. 2015. *Qui est Charlie?* Paris: Seuil.

Toobin, Jeffrey. 2012. *The Oath: The Obama White House and the Supreme Court.* New York: Doubleday.

"Topics of the Times." 1918. *Times-Republican*, Marshalltown, Iowa, July 5, p. 6.

"To Strike Germany from Map of US." 1918. *New York Times*, June 2, p. 56.

Townsend, Mark. 2021. "How CCTV Played a Vital Role in Tracking Sarah Everard – and Her Killer," *The Observer*, October 2.

Toynbee, Polly. 2015. "On Charlie Hebdo Pope Francis is Using the Wife-Beater's Defence," *The Guardian*, January 16.

Trading with the Enemy Act. 1917. An Act To Define, Regulate, and Punish Trading with the Enemy, and for Other Purposes, 65th Congress, ch. 106, sec. 19, pp. 425–426, enacted October 6, *United States Statutes at Large*.

Treaty of Guadalupe–Hidalgo, 1848, Article IX.

Trudeau, Garry. 2015. "The Abuse of Satire," *The Atlantic*, April 11.

Trump, Donald. 2016. Tweet, March 12, available at: twitter.com/realDonaldTrump.

2020a. "Transcript: Donald Trump's RNC Speech," CNN Politics, August 28, available at: www.cnn.com.

2020b. "Executive Order on Preventing Online Censorship," May 28, available at: www.whitehouse.gov/presidential-actions/executive-order-preventing-online-censorship.

Tufekci, Zeynep. 2020. "The Pandemic is No Excuse to Surveil Students," *The Atlantic*, September 4.

Twitter. 2020. "Rules and Policies," available at: help.twitter.com.

Twitter. 2020. Terms of Service, available at: https://twitter.com/tos?lang=en#restrictions.

United Kingdom. 2012. Protection of Freedoms Act, available at: www.legislation.gov.uk.

United States Code. 1928. *Supplement I to the Code of the Laws of the United States of America.* Washington, DC: United States Government Printing Office.

United States House of Representatives, Committee on the Territories. 1911. "Report on the Constitutions of New Mexico and Arizona," Report No. 33, 62nd Congress, 1st Session, May 12.

*United States Statutes at Large,* available at: www.govinfo.gov.

*United States Statutes at Large. A Century of Lawmaking for a New Nation: US Congressional Documents and Debates, 1774–1875.* Library of Congress.

Upshaw, William D. 1925. "The Child and the Motion Picture," 67 *Congressional Record,* July 2, 1926, p. 12842.

Usher, Shaun. 2015. *Lists of Note.* San Francisco: Chronicle Books.

"Uttered Against President." 1917. *Fulton County Tribune,* July 6, p. 6.

Veit, Helen E., Kenneth R. Bowling, and Charlene Bangs Bickford (eds.). 1991. *Creating the Bill of Rights: The Documentary Record from the First Federal Congress.* Baltimore, MD: Johns Hopkins University Press.

Virginia, State of. Code of Virginia, § 18.2-282, Pointing, Holding, or Brandishing Firearm, Air or Gas Operated Weapon or Object Similar in Appearance; Penalty.

Warren, Samuel D. and Louis D. Brandeis. 1890. "The Right to Privacy," *Harvard Law Review* 4(5) (December 15): 193–220.

Webb, Edwin. 1916. Debate on Presidential Threats Bill, 53 *Congressional Record,* p. 9377, 1916.

Webb, Ralf. 2021. "He's a Poet and the FBI Know It: How John Giorno's Dial-a-Poem Alarmed the Feds," *The Guardian,* October 18.

Webster, Noah. 1828. *An American Dictionary of the English Language.*

1833. *The Holy Bible, Containing the Old and New Testaments, in the Common Version. with Amendments of the Language.* New Haven, CT: Durrie & Peck.

Wellemeyer, James. 2020. "Conservatives are Flocking to a New 'Free Speech' Social Media App that has Started Banning Liberal Users," NBC News, July 2, available at: nbcnews.com.

Whiting, Brent. 2013. "Run-of-the-Mill Phoenix Rape Case Made Legal History," *Arizona Republic,* May 27.

Willis, Clyde E. 2002. *Students Guide to Landmark Congressional Laws on the First Amendment.* Westport, CT: Greenwood.

Wills, Garry. 1995. "To Keep and Bear Arms," *New York Review of Books,* September 21.

Wilson, Woodrow. 1915. "Americanism and the Foreign Born," Address at Convention Hall, Philadelphia, May 10.

1916. "Address of President Wilson to the Citizenship Convention," Washington, DC, July 13.

Wrede, Steven. 1979. "The Americanization of Scott County 1914–1918," *Annals of Iowa* 44: 627–638.

Young, Art. 1917. Cartoon. *The Masses*, August, p. 33.

Zangwill, Israel. 1909. *The Melting-Pot*. New York: Macmillan.

Zimmer, Ben. 2012. "The Fight Over Defining Marriage, Literally," *Boston Globe*, June 10.

# Cases Cited

*Abrams* v. *United States*, 250 US 616 (1919).

*Adam Silva et al.* v. *St. Anne Catholic School, Wichita, Kansas et al.*, Complaint, 08-1143-JTM (2008).

*Adam Silva et al.* v. *St. Anne Catholic School, Wichita, Kansas et al.*, 595 F.Supp. 2d 1171 (2009).

*Andrews* v. *State of Tennessee*, 50 Tenn. 165 (1871).

*Arizonans for Official English et al.* v. *Arizona et al.*, 520 US 43, 1997.

*Aymette* v. *State of Tennessee*, 21 Tenn., 2 Humphreys 154 (1840).

*Bethel School District No. 403 et al.* v. *Fraser, a minor, et al.*, 478 US 675 (1986).

*Bostock* v. *Clayton County, Georgia*, US Supreme Court, No. 17-1618, June 15, 2020.

*Brandenburg* v. *Ohio*, 395 US 444, 447 (1969).

*Brogan* v. *United States*, 522 US 398 (1998).

*Brown* v. *Board of Education*, 347 US 483 (1954).

*Burstyn* v. *Wilson*, 343 US 495 (1952).

*Cabell* v. *Markham*, 148 F.2d 737 (1945).

*Clark* v. *United States*, 250 F. 449 (5th Cir. 1918).

*Cohen* v. *California*, 403 US 15 (1971).

*Debs* v. *United States*, 249 US 211 (1919).

*Dennis* v. *United States*, 341 US 491 (1951).

*Dickerson* v. *United States*, 530 US 428, 443 (2000).

*District of Columbia* v. *Heller*, 554 US 570 (2008).

*Elonis* v. *United States*, 575 US ____ (2015).

*Elonis* v. *United States*, Government Brief in Opposition to Petition for *Certiorari*, 2014.

*Elonis* v. *United States*, Third Circuit Court of Appeals rehearing; Oral Arguments. 2016.

*Elonis* v. *United States*, Third Circuit Court of Appeals; opinion, 2016.

*Engel* v. *Vitale*, 370 US 421 (1962).

*English* v. *State of Texas*, 35 Tex. 473, 14 Am. Rep. 374 (1872).

*Escobedo* v. *Illinois*, 378 US 478 (1964).

*Federal Communications Commission* v. *Fox*, 132 S.Ct. 2307 (2012).

*Federal Communications Commission* v. *Fox*, 567 US 239 (2012), Oral Argument, January 10, 2012.

*Grove Press, Inc.* v. *Christenberry*, 175 F.Supp. 488 (S.D.N.Y. 1959).

*Hazelwood School District et al.* v. *Kuhlmeier et al.*, 484 US 260 (1988).

*Heidi Zamecnik and Alexander Nuxoll* v. *Indian Prairie School District #294 et al.*, 636 F.3d 874 (2011).

*Hodge* v. *Talkin*, 13-5250 US Court of Appeals, District of Columbia Circuit.

*Hollingsworth* v. *Perry*, 570 US 693 (2013).

*Jacobellis* v. *Ohio*, 378 US 184 (1964).

*Kessler* v. *City of Charlottesville*, Civil Action No. 3:17CV00056. U.S. District Court for the Western District of Virginia, Charlottesville Division. August 11, 2017.

*Knight First Amendment Institute et al.* v. *Donald J. Trump et al.*, No. 18-1691, US District Court of Appeals for the Second Circuit, 2019.

*Lander* v. *Seaver*, 32 Vt. 114 (1859).

*Lau* v. *Nichols*, 414 US 563 (1974).

*Mahanoy Area School District* v. *B. L., a Minor, by and through Her Father, Levy et al.*, No. 20-255 (2021).

*Masses* v. *Patten*, 244 F. 535 (1917).

*Masterpiece Cakeshop* v. *Colorado Civil Rights Commission*, 584 US___ (2018).

*McDonald* v. *City of Chicago*, 561 US 3025 (2010).

*Nicholas K. Meriwether* v. *Trustees of Shawnee State University and Jane Doe*, No. 20-3289, US Court of Appeals for the Sixth Circuit, March 26, 2021.

*Meyer* v. *Nebraska*, 262 US 390 (1923).

*Miranda* v. *Arizona*, 384 US 436 (1966).

*Miller* v. *California*, 413 US 15 (1973).

*Morse* v. *Frederick*, 127 US 2618 (2007).

*Mutual Film Corporation* v. *Industrial Commission of Ohio*, 236 US 230 (1915).

*New York* v. *Quarles*, 467 US 649 (1984).

*New York State Rifle and Pistol Association* v. *Bruen*, S.Ct. 20-843, due in 2021–22 term.

*Nix* v. *Hedden*, 149 US 304 1893.

*Nunn* v. *State of Georgia*, 1 Kelly 243 (Ga. 1846).

*Nwanguma, Kashiya, et al.* v. *Donald J. Trump et al.*, Civil Action No. 3:16-cv-247-DJH, Louisville Division, US District Court, Western District of Kentucky (2016).

*Nwanguma et al.* v. *Donald J. Trump et al.*, 2018. File No. 18a0202p 06, US Court of Appeals for the Sixth Circuit, September 11.

*Obergefell* v. *Hodges*, 135 US 2071 (2015).

*Olmstead* v. *United States*, 277 US 438 (1928).

*Pacifica* v. *Federal Communications Commission*, 438 US 736 (1978).

*Parker et al.* v. *District of Columbia*, 478 F.3d 370, 401 (2007).

*Partridge* v. *Strange and Croker*, 6 Edw. 6 Rot. 522 (1553). In Plowden, 1792.

*People* v. *Bruce*, Municipal Court for San Francisco and San Francisco County, F54134, March 5, 1962.

*Ragansky* v. *United States*, 253 F. 643, 645 (C.A. 7th Cir. 1918).

*Regina* v. *Hicklin*, L.R. 3 Q.B. 360 (1868).

*Regina* v. *Penguin Books Ltd.*, Crim. L.R. 176 (1960); also known as *Queen* v. *Penguin Books Ltd.*

*Roe* v. *Wade*, 410 US 113 (1973).

*Roth* v. *United States*, 354 US 476 (1957).

*Salinas* v. *Texas*, 133 S.Ct. 2174 (2013).

*Schenck* v. *United States*, 249 US 47 (1919).

*Silveira* v. *Lockyer*, 312 F.3d 1052 (2002).

*State of Vermont* v. *Max Misch*, 2021 VT 10, No. 2019-266.

*Terminiello* v. *Chicago*, 337 US 1 (1949).

*Tinker* v. *Des Moines*, 393 US 503 (1969).

*United States* v. *Dennis*, 183 F.2d 201 (1950).

*United States* v. *Dzhokhar Tsarnaev*, Criminal Action No. 13-MJ-02016-MBB (2013).

*United States* v. *Eastman et al.*, April 25, 1918.

*United States* v. *Emerson*, 270 F.3d 203 (2001).

*United States* v. *Hall*, 1918 248 F. 150 (1918).

*United States* v. *Masses Publishing Company*, 252 F. 232 (1918).

*United States* v. *Metzdorf*, 252 F. 933 (1918).

*United States* v. *Miller*, 307 US 174 (1939).

*United States* v. *One Book Called "Ulysses"*, 5 F.Supp. 182 (S.D.N.Y. 1933).

*United States* v. *The Spirit of '76*, 252 F. 946 (S.D. Cal. 1917).

*United States* v. *Stickrath*, 242 F. 151 (1917).

*United States* v. *Tsarnaev*, No. 20-442, 2022.

*United States* v. *Windsor*, 570 US 744 (2013).

*United States* v. *Zimmerman*, cited by Henry J. Gibbons and Henry John Nelson, "Brief for Plaintiffs in Error," *Schenck* v. *United States*, 1918, pp. 10–11.

*Virginia* v. *Black*, 538 US 343 (2003).

*Village of Skokie* v. *National Socialist Party of America*, 69 Ill.2d 605, 619 (1978).

*Watts* v. *United States*, 394 US 705 (1969).

*Watts* v. *United States*, 402 F.2d 676 [D.C. Cir. 1968].

*Whitney* v. *California*, 274 US 357 (1927).

*Wisconsin* v. *Breitzman*, Court of Appeals, 2015AP1610-CR 2016.

*Yniguez* v. *Arizonans for Official English*, 69 F.3rd 920 (1995).

# Further Reading

In addition to the extensive section of works that I have cited in this book, readers who are interested in exploring some of the topics in language and law that I have not had space to cover, or who would like to read about some of the issues covered here, might find the following titles useful. I have arranged them in general categories loosely following the order of the book.

**Forensic linguistics**: Malcom Coulthard and Alison Johnson, *An Introduction to Forensic Linguistics* (Routledge, 2007), offers a beginner's survey of legal textual analysis, legal style and register, the language of the courtroom, and the use of language as evidence in legal cases. Their more complete *Routledge Handbook of Forensic Linguistics* (Routledge, 2010) contains essays by various scholars discussing aspects of forensic linguistics in greater detail.

**Explaining the Constitution and the laws**: The Library of Congress publishes a regularly updated explanation of all parts of the US Constitution, in plain English, "based on a comprehensive review of Supreme Court case law and, where relevant, historical practices that have defined the text of the Constitution ... useful for a wide audience: from constitutional scholars to those just beginning to learn about the nation's most important legal document." It is available online at: constitution.congress.gov.

In addition, Cornell University Law School's Legal Information Institute makes available online a host of primary and secondary legal sources, including fully annotated texts of the Constitution, the US Code, Supreme Court decisions, and presidential executive orders, in addition to a number of state legal resources. Its text of the Constitution contains links to explanations of all the articles and amendments. It can be found at: www.law.cornell.edu.

**On legal interpretation**: In his *Interpreting Law: A Primer on How to Read Statutes and the Constitution* (Foundation Press, 2016), the legal scholar William Eskridge provides a broad, sensible, and readable overview of the practical ways that lawyers and judges read and interpret law, along with a close examination of pertinent hypothetical examples.

**On the Constitution**: Legal scholar Akhil Reed Amar has written a number of detailed accounts of the origins and meaning of the US Constitution. A good one to start with is *America's Unwritten Constitution: The Precedents and Principles We Live By* (Basic Books, 2015). Historian Jack Rakove has a number of books and articles that cut through contemporary political biases to help us to understand how to relate the constitutional discussions in the founding era and their relationship to present-day concerns. A good place to start is his *Original Meanings: Politics and Ideas in the Making of the Constitution* (Alfred A. Knopf, 1996), winner of the Pulitzer Prize in 1997. Another important corrective to today's fraught constitutional debates is historian Jonathan Gienapp's *The Second Creation: Fixing the American Constitution in the Founding Era* (Harvard University Press, 2018).

**On the Second Amendment**: A hot topic like this is fraught with political agendas, historical distortions, and a significant amount of anger and misinformation. One useful pre-*Heller* resource is "The History and Politics of Second Amendment Scholarship: A Primer," by Carl T. Bogus, in the *Chicago-Kent Law Review* 76(1) (2000): 3–108, available online at: scholarship.kentlaw.iit.edu. See also Saul Cornell, *The Second Amendment on Trial: Critical Essays on District of Columbia v. Heller* (University of Massachusetts Press, 2013), for a collection of post-*Heller* essays on the subject.

On a topic of growing interest in legal studies, corpus linguistics, particularly as it relates to the interpretation of the Second Amendment, see Thomas R. Lee and Stephen C. Mouritsen, "Judging Ordinary Meaning," *Yale Law Journal* (2018): 788–879. James Phillips and Joshua Blackman have also published several studies of Second Amendment corpus analysis, the latest being James Phillips, "Some Thoughts on Methodology," a post for the Duke Center for Firearms Law, available at: firearmslaw.duke.edu. The Duke Center also maintains a database of early English and American firearms legislation.

**On free speech**: The American Civil Liberties Union offers links on its website, ACLU.org, to resources on a variety of free-speech topics, including internet speech, student speech, employee speech, intellectual property, and the rights of protestors. The American Library Association, at ala.org, also offers a number of useful links about the freedom to read, book banning, content filtering, and academic freedom.

**On political speech**: Lee C. Bollinger and Geoffrey R. Stone (eds.), *The Free Speech Century* (Oxford University Press, 2018), presents a collection of essays by prominent legal scholars tracing the evolution of First Amendment doctrine from *Schenck* to the present. Two studies of *Abrams* v. *United States*, one published shortly after the trial and one more recently, offer a close-up look at the political vagaries that impacted that Supreme Court decision. The first is Zechariah Chaffee, "A Contemporary State Trial: The United States Versus Jacob Abrams et al.," *Harvard Law Review* 33 (1920): 747–774. And the second is Richard Polenberg, *Fighting Faiths: The Abrams Case, the Supreme Court, and Free Speech* (Cornell University Press, 1987). Geoffrey R. Stone, *Perilous Times:*

*Free Speech in Wartime, From the Sedition Act of 1798 to the War on Terrorism* (W. W. Norton, 2004), offers a through and well-documented history of the successes and failures of the First Amendment in times of national stress.

**On obscenity**: Christopher Hilliard, *A Matter of Obscenity: The Politics of Censorship in Modern England* (Princeton University Press, 2021), recounts in detail the development of obscenity law in the United Kingdom and the United States from *Hicklin* to more recent times.

**On threats**: Speech Act Theory, as articulated by J. L. Austin, in *How to Do Things with Words* (Harvard University Press, 1962, 2nd ed. 1975), and developed in more detail by John Searle in *Speech Acts* (Cambridge University Press, 1969, rpt. 2012), suggests a relationship between promises and threats that hinges on whether the listener desires the outcome of an utterance (thus making it a promise) or does not desire that outcome (making it a threat). As subsequent discussion has shown, the distinction between the two is not so simple. Paul T. Crane discusses in detail the history of legal treatment of threatening language in "'True Threats' and the Issue of Intent," *Virginia Law Review* 92 (2006): 1225, 1229–1234. Cornell's Legal Information Institute offers a concise discussion of *mens rea*, or criminal intent, one of the thorniest issues in threat cases, taken from the Model Penal Code (1961, rev. 1981), at: www.law .cornell.edu/wex/mens_rea.

**Official language**: Douglas Kibbee, *Language and the Law: Linguistic Inequality in America* (Cambridge University Press, 2016), offers a wide-ranging introduction to the problems posed by language variation in the United States from the founding era through today's English-only movement, with focused discussions of language in the schools and in the workplace. See also Geoffrey Nunberg, "Lingo Jingo: English-Only and the New Nativism," *The American Prospect* (July/August, 1997), pp. 40–47. For an excellent study of the treatment of language variation in American schools, see Anne Harper Charity Hudley and Christine Mallinson, *Understanding English Language Variation in US Schools* (Teachers College Press, 2010).

**Technology, privacy, and speech**: There is no better place to start than "The Right to Privacy," the classic essay by Samuel Warren and Louis Brandeis, *Harvard Law Review* 4(5) (1890): 193–220. For a look at the impact of social media on privacy, see Siva Vaidhyanathan, *Antisocial Media: How Facebook Disconnects Us and Undermines Democracy* (Oxford University Press, 2018). For more general studies, see also Jonathan Zittrain, *The Future of the Internet – And How to Stop It* (Yale University Press, 2018), and Timothy Wu, *The Master Switch: The Rise and Fall of Information Empires* (Alfred A. Knopf, 2010).

# Index